T0374363

Wisdom of the Archangels

Margaret Doner

WISDOM OF THE ARCHANGELS

iUniverse books may be ordered through booksellers or by contacting:

iUniverse
1663 Liberty Drive
Bloomington, IN 47403
www.iuniverse.com
844-349-9409

ISBN: 978-1-4502-6353-5 (sc)
ISBN: 978-1-4502-6354-2 (e)

Print information available on the last page.

iUniverse rev. date: 02/24/2021

ACKNOWLEDGEMENTS

I wish to thank all my Lightworker friends for their support and love. You know who you are. The community we have created is astonishing—truly a vision for the New Earth. I am blessed to be surrounded by so many people who are not afraid to do the inner work necessary to clear the old karma and stories so that more Light can be received. We are all truly blessed. We stand together in service to the Light. It takes a community to create change; alone we can't do it, but together we can. As we awaken to the truth of ourselves we awaken the world. I love you all.

ACKNOWLEDGMENTS

Table of Contents

Introduction

Nothing has been more exciting and wonderful for me than to realize over the last few years that the realm known to most of us as "angelic" has become more and more accessible. It's not available to just a few—it's available to all equally. Rather than being relegated to "fantasy" it has now become a reflection of our Highest Selves. As more and more people awaken from the "slumber" of separation and despair and remember through personal experience and scientific discovery that Unity Consciousness is not merely a meaningless term but an actual provable reality, they also awaken to "other realms." "We are not alone" gains new meaning on all planes of existence.

From Masaru Emoto's, *Hidden Messages in Water,* and the revelations of the book, *The Secret,* we are learning that our thoughts literally create our reality: the Universe "out prints" our individual and collective consciousness. That is why "ask and you shall receive" is a real truth. But we also have come to realize that we are asking and creating from a place of unawareness. Our individual and collective consciousness has been programmed over time with belief systems of lack, greed, fear, hatred and judgment, and often we are creating from these old paradigms without even realizing it. We are asking from our lower selves instead of our Higher Selves. Such understanding has lead many of us to look at our "past lives" and at how these lives are carried forward to impact our current lives and to become aware of the frequency control that has been put over us like a veil to keep us "asleep."

If the 2012 experience is about anything it is about "waking up." But like all "wake up calls" for many people this one is quite a rude awakening. We are being called to "look in the mirror" and rather than blaming others for the dark cloud around us, we are being called to realize that we must look at the part of ourselves that has called this dark cloud to us. Personal responsibility goes hand-in-hand with being a co-creator with God—no more blaming God when we don't get what we want or when we don't like what we have co-created.

What the angels say is that our job is to lift our consciousness to the place where we too are "Christed Beings"—this is not about organized religion as we have defined it. Christ and all Enlightened Ones on Earth have shown us that we too can create miracles; we just have to release our doubt and fears and bring our Divine Self into union with our physical human self. Perhaps that is not as impossible as it sounds. Inside each and every one of us is the spark of Divinity—it's up to us to awaken it.

We have been imprisoned in ways that we are just beginning to realize—but it doesn't mean that we have to accept this false imprisonment. If we unplug from the third dimensional matrix and "plug in" to our Higher Selves we are liberated from anything that anyone can throw at us. But, freedom does not mean denial. Before you can fix something you have to know what's broken. That's why I believe the healing is in the "shadow"—both the individual's shadow and humanity's collective shadow. Know Thyself. The symbol of the Yin/Yang includes both dark and light; within the dark is a dot of the light, within the light is a dot of the dark. You cannot be whole and only embrace knowledge from one side of the equation or another. Integration is the idea which runs throughout this entire book—your wisdom has been gained through a wide variety of experiences, through many lifetimes. If you embrace only some of your Selves you can never be enlightened. Enlightenment is to hold it all in the light of higher knowing.

Through many private channeling sessions my clients and I have been pushed to awaken to our "other selves," to release the illusion of linear time, and to remember that we are multi-dimensional beings alive on many planes of existence. It is liberating. It is exhilarating. This is truly who we are. As we move closer and closer to the 2012 End of Days (or as I like to think of it The Beginning of Days) it is up to each one of us to co-create a vision of Heaven on Earth and remember that the world is a reflection of our beliefs—if we want love and abundance for ourselves and others then we must live it day to day.

"Be sure to run over your inner victim on the way to inner Mastery," says Merlin.

PART I
HUMAN KARMA STORIES

I have divided this book into two main sections. This first section is entitled *Human Karma Stories* because it focuses on the human condition and the karmic stories which everyone carries within them, whether they are conscious of these stories or not. I have been doing past life regression since 1994—I studied and graduated from Roger Woolger's, Ph.D. (author of *Other Lives, Other Selves*) program in 1996. There are main themes in the human stories or dramas: abandonment, responsibility for the safety of others, guilt, betrayal, poverty, disloyalty—the list is quite long. But, they are universal. Everyone has them and reacts from the accumulation of their past life stories and dramas whether they are aware of it or not. If the past life is unrecognized and unresolved the drama drives the present life. The person can try and try to be a "Master in the Now Moment" but it will elude them. To truly be in the "Now" one must be clear in the past and the present both.

From the point of view of your Higher Self or "Oversoul" these lives are not linear and disconnected. They are all you and they just occur in different places. Integrating the human is a major theme of this entire book—the angels believe that it is essential to achieving wholeness and happiness. The idea of soul retrieval is just that: picking up the pieces of your selves that are scattered throughout time and space and re-owning them. Loving all of you is to love the dark, the light, and the abandoned pieces as God loves all of you.

CHAPTER ONE

GROUP KARMA

CHANNELING FOR FIVE WOMEN GROUP

ANGELS: It is with great delight that we have this opportunity to speak with you, to work with you in this way and to share with you. As always, we introduce ourselves as Ariel, Michael and Gabriel and remind each and every one of you that all of the angels are available to each and every one of you, as we are not exclusive but come when called.

It is important that we begin today by stating and reminding each of you that you live in a benevolent universe. At this time in human history many of you are forgetting this, while simultaneously, many of you are also remembering the Truth of this statement. What we mean by the fact that you live in a benevolent universe is the idea that you create or co-create your own reality, and that you are not being given things to punish you, to harm you, or even, to harshly judge or teach you, but you are given things as a result of your own consciousness desiring and calling forth to you what it is that you believe you either need, want, desire or at times fear, on some level.

Although it is hard to imagine that you call to you some of the events that you see around you or that you have experienced, you must understand that in order to step into a responsible or victimless attitude it is necessary to understand that many human beings, and that includes yourselves at times, are creating from past trauma. The human species is in fact a traumatized species. Once you have been traumatized and have awakened fear inside of your consciousness or your collective consciousness, it is easy to reawaken it, and in the reawakening of it, to re-attract the experiences that you fear most.

It is for this reason that those of you who are choosing to move ahead as spiritual beings and choosing to co-create your reality must become aware of who you are on deeper and deeper levels. This awareness allows you to attract to you what you want and to be aware when you are attracting things to you which you don't want. If you can root out and release old traumas or places of fear—whether from previous lives or the current lifetime—you are more likely to be manifesting from a cleared palette—a cleared energy field. Then you know that the "magnet" you are is creating and consciously drawing to you the experiences which support your soul's growth and highest vision.

We do not believe that it is necessary, in a sense, to always have what human beings think of as good or positive experiences to create growth, for humans have also been using experiences of pain and difficulty to bump themselves into a higher level of awareness or consciousness. Often times, however, you will find that your painful experiences, if they come too fast and too hard, become so overwhelming with darkness that you cannot release the pain or the darkness, you cannot transform or transmute the consciousness, and you become overwhelmed by the darkness. Thus, you create more darkness for the self and more experiences that are painful for you.

This idea of moving into higher consciousness means increasing your own vibrational rate. Because your own vibrational rate is increasing, your ability to create and to draw and magnetize to you is also increasing. Because of that, it becomes even more important that you become conscious and that you create and understand and align with the Bigger You: The You who is divine and infinite, and is expansive and knowing. As you become aware, root out your smaller self and replace it with your Higher Self.

This cannot always be done simply by saying, "I will it away." Sometimes the wounding is so deep that it will take much time and many different methods of healing for you to release the wounding, to let it go, to clear out the puss, in a sense, from the wound, so that it becomes clean and you don't attract places and things to you that are magnetized by that wounding. The first step is always to understand and to recognize it. It is for that reason that you must be very brave to take a journey to higher awareness, a spiritual journey, and you must be willing to look at yourself with a very fine microscope, and be willing to be honest with yourself about what you are creating, about who you are, about where in fact you pass judgment on yourself, where you pass judgment on others and to be willing to look at your fears. You must be willing to look at your limitations and to notice your self-conversation every day. Where is it that you say, "I'm no good?" Where is it that you say, "I can't do that; I can't have that; the world is a very bad place; the world is a dangerous place; I must always protect myself?" Where is it every day that you call those beliefs to you? You can be assured that if you are operating from those places that fear begins to arise. And where fear arises, energy is magnetized.

At this time, as many of you are aware, there is this thing going on that humans call the ascension of the earth. There seems to be an awakening and an awareness and simultaneously many of you are seeing a microscope turned on to look into your own darkness and to the shadow part of the human race. We like to let you know that this is because those places must be looked at, those places must be recognized, must be admitted to and must be transformed consciously, with knowledge. Something outside of yourselves is not going to just come in and wash it all away so you don't have to ever think about or deal with the things that are disturbing to you or that are blocking you.

But because you are, from our perspective, Masters, it is not our job here in the angelic realm to tell you what to do. It is not our job to live your lives for you, but it is our job to help you know and understand and recognize your Higher Self and to wed your Higher Self, your Mastery, with your human self. It is our job to help you root out those places where you still believe in your limited self, your limitations, where you might be still calling to yourself fear-based thoughts of illness, fear-based thoughts of poverty or loneliness, and to help you to transmute and transform those places into something that makes you feel better, not to just paint over those places and whitewash them and pretend, by putting some "sugar coating" over your wounds and let the wounding seep down inside of you. That is not what we're here to do and it is not what the energies of the ascension are here to do. The frequencies of the ascension are here to bring the wounding to the surface, to help transform it and transmute it, and then to call forth a higher frequency, which some of you have dubbed the fifth dimensional realm or fifth dimensional frequency.

We explain to many people that when we speak of dimensions, we are speaking of levels of consciousness. This is very important for you all to understand, and perhaps you will ask a question about how to raise your consciousness and what consciousness is and how to live in a higher consciousness, so that you can be happy while on the earth and not feel fear or be frightened about those things which you consider to be impending or a danger.

So, we welcome you here today and we understand that as each one of you transforms yourself and becomes your angelic self while in human body you also assist all others to come closer to their angelic selves. Rather than thinking of that as being a fantasy or something unattainable, we ask each of you to be willing to make the step and to leap into your angelic selves and look at and recognize where it is that you might be holding yourself back from believing that it is indeed possible to be a human angel.

We invite your questions. We thank you so much because, as we like to explain to human beings, we also learn and there is a realm here that is real and a realm here that is conscious, a realm here that is growing. Just as we are given the opportunity here through our task, which is to assist and to learn from the human race, you also are given the opportunity and the task to assist and to learn from us. So we see it as a mutual sharing and growing, and we thank you for sharing and growing and believing in this realm and the possibility of this connection and in the co-creation between the angelic and the human race.

DARLENE: My question is: the five of us friends—I probably can't remember how each one of us came into each other's lives. But my question is: are we karmically connected somehow? What keeps us together? What brings us together?

ANGELS: Well, one of the things we first notice about all of you—and as you look around the room, you will notice it as well—is that there is not much overlapping in who you are. Each of you is holding a very distinct and separate point on the pentacle star. Do you see what we're saying? Each of you has the responsibility to hold a point, to give you an image, if you would align yourselves as that star, you each are holding a different energetic point that when brought together, makes a geometrical formation which holds a consciousness greater than each of your individual parts. We're going to just stop for a moment, pause, and ask if you understand that first image we gave you.

DARLENE: I do.

ANGELS: Okay. So in other words, what we're saying is the whole is greater than each of your individual parts. Do you understand that?

DARLENE: Yes.

ANGELS: You feel that, yes? You understand how, when you're brought together, you can see a different aspect that's very distinct, that you're each holding. You each have a strength and a gift and an energetic ability and also weaknesses that are very distinct. It's not like—some groups get together and they all feel that they are similar, in a sense. In your case, the strength of this particular alignment or group is your differences. It is the differences in all of you that strengthens you and makes you greater than you are individually. That is one of the reasons that you have called one another together is to make this geometrical star, this five-pointed star.

Now, the next thing that's very important for you to understand about the vibrational energy of five is that the vibrational energy of five is the energy of change. It's an unstable vibration. Do you see what we're saying? Do you know that, that five is unstable? Four, for example, is very stable.

DARLENE: Yes.

ANGELS: Five is the energy of change. When you see a five or 555 somewhere it means change. It means something is changing and transforming. What we feel, with the energy of this five is that you all call each other together to bring a different frequency. You each carry very different frequencies that when brought together create the alchemy of great change for each of you. You stimulate each of you to grow, to move—at times it can bring disagreement or energy that's not similar but that makes you think or look at something and to grow and to create and to make something bigger than who you are alone.

From a karmic perspective, from a past life perspective, your energies, when combined, always have been involved in situations or times where there has been change or stress or debate or shifting. When you come together as a "fivesome" no matter where it is in time or space, the energy combination always is involved at times of great shifting and change.

For example, one of the times you all came together was in a small town, a small village. One of the things happening in that town at the time was that there was what many of the men felt was a female uprising—the energy of the women was becoming unstable in that town and dissatisfied. One of the things that you had karmically agreed to do energetically was to reincarnate in that town again as that "fivesome" and use the energies that you all carry to stimulate change in the town for the betterment of the women who lived in the town. The idea of a suffragette movement would be similar. The five of you brought the idea that, "We're not going to be the slaves of the men anymore; we deserve to have a say; we deserve to be real people and not to be the slaves of men." Your energies combined in that experience to be radical and revolutionary; but that is the energy of your "fivesome," from our perspective. We're going to ask you how you resonate with that concept.

DARLENE: I'm thinking Witches of Eastwick.

ANGELS: Right, because that was the energy. What is thought of as witch energy.

DARLENE: The revolt.

ANGELS: Right. And that is why we mentioned the pentagram, you see. That is a very nice way to simply put it. We always like to find simple human ways to express complicated things. So we're going to say okay, we'll go with you there. We like that.

DARLENE: Knowing each of us, I can see—

RHONDA: We're five strong, different personalities.

LAUREN: Yes.

JENNA: All leadership, right, every one of us.

ANGELS: So, there's always—when you're together, there's always some kind of conflict or resolution or searching. It's a sense that when you come together and make a greater part of a whole you're going to be stirring the brew. Perhaps that is the best way for us to again simplify it. You have the potential to stir things up but for better. You all want, in your own way, to change the world and to create something better.

Each of you holds a different energy and you can see the one who is very down to earth and more practical and you can see the one who is a little more fiery and angry, you know? And you can see one who tries to keep the peace and so forth. You can see that you combine and it helps to not only stir things up but also, if one of you acted out of an extreme pull, it wouldn't be as successful. With all of you, you balance each other out. You make the "stirring up" possible without destroying any of you individually.

Do you see what we're saying by that?

DARLENE: Yes.

ANGELS: We mean if you tried to do it alone, you'd be destroyed. So, you stir, you balance, and you create change. That's the best way for us to summarize it.

RHONDA: Could you explain the energies of each of us?

ANGELS: Well, all of you know your energies. No one, of course, perhaps wants to admit to where their place is necessarily, but we're going to—perhaps we'll just start with you. Do you want to start with you?

DARLENE: Absolutely. Sure.

ANGELS: Okay, so let's just talk about what your energy is like and where you hold your energy and how you hold your energy. You're capable of getting riled up and you're capable of feeling strongly. Let's see, what is the word we're trying to find? Just give us a second to get the human word. You have a strong sense of right and wrong and you're capable—there is one human word we're struggling for. We will get it—of having—indignation is the word that we're looking for. You're capable of holding the indignation.

Do you understand that? Do you understand that word?

DARLENE: Well, you could explain a little bit more, please?

ANGELS: Okay. Well, how do you see indignation? We see it as you have a strong sense of what's right and wrong, and when something wrong is being done, you hold "that is not right!" Do you see what we're saying? That is not right! You shouldn't do that! You shouldn't do that! That is what we see is your point in the star. Do you understand that?

DARLENE: Yes.

ANGELS: Does that resonate for you?

DARLENE: Yes.

ANGELS: Okay. So, that's your point. So, go ahead, whoever wants—perhaps you don't all want to know your point on the star. But if you do want to know your point on the star, please speak so that we—

RHONDA: Yes. We'll go around the table, so I'll be next. We'll take my point on the star.

ANGELS: Well, you are one who tries to calm and to pacify. So, when the indignation, which is good, comes up, you're the one who says, "But wait, let's see if we can work this out." That would be your point in the star. Would you understand that?

RHONDA: Yes.

LAUREN: How about me?

ANGELS: Well, you laugh at yourself, yes? Yes, you do. And it's an interesting energy. You have a very interesting energy because in some ways, it's contradictory in you. You carry two kinds of contradictory states at the same time. One of the things that you have tended to do... We're going to use old stories—an action, in other words, to explain.

In the past life we mentioned, when a woman was being abused—you're down to earth, you're practical, and you see the problem. You would see when there was something happening. You would want to go in and you would want to change it, but you had a belief system that there was a way to do it—in other words, you would say, "Let's do it behind the man's back." You wouldn't go to his face because you'd say, "That's not going to get us anywhere." You have that practicality. You told the others, "Listen, if we go right in there, we're going to stir up things so badly that we may not succeed, we may not be able to help her." So, you were practical.

This is how you dealt with the situation in the past life. You said, "I'm going to go in there, I'm going to help the woman, with the idea of being a midwife. I'm going to help her, but I'm going to have to help her behind the back of the man." You would figure out a way to do it anyway. You'll do it anyway. You'll always do it, but you're going to figure out how to get it done. Even if it means diversion, if it means using humor or something like that, you will use it to get the job done that you need to get done. That would be how you would approach the problem.

Do you understand what we're saying?

LAUREN: Yes.

ANGELS: It's not that you don't experience indignation, certainly you do. Not that you don't find peaceful means at times, certainly you do. Not that you're not capable of using humor, certainly you do. But you will use and figure out what to do that will get what you want done at the time, utilizing and trying to bring everything together, in a sense almost acting or assisting the synthesis by using the perfect method. You're more grounded than some of the others. Do you see what we're saying?

LAUREN: Uh-huh.

ANGELS: Okay. So there's no one word but it's more of an action. If anyone else would like to ask, that would be fine.

JENNA: That would be me.

ANGELS: Well, we're going to put it this way. It's kind of funny. You're the brains of the operation. Sometimes that gets in your way, and you know that, yes? Do you understand what we mean by that? Because you come at things from a place of—well, you're going to look at the other side. You're not going to take something at face value. That is why we call you the brains. Whereas the peacekeeper would want to operate perhaps sometimes from a place of idealism, it would be your job to bring in points that would perhaps not be seen by the others. Do you understand what we mean?

JENNA: Yes.

ANGELS: We're going to put it this way. It's a silly way to put it but it's your job to remind the others at all times of the shadow ever lurking, you know? Don't forget to look at that, be wary and know and think, don't leap. The brains. So, we're going to ask if there is another that wishes to speak.

RITA: Yes, I wanted to know about my part.

ANGELS: Well, it's interesting because you have held what is essentially the purity in the point. By that, it's very interesting because in the life we spoke about where you were all together; you are like the conventional woman. You were the woman of the town that everyone looked up to as being the good housewife and being the good one. You struggled with joining forces with the rabble rousers. But at the same time you are the conduit or the link between the townsfolk and the rabble rousers. They needed to have someone who understood the town folk. Do you see what we're saying? Who understood? And everyone looked at you in the town as being so pure and the good one, that no one suspected that you were part of this group. That is what we mean by kind of holding what was thought of as the pure point. Do you see what we're saying?

RITA: We see.

ANGELS: So, each of you has these abilities but when you combine them, they create this beautiful star, and the star perpetuates change and creates a much greater energy. We salute you for doing this.

CHAPTER TWO

INDIVIDUAL KARMA AND FORGIVENESS

MEREDITH S.

ANGELS: We are so delighted to have this opportunity to speak with you and to work with you in this way. This is the Archangel Ariel who is speaking with you. As you are aware, the angels Gabriel and Michael are also with this conduit. However, any angel is available to you if you wish to call upon an angelic energy specifically.

We wish to begin today by speaking to you a little bit about some of the wounded places that you have. It's not that we wish you to live there, it's not that we wish to in any way hurt you or harm you, but it is our belief system that if we can expose for you and help you to remember some of the places that you're still wounded, some of the pain that you still hold, that you can release it, that you can move past it. It's difficult, particularly for an individual to see some of the more wounded places because it is the natural instinct of a human to run away from what hurts and to want pleasure.

Often times, in running away from the pain or the hurt, the part of the self that is wounded begins to feel quite orphaned. It gets lonely; it gets sad, its pain increases. So, it's the idea that if you embrace those wounded or painful parts of the self and are able to address them and look at them, then they become unified with you and they are no longer an irritant. They can be healed, they can be forgiven, they can be integrated, and they can ultimately become your teachers. And it is the idea that these places can help teach you that frees you from holding them as wounding and helps you to embrace these places as something positive, as a blessing.

We're going to go right to what we see as one of the most painful woundings which is still carried deep within you; and it is from what humans call a past life. We will talk to you today about the idea of past lives and help you to understand that from the perspective of your soul, since there is no past, or future, since the soul is out of linear time, the wounding and the experiences and the knowledge and the teachings that you receive from what appear to be past lives are very present life as well.

The deepest wounding comes from a life as a small child. In that life, you were a boy, and your family was living in a very simple house, what you would think of today as a cottage or a cabin, that kind of simplicity. You were not wealthy. You lived simply in your cottage. And for the earliest part of your life, it was actually quite a good life, an innocent and sublime life, and you enjoyed very much how you spent your earliest years.

There came a time in that life where attackers, invaders if you will, came and they slaughtered your family. But what happened to you that made it even worse for you was that you hid. You were able to hide and they did not find you. You crouched down and you hid. As you crouched down and hid in the corner behind things, quietly, unfortunately, you were also witnessing and experiencing through your ears the sounds of the brutality, and it paralyzed you. You never recovered emotionally, as you can imagine, although you lived. You were so traumatized that you were the living dead.

That imprinted upon your soul the belief system, which had already been set up through other lives, but sealed for you the belief system of how unsafe the world is and how painful it is to be alive. It sealed in your soul the idea to protect yourself and to hide and to stay small. When you are not incarnate, when you are what humans would call between your lifetimes or in a spiritual body, you resist incarnating, embodying. It's not what you look forward to. Again, it's the idea that it makes you feel unsafe and you want to just hide where it's safe.

So, we begin with what we see is that deepest wounding; everything else that you experience or that you go through comes from that most deepest wounding that you still contain within you—that emotionally paralyzed child. You want to learn to overcome it. You've tried to overcome it with your intelligence, with your mind, with your mental prowess. But, no matter how much you learn or you study or you try to understand, there's still that wounded child that wounded self part of you that doesn't know how to be safe on this planet.

Now that is a universal, we understand. It is a universal. From our perspective, every human being is doing what they do because they think that they are going to be safe if they do it. Whether it is to be aggressive and to fight or whether it is to hide, it is the individual's reaction to the events of their lives that cause them to react in a certain way, to create the situations that they believe will make them safe in an unsafe world.

Your way of coping, your method of coping is your own. It is your particular signature, and that signature at times is an overcompensation of the mental body trying to hold on when the emotional body starts to shake or feel unsafe. The mental body tries to convince it that it's safe and figure out ways to be safe. But from our perspective, if we were just to jump into a life, if you will, an experience that your soul has had that has deeply wounded you, we would point to the one we just mentioned.

We're going to just pause for a moment and ask if you're with us so far, if you understand why we might have chosen to begin in this manner.

MEREDITH: Yes, it makes sense based on how I feel about life. I think it makes a lot of sense.

ANGELS: Okay. So what we want you to understand is that as painful and difficult—and we're going to ask you to close your eyes for a moment and go ahead and imagine an image for yourself of what that life might have been like for you, that small boy, that experience—where would you have been crouching? What position would your body have been in? See an image and describe it to us.

MEREDITH: I think I see a small boy crouching, just scrunching up as tiny as you can make yourself, in some kind of piece of furniture that was against the wall. I don't know. That's the only image I'm getting, that it was inside.

ANGELS: That's good, yes. Can you understand and feel, as you begin to recreate it, the shakiness in the body a little and the fear? But the idea that as you try to push away all the frightening things that your ears still could hear. Do you understand that feeling? You couldn't keep the ears from knowing or hearing what was going on.

MEREDITH: Uh-huh.

ANGELS: So, some of it did enter, no matter how small or how tight you squeezed your eyes, that feeling, there was still a knowledge that something horrible was happening that you didn't want to witness.

MEREDITH: Right.

ANGELS: Can you understand how today, in this life, sometimes that's how you feel, that you want to just scrunch up and hope that perhaps something bad will just pass you by?

MEREDITH: Yeah, and I think that I'm very emotionally closed off sometimes. One of the things that bothers me about myself is that I feel like I don't have a lot of compassion for other people. I feel like there's some kind of like emotional blockage or stoppage, and I don't know if that is related to this past life.

ANGELS: You can see that this would be it, yes? Can you see? What would happen to that child? Let's help you to recreate that. What would happen when—do you understand what now is called post-traumatic stress disorder?

MEREDITH: Uh-huh.

ANGELS: Now? As a modern word?

MEREDITH: Right.

ANGELS: Well, think of your post-traumatic stress disorder in that life.

MEREDITH: Yeah.

ANGELS: Although it wasn't understood. What happens to a small boy when he witnesses, no matter what culture, what life, when he witnesses brutality and the slaughter of his family? What happens when he awakens is that he is numb.

MEREDITH: Yeah.

ANGELS: He's numb. It's too painful to feel, isn't it?

MEREDITH: Yeah.

ANGELS: Too painful to hold. It shuts down the emotional body.

MEREDITH: Yeah.

ANGELS: We're trying to get you to understand there's a good reason for why you are the way you are, and that you should feel gentle with yourself, okay?

MEREDITH: Uh-huh.

ANGELS: Not to judge yourself.

MEREDITH: Yeah, because that's what I do.

ANGELS: Yes, and we're trying to help you to understand that you are suffering from post-traumatic stress disorder still. Okay? You're the one who huddled in that little ball that we showed you.

MEREDITH: Exactly.

ANGELS: That goes into the coma.

MEREDITH: When I was in first grade—I think it was—I didn't talk at school for an entire year.

ANGELS: That was your story. Do you see why that would happen? We told you, you didn't speak? Do you remember that boy? That's how old you were, do you see? You were repeating that trauma.

MEREDITH: Oh, okay.

ANGELS: Do you understand how that happens?

MEREDITH: Yeah.

ANGELS: So, instead of thinking, I must be a bad person, it's not that. It's that you're a very good person who experienced something very bad, and that made you do what you had to do to make yourself feel safe. Then you're going to stop judging yourself so harshly, and that is the first thing we want you to stop doing. We're hoping we're going to help you to understand yourself better, so you have more compassion for yourself as well, okay?

MEREDITH: Okay.

ANGELS: That would be good, right?

MEREDITH: Yeah.

ANGELS: In order to love others, you want to love yourself.

MEREDITH: Right.

ANGELS: Now if you can imagine and see and feel how wounded that part of you is, what would happen then is this feeling that something bad—a constant fear that something bad is going to happen, befall you, a feeling that humans somehow can't really be trusted, or at least—even though maybe not all humans but you're never quite sure who the ones are, you know?

MEREDITH: Right.

ANGELS: The other feeling is that it's too painful to love that deeply, because what we want you to understand is that that life began, as we said, quite idyllic, quite innocent. So, the trauma was even more horrifying because it wasn't that you were born into a life of poverty, a life of brutality from a parent or anything. The life started out well, you see, in innocence. To have such a horrible event come out of innocence is the most traumatic thing that a human can endure.

What happens when a human endures such a thing is that there are all these mechanisms and reasons that they shut down. They try to cope with some protection. It's completely understandable that how you are coping today is a direct result of what you experienced yesterday, in a sense, in another life. So, step one, if we're to give it an easy progression for you so you can hold it, step one in your healing is the understanding where you're wounded, okay? We're just starting with step one for you, okay?

MEREDITH: Uh-huh.

ANGELS: Once you understand step one, where you're wounded, step two has to be what? How can I get past the wounding, right?

MEREDITH: Yeah.

ANGELS: We're helping you as quickly and efficiently as possible. But understand that even today, as today is an awakening for you to understand deeply what your wounding is and what will be necessary for you to release the wounding, it does not mean that it will happen in the hour or two that we have today, but it means it will be the beginning of helping you to get there, okay?

MEREDITH: Okay.

ANGELS: You understand that, correct?

MEREDITH: Yeah.

ANGELS: Okay, good. When we start to understand all of the emotional trauma and responses and protections and consciousness, and the fear-based consciousness and the belief systems that would come out of such an event—

and you're not only coming from one life, you have others that are in there as well. We are just picking that most traumatic one.

The second thing that has to happen is the healing of it; and one of the things that needs to be healed is the old quandary, the old universal quandary, "How did God let that happen?" Also anger that you have to return to the earth in another incarnation. It's that you don't want to. You understand that, yes?

MEREDITH: Yes.

ANGELS: You do know that. You can remember that part of you. So, when you feel pushed and your guides tell you, "you have to go back," there has been tremendous resistance and tremendous anger, and you don't get it. You don't want to, and you feel—almost a similar feeling would be of a child who had been pushed out of the nest or that feeling of just abandonment by the parent in a sense. Why are you pushing me back to something so horrible?

One of the things that needs to be healed in you is the understanding of why you are being pushed back on to the earth, because until you can find some value in your experiences here and begin to understand why it is you would be returning here, the anger will make it too difficult for you to learn while you're here because the resentment will block the learning. Do you see how that can happen?

MEREDITH: Uh-huh.

ANGELS: You've seen it in a child, right? When you try to tell a child something and teach them, if they're resenting your authority, they don't learn it.

MEREDITH: Right.

ANGELS: That's kind of how you are with your guides sometimes.

MEREDITH: Oh, wow!

ANGELS: Do you see what we're saying? It's like you're pushing me here and you know what? I'm so pissed at you for putting me here that really, I really don't want to hear what you have to say.

MEREDITH: Oh, that's funny.

ANGELS: Because I've been in—you put me in peril. First of all, we're going to talk for you in your anger state, and that would be from that boy. It would be, "Hey, you know what? How can I trust you again? Look what you did to me! You put me on the earth as a young boy; you put me in innocence, and then what happened? You slaughtered my family and you tortured and traumatized me. Like I'm supposed to trust you guys again?" You see?

MEREDITH: Yeah, that makes sense.

ANGELS: That's still a part of you, and understandable. Your guides are hoping that we will convey to you today that they understand, okay? It's not you against them. So, if you can just remember that there's a couple of big, big metaphysical principles here that might help you a little bit, okay? To help you to move past that place, so you can get on with your life and your learning and drop that resentment and anger and heal that old wound.

Now, one of the big things that you haven't taken into account or you haven't wanted to look at is the realization—and it's not easy—that you yourself did a similar thing to others in one of your previous lives. In other words, it was a karmically-induced situation. For the Higher Self, it doesn't really matter where the karma starts. It's an agreement or it becomes quickly an agreement of souls in a strange energetic way, to create experiences that will teach or will give the soul some kind of knowledge.

Often times what's happened, however, is that once souls get on to the earth, what happens is that the circumstances around them, the amount of fear, the amount of separation from God has traditionally really created some even worse situations than were agreed upon. Now, where this karma came from for you was as a soldier yourself, in a life a long, long time ago. What happened was—you were not yourself a brutal person, a brutal man. You yourself were not. But you got caught up in the acts of brutality that were being done by the others. In other words, you're surrounded by brutality—you take a village by force. Let's help you to understand it in this way. Soldiers come into a village and it happens from Vietnam to Iraq to the Roman Empire to every single possible war.

MEREDITH: Right.

ANGELS: Soldiers come in and they take a village. Some of the soldiers are extremely emotionally wounded. They're very, very wounded. They themselves were brutalized as children. So, this madness and this anarchy have given them a perfect vehicle to release their own anger and fear and rape and so forth, correct? It gives them a chance to work that out.

MEREDITH: Right.

ANGELS: There are others who get caught up in the moment of it, you know, who just go with the guys. There are others—as you were in that situation—who got pushed into brutal behavior. What happened to you—it was very unpleasant. We're going to tell you the exact scenario, okay? What happened is a group of the soldiers you were with go into a home and they raped a woman there, and they forced you to rape her. You did have an erection because you were watching the rape. Your instinct, your animal side couldn't help to have the erection, okay? So, it was stimulated. You did not want to participate. It was a horrible situation for you emotionally. You feel absolutely terrible that you even had the erection and that you were watching. You couldn't walk away or you yourself probably would have been raped or abused by these very—to use a human word—terrible men.

They pushed you and forced you to rape this poor woman. This woman, when you raped her, you looked at her and you saw her face, and it singed your soul. You actually got a lot of self-loathing from that event. It was a terrible situation for you. That woman hated you. You could see why, yeah?

MEREDITH: Yeah.

ANGELS: Because of your guilt, you allowed her to come back many times and do abusive acts to you, because it was as if you paid back that karma over and over many times, and that is not unusual. Guilt draws the energy back over and over and over. In other words, it's common for one act of karmic violence to create far more than one act of retribution. The energy each time gets so much worse with each act.

MEREDITH: Wow!

ANGELS: You could see with each act, more energy chords are given between the two. Very often it will be a revenge karma back and forth that is created through many lifetimes. And sometimes, it will be a guilt-ridden victim that will be victimized over and over. You allowed this woman to act out her rage karmically on you many times, okay? So, that's why it happened to you.

It *didn't* happen to you as a boy because it came from nowhere. It *didn't* happen because God created this horrible situation and your guides were punishing you, okay? It came from this karma and this wounding in you and in this woman, this terrible wounding, and how you carried your own guilt and self-loathing and trauma and kept building upon it in lives, until the point where that life we mentioned as the boy. And what happens? Your heart just shut down. That was it. That's enough. I can't take it anymore. You could see, right?

MEREDITH: Uh-huh.

ANGELS: So, you die, you come into heaven and you say, "I'm not going back there, I can't do this, it hurts too much. If I go back, if you force me to go back, I am never going to experience that again. I am never going to allow myself to feel, to care, to experience, because it has wounded me so many times." In a brief but very intense summary, we are showing you who you are, okay? Are you okay with this? Because we know it's not a pretty story.

MEREDITH: Yeah.

ANGELS: But it resonates, yes?

MEREDITH: Yes.

ANGELS: That place is hard to look at but it will free you, and that's why we do it, okay?

MEREDITH: Right.

ANGELS: We do it to help you, because we want you to understand that today, who you are is just a fraction of the totality of you. If you want to become the Greater You, the parts of you that are holding this fear and this pain just need to be forgiven and released, so you can move past it and it won't haunt you anymore, okay?

MEREDITH: Yes.

ANGELS: Our job is to help you move past it. We agree with you and your guides agree with you, it's time to let that old story go. You don't have to create it anymore. There's no reason for you to be holding in your energy field any of that which might draw it to you. Energy fields are magnetic. You've heard the idea of a law of attraction, you know?

MEREDITH: Yeah.

ANGELS: That's why sometimes people attract things to them that they think they don't want but it's coming from old, what we would call old story, unconscious story.

MEREDITH: Okay.

ANGELS: They are really attracting their fears that they've carried through from old karmas and past lives. The time for you to finish that story is over and we're here to tell you that it's safe for you now to open your heart again and to love because it's okay. You're not the same soul you were. You're much wiser. You have been through the mill, so to speak, and now it's time for you to remember the higher truth of who you are and to integrate into your human body more and more and more of the spiritual self.

What you need to do is to really work through the feeling that you can be safe on the earth and you can be open-hearted, and that there's a way to do that and to be a human, and also to be beautiful, to be spiritual and to love. Because at your heart, that's what you truly want, yes?

MEREDITH: Yes.

ANGELS: That's what you want. But it's hard for you to convince yourself, due to your past lives, that either that's really possible or that it's safe to do it. It hasn't helped you, either, because there's that image that—certainly the whole collective human race carries but certainly many in the western world carry—which is what happened to that being that you consider to be the most open-hearted, loving being, Christ. You say, well, look what happened to him, so prove to me that it's safe here. You're going to have to do some good talking, Angels!

MEREDITH: Right.

ANGELS: Because I'm not seeing it.

MEREDITH: Right.

ANGELS: So, we have a sense of humor with you. We want you to know you have to laugh a little about these things because otherwise, they become so heavy for your heart, it's hard for you to transmute them, you know?

MEREDITH: Okay.

ANGELS: It's a tough place and we're in agreement, it's a tough place. But you're alive today, in this place, at this time, as a human, to participate in what is called the ascension of the human race. You've heard of this time that you're in?

MEREDITH: A little bit.

ANGELS: Do you know that you're in a special time? You are. One of the things that shows to you that it's a special time is that there are so many humans that are awakening to spirituality, that are being given opportunities, such as the one you're being given today, to look past what previously hadn't even been possible for them to look at. Do you know what we're saying?

MEREDITH: Yes.

ANGELS: If this opportunity had not been given to you then you would just be stuck in the body, repeating, as you had for so many lives, all that old karma. You would be wondering, "Why am I here?" and "Boy, this isn't much fun at all." This is a time of awakening and the time of the great clearing or cleansing. All the wounds, either individually or collectively, are being brought up to help you clear them, so that you can begin the next step or stage of human evolution. That next stage or step of human evolution is hooking human beings back up into their divine selves and giving them the mastery to realize that they are co-creators, that they are capable of creating heaven on earth, and that all that painful experience doesn't need to bring you down, if you allow it just to teach you, empower you, you see it as a blessing, you don't resent it, you use it to make you wiser. You step now into the next stage of human development, which is what is called the ascension.

That is really what people are talking about when they talk about the 2012 time, is this idea of ascension. That's how we see it. So you have invited this experience today with us, whether you realize it or not, to pull up the wounding of the past, so that you can see it differently, let go of it, and open your heart and bring in more of your divine self, and teach others how to be safe upon the earth as divine, co-creative beings.

That's a lot, isn't it?

MEREDITH: Yeah, but that's good.

ANGELS: That's good, isn't it?

MEREDITH: Yeah. I'm glad that I'm finding this out because I really didn't know.

ANGELS: It will help liberate you in interesting ways, as you start to feel a little lighter. One of the things we want to teach you as well in Step 2 about how to heal is the idea of forgiveness. Now, you've got to forgive yourself, as we said, for what you did to that woman when you raped her. Because you were more sensitive than the others, you actually even took it harder. Can you see why that would be so?

MEREDITH: Oh, yes, absolutely.

ANGELS: Even if you didn't instigate it, you felt responsible for it. So, you've been carrying the responsibility for all of those soldiers and all of those souls.

MEREDITH: Wow!

ANGELS: You need to forgive yourself. It's okay. You did it. It was a situation human beings have been doing over and over, billions and billions and trillions and gazillions of times, and it's time for the wounding to heal. It's time for the forgiveness to begin. When you forgive yourself and you ask her to forgive you, you break the bonds of karma. That's what Christ taught you when Christ said, "Forgive them, they know not what they do." Christ was teaching the human race that forgiveness is what breaks karma. By his ability to forgive those who wounded him, he broke the bonds of karma instantly and he was able in a sense to ascend and not have to be relegated back to human incarnation cycle. Everything that Christ did, he did to mirror the experiences that you as human beings would have, so that you could learn from his way of experiencing or enduring, and teaching you that you do live again, you rise again, and you can burn even the most horrendous karma with forgiveness and God consciousness and heart.

The reason that that crucifixion was allowed to be an experience for some people is because they needed to understand and learn that even the worst circumstances can be transmuted. If Christ had just lived and lived quietly, a beautiful, peaceful life, he would not have gone down in history the way he did. It was necessary for some human beings who were going to suffer to feel that they weren't suffering alone, that Christ suffered, but that he also—the part that often gets lost is that he was teaching you with his forgiveness of them that you need to forgive yourself and to forgive others so that you can be free and liberated from your karma.

So, Step 2, in order to liberate you and open your heart, is going to be deep forgiveness work. So, each time you get angry at yourself, you will be helping to forgive yourself by saying, "It's okay, I'm just reacting from my old wounding. I'm going to breathe, I'm going to meditate, I'm going to draw up the images of what life that comes from and I'm going to release it and forgive it, so I can step out of the past and move forward." That is what we believe and that is what we teach that is most useful to the human race.

You would be welcome to ask any questions.

MEREDITH: Okay. Since you were just talking about past life—raping a woman—in this life, I often feel totally disgusted with sex, with sexual intercourse, and I've never known why.

ANGELS: And now you do, yes?

MEREDITH: Yeah. I don't have a sex drive. I don't think I do, anyway. I've always considered I'm just different than everybody else. I feel like I'm asexual. First I used to think I was homosexual, since I'm not really attracted to men, but then I wasn't really attracted to women either. I just am not attracted to the sex act, which is very hard to get by in this life.

ANGELS: You could see how that wounding is the answer to your question.

MEREDITH: Yes.

ANGELS: But also, just to let you know, as that small boy, one of the things that happened to your mother was that before she was killed, she was raped. It's deeply woven into the story.

MEREDITH: Okay.

ANGELS: So, rape is the reason—both when you have raped, and you heard and witnessed rape. Sex for you had been very deeply imprinted as a violent act, and it's why you feel that way. As you release these stories and you move past them you start to bring life back into your lower chakras, of course which also hold not only sexuality but the desire to be on the earth, you know?

MEREDITH: Yes.

ANGELS: Once you bring light back there and you start to feel that you're going to come to the earth in a new way and shed the skin of the old, you'll feel a warming taking place. You may not ever be as sexual as some but you'll feel, okay, now I get it. I can let it go. And you'll realize that maybe there are ways that you haven't explored sexuality that can change your mind, once you let go of these old stories. Don't judge yourself; it's okay. We just wanted to let you know that you can see how it's a perfectly logical way to feel, given your karma, yeah?

MEREDITH: Yeah.

ANGELS: Again, that will help you release your self-judgment and it will help you to understand yourself, so you can love and forgive yourself for that as well.

CHAPTER THREE

INDIVIDUAL SOUL KARMA

BRENDA W

#1

(This is the first of three sessions with Brenda)

ANGELS: We have been looking forward to this opportunity to speak with you and we are delighted to be able to converse with you in this way today. As you are aware, the Angel Ariel, the Angel Gabriel and the Angel Michael are with this conduit and have agreed, if you will, to serve through this conduit in this manner, as a link or a guide to assist human beings to find their true heart, their true center, and to help them to understand better how to link or connect their Higher Selves to their physical selves, how to bridge, if you will, the divine to the physical, so that so much disharmony and so much insecurity and fear does not run so rampant upon this earthly plane.

Speaking with you at this time is primarily the Angel Ariel, although Gabriel is also lending energy. We are delighted, as you had been informed, to work with you and to speak with you about the idea of trust and how it links to faith and how that links to the concept of surrender. We are aware that you understand that these ideas of trust, faith and surrender are interwoven, interlinked, and you are aware that there is a different template involved when discussing them as human or physical experiences and when discussing them as divine or spiritual experiences.

When a human being has difficulty with these concepts it is because they are confused—through past life karma or experiences and also present life ones—as to how to work with these concepts in the human framework and also how to work with these concepts in the spiritual framework. Often they try to apply either the same lack of trust to a spiritual experience or they try to apply surrender of spirit to the physical, and they find that the same rules in the physical and the spiritual plane cannot be applied. Then they get hurt or disappointed or betrayed through the incorrect application of these words or these concepts, trying to apply them equally in both realms, physical and spiritual.

We had given this conduit an image to work with you on, which is the idea we wanted to discuss with you about a tightrope or a tightrope walker. Now, one who works in this arena, this area of getting up on to a wire and walking it without a net appears to other humans sometimes as foolish. Why would someone do such a foolish exercise in trust or faith? Sometimes some interpret this as extremely brave and others see it with a more calculated eye, that this being is so well-practiced in areas or arenas where they were safe that they aren't taking such a risk at all.

To some extent, all of these are true; all of these interpretations of the act of faith and the act of trust are involved in tightrope walking. They are all true. But what we want to begin with is this concept or this idea of practice. First of all, we're going to divide our work today with you on the physical/human level first and then we will be speaking of these same concepts for you on the spiritual level.

The human/physical level has been for human beings an area where you have had to refine and to practice and to learn where to place your trust. Early on in the soul's growth, the experience of placing trust incorrectly, of trusting naively would be the idea of one just trying to walk a tightrope fifty feet up, never having done it previously, never having practiced. Often what happens in the earliest incarnations of course is that because the soul doesn't even know the concept or the idea of falling, or what will happen to it, it goes out on the wire and it trusts without a net, without practice, without caution, and gets pretty banged up, pretty bruised up.

Through a soul's journey, through what we call the infant and baby soul, and even the young soul experiences, is that those bruises, those knocks, those pains to the heart and the mind and the physical body start to make one very cautious. Often one decides, if we are to continue with our analogy, "Well, I'm not going to even go out on that rope again, I'm not going to go on the tightrope because I feel that it's just going to hurt me, it's just going to hurt me."

Because one has been so damaged, so hurt, one goes into withdrawal, then what happens is there is a sense of severe loneliness and isolation which occurs to the human, and its soul and its heart becomes mistrusting but ultimately extremely lonely. After perhaps a few lives where this cynicism or loneliness has manifested, the soul then decides that doesn't work, either. And after a great deal of pain in that arena, the soul decides that perhaps what it needs to do is be a little wiser and a little more cautious with trusting but perhaps withdrawing and becoming cynical about all humans or about religion or God, perhaps that isn't the way to go. Perhaps there's another way to walk this tightrope of trust and faith and to do it carefully and cautiously and with a great deal of foresight and practice.

All those times that you have been hurt and bopped around, fallen off the rope and fallen down and harmed yourself or been harmed by others, have led you, we hope, to become an expert as you step out on to that rope, knowing exactly, without looking, how to place each foot, cautiously, with a sensitivity that is coming from deep within the heart. You'll notice that the tightrope walker does not look at the wire, does not look directly down at their feet, for if they did, they would fall.

Instead they work with a combination of a heart-centered consciousness, a high spiritual and kinesthetic consciousness, and their gaze is outward, outward, far ahead of the Self. It is with that that they are able to slowly and carefully and cautiously work their way across the wire. This is a good way to summarize quickly the way to discuss your soul's journey. We're talking of course about many lives that we're summing up in a little ten or fifteen minute discussion. But it is a way for us to talk to you and summarize quickly and succinctly the idea of where you are, we believe, and how and why you got there. Ultimately the Master then does not even touch the rope. That is when we will get to the spiritual side of the equation; but let us stick with the physical side and what it is that has happened to you.

As you probably have realized about yourself, deep down, buried inside of you is a very, very sensitive, good and trusting soul. You are aware of this, yes? You know this about yourself; that this is truth for you, yes?

BRENDA: Yes.

ANGELS: We believe you can imagine that in your earlier incarnations you were a very eager and trusting soul who was so excited to be walking that rope without practicing enough. You were trusting humans without looking more deeply into the situation and believing in them perhaps too quickly. Yes, you understand that that might be so?

BRENDA: Yes.

ANGELS: What we are going to say is that the heart of your wounding would be summarized by a word called betrayal. The betrayal comes from putting trust in one who you feel did not live up to or return the trust in a way that it should have been returned.

You also expected a lot of other people. Your expectations were very high. Let us give an example, one that really did wound you in your death. You died with a situation—let's give you this image: You're a male and you are on a battlefield. You are wounded and your dear friend, your comrade and soldier is next to you.

He has said, as he has seen you wounded, "Stay here, I will return for you; don't worry. I will come back and I will get you." He did not return. He ran away and you did not know what happened. You did not know if he had been killed, you did not know for certain, but you sensed that he had gotten afraid, that he had run away and left you there, and left you there to die a slow and painful death. That in many ways is a good summary, this feeling that you were let down by this friend of yours, this comrade. You thought, as you died slowly, 'Did he abandon me? Did he himself feel afraid? Did he die, did he get killed, and why has he abandoned me? Perhaps he was just lying to me.'

If you could see how your mind went through all these different scenarios. You see that idea? You can see how today, you do a similar thing, yes? You have many scenarios that you like to sift through. You understand what we're saying, yes?

BRENDA: Yes.

ANGELS: That's not unusual for you, this idea of scenarios and trying to figure out. Had your friend been killed and he couldn't come back or had he just forgotten about you? It still wounded you in your heart as a sense of betrayal.

Often, these scenarios, these thoughts have happened after the betrayal. Often, you have beat yourself up, not so much in the one we're talking about but other lives, you kind of beat yourself up. You said to yourself, "Why didn't I see this earlier, why didn't I think about this?" This is kind of what we would call a little karmic patterning for you. You go through all these scenarios. Why did I trust him and so forth? But in your earlier lives, rarely did you question others beforehand—you trusted blindly and then you were hurt.

Let us give you another example: It was quite easy in your earliest incarnations as a female to be talked into things with flattery. That was a way that often you found yourself in not a very good situation. For example, if a man wanted to seduce you and even do so without your consent, what humans call rape or take you without your consent, he would often use flattery first. This is, of course, a time-worn tradition on this planet. But it worked with you quite often. In other words, you didn't have enough of a sense that perhaps first of all, it wasn't sincere, and second of all, you were hungry enough for the flattery that it took you away. It did, in fact, when you were a female body, get you in a number of situations that you regretted, where you allowed a young man to flatter you to his own ends, and once having gotten what he wanted, to abandon you.

It also was a difficult situation for you in a previous life, where you left your own family. The marriage was against what your family wanted for you. You believed this young man when he told you of his love and said that he would be by your side forever. You even turned your back on your own family because you said, "I love him. Father, even if you do not like him, he is going to be my husband and I will go with him." Unfortunately, that did not turn out so well for you. You traveled away with him, but at one point he actually abandoned you and left you at a seaport and went off with another woman, leaving you there. And unfortunately, you turned to prostitution to survive.

So, you have had a number of cuts and bruises, if you will, to the heart through your many lives. You came from those earlier cuts and bruises, and then in later lives you become a little hard-hearted, a little more cynical. You can understand that side, too, at times, how that's easy to waiver into. You see what we're saying, yes?

BRENDA: Yes.

ANGELS: After being hurt, it is going to be quite common for the soul, the human then to incarnate with the opposite feeling. You became a little hard-hearted. Your mental recorder plays the theme: "Well, you can't trust humans. You see, you can't trust them." You actually got pretty wealthy in your lives when you did this. You became a wealthy merchant in one life because in that life, you went at every single person who was dealing with you with the idea, "I'm going to outsmart them. I am going to get them before they get me." It did lead you to a fairly successful career, if you will, but of course, the heart was quite lonely again.

So, what we sense is that in order for you to get to the point you long for, which is to have a comfortable heart, to be at peace, you need to be stop wavering between one extreme or the other. You're in a quandary because you're wondering: can it be possible for a human being to be on this planet and make themselves vulnerable enough to trust another human and not suffer the consequences of abandonment or a broken heart?

We're going to just stop here for a moment and we're going to ask you if you understand our message so far and perhaps might have a comment about what we have imparted to you.

BRENDA: I think I understand. I would say that the kind of betrayal and the kind of neediness, you know, not necessarily feeling my own worth. I do understand.

ANGELS: It is fine for you to say this and we would suggest—we're going to put it this way: We would love to see you have more self-assurance. You see that idea? Not just your own worth but self-assurance, that when you say something or when you believe something or when you feel something, that you will trust it in yourself that you have the wisdom to make a correct choice.

Now, you can see where all these earlier lives we showed you, you see, would weaken that. You see that?

BRENDA: Absolutely.

ANGELS: Well, you say, "Boy, I really didn't know how to pick 'em." You know that idea?

BRENDA: Right.

ANGELS: When we mentioned that you then had to become a prostitute—that was a very painful life for you. We would say one of your most painful lives: the betrayal, the loss of the family, the betrayal of the loved one leaving you, and then turning to prostitution. From this place you sank even deeper into the idea that men are not to be trusted. Then that moved to: human beings are not to be trusted because you saw the women you associated with turn on one another. It wasn't even a male issue for you. It became a human issue for you. But, deeper inside, it even became an issue for your own self-assurance or trusting yourself.

When you say something, go ahead and stand up for it, stick up for it and let it sit and don't back down from it quite so quickly because you've done a lot of lifetimes and you've gained a lot of wisdom from those, but you need to apply the wisdom without doubting it or being afraid. We're going to put it this way: You've earned it, okay?

BRENDA: Okay.

ANGELS: You've earned your wisdom. Yes, perhaps maybe when we were looking back at these other lives we talked about, where you were more of a baby soul, we might say, "Well, you hadn't quite earned your wisdom yet." But at this point, it's not that you haven't had the experiences of the soul, but instead you haven't allowed them to guide you because you don't believe in your own ability to utilize them wisely and to stick up for yourself, you see.

BRENDA: Yes, I do. I see that. I see how in some ways, there have been a few experiences in this lifetime that, as I've gone back to look at, have mimicked that betrayal, that sexual betrayal, that feeling of not trusting myself and knowing what happened and therefore, certainly not trusting anyone else with that information but letting me continue to knock myself down and telling myself that I can't trust what I've seen, I can't trust what I feel, I can't trust what I've experienced.

ANGELS: Yes, and you can see by just the few examples we gave you of your previous lives, how they mimic so clearly your current one.

BRENDA: Yes.

ANGELS: What's happening is that you're not letting the wisdom you've gained change you today, you see? In a sense, you're still re-experiencing but you don't need to anymore. Do you see what we're saying?

BRENDA: Yeah, okay.

ANGELS: It's like you've already taken those steps on the tightrope. You know that section of the rope by heart. Your feet can walk that very clearly, but you don't believe that you can. You don't believe that you know enough, and we're trying to let you know that you do.

The other thing that we want to address is that you're also extremely hard on yourself, not only during the life where you suffered the betrayal but you tend to beat yourself up after death; in between lives. It's very hard sometimes in the astral plane or the Bardo—or whatever word you want to use for after death—for your guides to reach you and to work with you initially because even there, you have trouble and you feel, "Oh, I messed up so badly. Look what I did! I'm so sorry!"

This is because your heart is so good. You've always wanted to make good for the world and have a good life. In the beginning, you had such simple desires. I only want to have a nice husband, you see, a nice family, a good life, and look what I did! So, you would blame yourself, you see. Even in the life we spoke about where you left your family and went with your lover, you didn't know where to stop blaming yourself. First of all, you blamed yourself for leaving your family. Second of all, you blamed yourself for choosing what you considered a poor lover, and then you blamed yourself for the act of prostitution. You died with so much guilt. It was difficult for your guides to reach you, you see, and help you heal some of that wounding.

It's important for you to understand that and re-touch the pure heart within you. We need you to kind of re-touch that and return to that part of yourself. Yes, you got a little bruised and bumped and people did take advantage of your naïveté and your simple goodness. But that goodness was good and that goodness is a good part of you. Let's remember to let that come back out. Let that shine. Let that heart be alive again.

Now you have the wisdom to know that you don't have to give your heart away to everyone, you see. You can love everyone as a "Christed being" would, as a being of Light would; but that does not mean that you give them power over you. You can see where we're going: In your mind you had interwoven the ideas of love and power. Surrendering to love meant giving up your power.

So, you can love with this good heart but at the same time, you can maintain and keep intact your own power center, your own sense of self. You do not give yourself away to love another, you allow God to love through you. If that being who is opposite you loves equally, with respect and without the neediness and the surrendering of power, then you are in a healthy, equal relationship, where love is returned equally and given equally, and there is no issue that you will feel afraid because you have not surrendered your personal power and you have not equated giving your heart to someone as giving it away and surrendering and making yourself weak or vulnerable.

We feel that you're beginning to understand, as if a light bulb is going off inside of you: I think I might do that. When I love, I might think it means that I have to give it all away or surrender, and this is not so. This is what we're hoping you'll be able to work on and change, so that you can truly let love flow through you, not from you in the way that you give yourself away, but through you, as God loves through you to the world. As God loves through you to the world, those who also love in the same manner, without these human power plays, will be attracted to you and will want to return love, and the power issues will dissipate or subside, for they won't be intact. You won't love from your power chakra, in a sense. You won't be surrendering and weakening yourself, either.

Do you understand what we're saying?

BRENDA: I do understand.

ANGELS: It's a matter of your being conscious when you give your love to another. You realize that your Higher Self must direct it, that your God Self loves all beings. Your God Self loves all beings equally. Your God Self will not ask you to weaken yourself in any way to love. This will allow you to have the open heart, so you won't be the cynical merchant that you had become, but it will allow you to love without pain, so you won't become the broken-hearted prostitute. Somewhere between that broken-hearted prostitute and that cynical merchant lies the ascended you; and that ascended you is the one who can love without it being about you but about it being God. This is actually going to take us into our next part of the discussion. We're going to stop for a moment because our next part is about the spiritual and how that got mixed up for you.

Let us, just for a moment, before we forget this train of thought, go to the next part of the equation. Well, how does trust, faith and surrender work with God, you see? How does that work with God? You have worked on that in other lives as well. It's a difficult one for the human because often, the idea of trusting, having faith and then surrendering to a human leads to pain, as we have shown you, and so it's hard for human beings to think that trust and then having faith and surrendering to God is not something which would require pain, you see?

Now, you had a life in a convent, okay? It was there that you tried to find a way to love with an open heart—it was your soul's choice to do this because throughout many of your lives men had hurt you so much and you had surrendered in love and been flattered. You found love painful so it was then a choice for you to try the life in a convent, which you can see would make sense for your soul. You thought, "Well, I want to still have my goodness intact but I'm going to try a safer route." So, when you chose to incarnate and have a life as a nun you thought that was going to be safer for you.

What happened were two things: One was there was a "coldness" about that life that was very upsetting to you. It felt to you that everything was done almost very coldly, you didn't feel that the hearts of many of the Sisters were very open. Now, you can look objectively and see why perhaps their karma led them to choose a convent for similar reasons that you had. It felt safer for them after lives of difficulty. But you wanted to trust and you wanted to be open, and you thought that if you eliminated the male factor, perhaps it would be safe to do that and to love God and to be in a community of women.

But what happened was there was a lot of fear, a lot of fear that you felt. You got afraid after a while in that life. You were so sweet, and you had that kind of trusting nature there. But your words would be scolded, you would be told you weren't perhaps loving Christ correctly or loving God correctly or doing things correctly. You always struggled with this feeling that you—I'm just not doing it right, I need to do it better. "I'll be more pious, I'll be better, I'll say these things better, I'll keep my mouth shut and I won't be so foolish."

Although you weren't concerned with giving your heart away to a male, it was there that you wrestled with: "Does God love me?" The others told you, "No, because you're not doing it right, God doesn't love you." You wanted God to love you, so you tried to do it better and right, but they never gave you the peace you were looking for in your heart. It wasn't a place of unconditional love, it wasn't a place of feeling free to just open your heart and be a loving being that you had hoped it would provide, and it didn't really do much to help you open your heart.

In many ways it did weaken you further because when you died in that life, you felt again that perhaps you weren't good enough. You didn't do it enough and you didn't do it well enough, and your guides were trying—your angels and your guides were trying so hard to reassure you and to open you up. You did surrender to them and you did allow yourself to be comforted in between lives before returning, but it still did not do what you had hoped it would do. You had hoped it would allow you to have an open heart on the earth without so much pain, but it did not work.

It was there in the next life that you started to think, "Well, forget it, I'm going to just start not trusting so much or I'm going to try to have to be cautious and learn how to read other people," and it started you on that path. That really did lead to quite a bit of loneliness, even to the point where, by the end, as a male, you wouldn't even want to be married. It was just about the money making and being a merchant and so forth. As we said, these are the two extremes.

So, how do you, someone who has been so wounded in the areas of trust and faith and surrender, as we said—how do you come to a place where you can really surrender to God? You know, how do you feel that you can do this and come to this trust and this faith? Okay, I'm going to just walk that tightrope, knowing that God is going to take care of me. What does that mean, when you hear people talk about that? You hear them talking about "Let go and let God." And you wonder—you like the idea but you're not quite sure you know how to do it.

Do you understand what we're saying?

BRENDA: Absolutely, absolutely. Thank you, absolutely.

ANGELS: Now we're on what we're calling the spiritual template. We're trying to help you hold all this information. We're giving you quite a bit, as you can see, in a short period of time, but we think we're doing a pretty good job of organizing it for you.

BRENDA: You are.

ANGELS: You're in the spiritual template now, "Let go and let God." Well, it's very hard for you to believe that there's a way to do this, that there can be a way. The first thing we want you to recognize and to understand is, first of all, let's get rid of any concept of God as mortal, okay, or as human or as having a human body or as being in any way a big man or a big woman or in any way having any human attributes. Let's strike that from your mind, okay?

BRENDA: Okay.

ANGELS: Do you think you can do that?

BRENDA: Yes, I can.

ANGELS: Okay, let's get that out of there. Let's instead define God as a flow of energy which leads all things, when unimpeded, to the perfect outcome. A flow of energy which leads all things, when unimpeded, to the perfect outcome, okay? Like a river without dams, okay?

BRENDA: Alright.

ANGELS: Now when people say, "Let go and let God," they're talking about—if it's going to work correctly, they're talking about a pure consciousness of perfection, of love and perfection that when not messed with, with human fear, will make perfect, synchronistic moments, will create the flow and synchronicity.

If it's a man or woman it gets into all sorts of messy areas, and it starts having too much religion and good and evil and punishment and who knows what else connected. So, we strike that from your mind and we replace it with: *A perfect flow of energy that you ride in synchronistic perfection to the perfect outcome.*

Now, what are going to be the things that block it and dam it up? What blocks the flow of God's perfect consciousness are accumulated fears that you've collected over your lifetimes that keep you from surrendering, from trusting. So now, how do you listen, you're asking, to the voice of God? How do you hear the voice of God to know it's God and not some lesser energy or some "dumb human" leading you the wrong way, you see? You see that issue in you?

BRENDA: Yes.

ANGELS: You've forgotten, in a way, how to listen with your intuitive and your heart center, and then when you do hear it, you second-guess. You don't trust yourself. Again, a block is created, you see? So, it's about, first of all, knowing and believing that there's this energy that's going to flow through you and lead you to exactly where you need to go. Now, we're going to give you something kind of concrete, and that is this: When you're on the flow of the energy, your physical, human body will feel differently than when you're off the flow, okay? That's one way to know you're on the flow and you're letting God guide your life, okay?

BRENDA: Okay.

ANGELS: Or Source or Chi or the Great Central Sun or whatever you need to call it. Your body, when in harmony with this energy, feels peaceful, receives messages, gets tingles, gets joyful. The heart gets very full, and there's a sense, a knowing in the crown chakra of perfection and rightness.

Now, let's say to give an example. We'll give a simple example. Let's say a situation has been presented to a human and the situation is—okay, we're going to make it simple. "I've been offered a job in Chicago; should I take this?" On one level, the human is debating with its mental facilities. They might think, 'Well, I'll be closer to my family, and it's more in line with what I want to do, so there's the plus. On the negative side, I won't make as much money, it might not be as secure, I'm not sure I like the idea of living in the Midwest and leaving my friends.' Then you look at this and you debate it with your mental, and you ping-pong back and forth and back and forth and back and forth, and you drive yourself insane, because you cannot answer the question that way.

There's only one way to answer it:

If the question is a human asking about a move or job change such as this, they imagine first themselves moving in that direction; feeling the energy flowing toward that. In this case, our example would be Chicago. The energy has moved itself there, and they feel themselves there, and they feel to see if their body feels fully relaxed and loose in that place. Then they go back to where they are and they feel what their body feels like, and they're going to get an image or feeling that it's tight there, it's tense. Hmm, the energy seems to be flowing towards Chicago.

Then they say to themselves: 'I'm not going. How does that feel? I don't take this opportunity. That opportunity is out there and it's let go of. I let it go and it will never return.' Immediately, the human being will have a reaction in their body. There will be something that feels bad, in the example we're using, that they're going to feel, uh-oh, there's a part of me that has a sense of feeling fear and regret or I didn't take something and now it's passed me by. Then they go back to the flow of the energy in that direction and they feel that it's flowing smoothly, and they say, "Okay, I feel the energy flowing me there, I know that God is saying to me, I need to be there, for whatever reason. I may not know all the reasons. There are people I need to meet out there, there are experiences I need to have, and I'm going to go there and I'm going to take them, and I'm not going to debate it anymore. I'm going to follow it." Then that's where you go.

Once you've made that choice, you feel that all of a sudden, the energy is correct. It's like the dams of energy open up and everything just starts moving. If it starts moving easily and flowing you there, you know you are on the way. If you had stuck there and debated and second-guessed and doubted, you would have never come up with a suitable answer or you may have acted out of fear, thinking I'm afraid to move, it feels so secure here, and staying, always with that gut aching inside that maybe you did the wrong thing but maybe not but maybe you did. You see?

So, trust the physical experiences to lead you, the sensations. Learn to read them, feel them, and do a similar exercise. The choices are being guided by energy flow, by the heart, by where you feel peaceful, where things are moving, you see, and let your mental body relax a little bit. Does this assist you?

BRENDA: Yes, it does.

FACING THE SPIRITUAL JOURNEY

BRENDA W.

#2

BRENDA: I have the opportunity to go on a spiritual journey and fear is completely—is a very strong component—and I am feeling the mental battle back and forth, back and forth. That's so much how I handle or deal with or do a lot of things. I get in my head and I battle it back and forth, for a variety of reasons. It makes it very difficult—I appreciate the sense of feeling that I don't—that in the past lives, I have not let my guides help me. I feel so very much like that now, that I block myself. I block—I do beat myself up, I don't trust myself...

ANGELS: We need to interrupt for one second...

BRENDA: Sure.

ANGELS: Because we'll lose the idea and we won't be connected to the correct point you're making. Then we'll let you continue. Now, the reason is because of martyrs, okay? You equated—we don't even need to go further than the one we've already pointed out, your life in that convent, okay?

BRENDA: Okay.

ANGELS: What did the martyrs do? They let God guide them and boy, they ended up boiled in oil, burned and crucified, you see? We want to let you know that's in you, okay? That's in you. So what's happening, you say? I'm going on a spiritual journey and if God guides me, what am I going to end up in? I'll be burned at the stake, I'll be boiled in oil or I'll be crucified, you see? That's the fear, okay? You see? We want to make you understand that there is a past life working here, okay?

BRENDA: Okay.

ANGELS: With the idea of, often times, when humans have gone on spiritual quests and journeys, the crusades, the Cathars, who were all burned, you know, at the stake and so forth and martyred, yes? Well, what happens to those poor souls, you see? They don't end up very beloved. They end up often punished for their quest, okay?

BRENDA: Okay.

ANGELS: What fear is coming up for you is just that, okay?

BRENDA: Okay. I'm thinking that my fear—I take my fear to, oh, I have to get in an airplane and I don't think I like to fly. It doesn't matter. A fear is a fear.

ANGELS: Well, yes, because it's the idea of course of trust and faith to be in that airplane.

BRENDA: Yes.

ANGELS: It's also the idea that, for you, this concept of going on a spiritual journey is very hard because it means really surrendering and opening one's heart, yes?

BRENDA: Yes, yes, yes.

ANGELS: So, that's very hard for you and you're afraid that you're going to not only get hurt emotionally but there's some fear also, as we mentioned, of where does that leave me? I haven't seen many good examples of people doing spiritual quests and ending up happier at the end of it. We're trying to make light of it so that you don't get so serious about it.

BRENDA: Okay.

ANGELS: By the way, it's okay. They're not after you this time around.

BRENDA: Okay.

ANGELS: Now, what we want to say and we want you to understand that the other thing that we need to talk about is the fear of death. We need to talk a little about death, and we think this will help you as well, okay?

BRENDA: Okay.

ANGELS: So, let's go on to the talking then, if you don't mind, of death, and we're going to ask you what happens when you die? What happens? You don't know what happens when you die, what's going to happen?

BRENDA: I don't know.

ANGELS: You do know but yeah, again, you're a little—you need a little more trust of what you're going to say. Rather than, I don't know, just go ahead and say anything. It's okay. What do you think maybe will happen?

BRENDA: I think that, you know, I will leave my body and I will go to the next level, wherever that is, wherever I'm supposed to go or do or be. I don't think about it. I think I work very hard not to think about it.

ANGELS: It's kind of like the old walking around the elephant in the middle of the living room.

BRENDA: Absolutely. Yes, absolutely. I don't—but I believe that it has—it is a question there for me. It is there, it has been there, and exactly that. I don't—it's a fear, it's an unknown. So I kind of just avoid it, but I let the fear of it impede my life.

ANGELS: What you're telling us—we want you to hear this—is that you're not particularly comfortable with being alive and you're not comfortable with being dead. So, there's no place that you've felt that's comfortable for you, okay?

BRENDA: Okay.

ANGELS: We want to address this because what we want more than anything for you is for you to feel safe, to feel self-assured and comfortable, okay?

BRENDA: Okay.

ANGELS: Death is a topic we knew we had to get around to sooner or later with you because it is the thing that you can't avoid and you should not be afraid of. In fact, the only thing to be afraid of with death is your own fear of it, because if you can begin your spiritual practices with what we had talked about, with an idea of coming into comfort with allowing the Light to flow through you, coming into comfort with allowing yourself to be connected to something greater than what you are—and realize that that energy, that force is guiding you, is guiding your lives, instead of your fear or your ego or so forth—by ego, of course, we don't mean it as being arrogant. You know that.

When you realize that there is this benevolent, beautiful Source of all that feeds this realm, this angelic realm, and that feeds all realms, you begin to realize that whether you're alive or whether you're dead, it is not that big a step, it is not that big a difference. In other words, it's really just a very small shift in the soul, in the energy. It's quite interesting.

We understand that many humans see it as a chasm. It is not. It is really a feeling that you will have of great liberation. It's as if suddenly, the energy of you which is so enormous and free and open has been cramped into this little body of this fear-based consciousness and so forth, and is liberated. At that shift, at that moment of liberation, the trickiest part is that next part for souls. That is what they create instantly at that moment of liberation. If they feel in that liberation, they feel themselves to be what you would call lost or there are fearful thoughts—if immediately, there's a thought that goes, uh-oh, I'm going to hell, then because it's pure consciousness, there's this feeling that all of a sudden, the consciousness can create something darker.

The idea is that if you, in your human body, are sure of your connection to All That Is, and if you, in your human body, are peaceful regardless of where you are, then the shift is relatively simple. All you do is feel this great liberation and you know you're Home. You know you're Home and you feel the Home. The minute you think and say to yourself, "I've come Home," you start to see and feel presence of the Light, of the energy of those who are dear to you, and you are welcomed by them. You realize and you remember quite quickly that this is where you belong, that this is the truth, and that where you've been, called the physical plane, is a short stay, a temporary stay.

The fear of looking at death as a chasm is quite incorrect. It will be a very easy shift, a shift of consciousness from what has been a blocked, closed and fear-based human consciousness to being more liberated. You'll immediately remember, "Oh, this is who I really am," and it will feel good. It will feel quite good to you.

You shouldn't be feeling that death is some huge thing. As you know, you have died many times. From our perspective, it isn't really death; it's a shift of consciousness. We view it as the soul says, "I'm going to shift into a denser form and now I'm going to shift out of that dense form, into a less dense or higher dimensional form." Then it says, "Oh, I think I'll go back and shift into a more dense form, called human." It's just consciousness shifting and playing back and forth.

It isn't even, from your soul's highest perspective, such a big deal. It really isn't. It is similar to when you shift from say, fifth dimensional consciousness to try your hand at sixth dimensional consciousness. It's really a shift of consciousness. It's the idea that you are creating a bigger deal about this thing you've labeled death than your soul believes it to be. At the moment of death, your soul will know its Home quite quickly and there's nothing to be afraid of. In fact, many older souls look forward to it. They're longing for the return because they feel so uncomfortable on the earth and they know the liberation of the soul from the human form. It's something that they are looking forward to and welcome when their time on the earth is at an end.

Now, let's tackle the idea of moving on a spiritual quest. If you are on a spiritual quest and you die during your spiritual quest, then it was in fact a choice you made. God doesn't "pull the string first." The human in alignment with the Higher Self "pulls the string" and God agrees, if you will. First of all, God is not coming down and just sucking you off the earth plane whenever He/She feels like it. That's not what's happening, so you don't need to be afraid of that. If you die while on a spiritual quest, if for some reason, your fear that the plane goes down and you die or your fear that you contract a strange disease and you die, or your fear that you get mugged or in some way, somebody harms you, or you get abandoned at that seaport and you die and so forth, if those were to come about, it would be because that was the perfect moment for your liberation—not that it would be a bad thing.

Now, you must understand that it is true that in your earlier incarnations, you created unconsciously. You allowed your human, your ego, as all humans do—it's not just you, it's absolutely universal. Every single human moves through this in their early incarnations. Their fears have dictated their choices and they've learned from that, but you're not there now. You're not there. You're old enough now and wise enough as a soul, you've gone through enough incarnations that you should have more faith in yourself and know that you will not be making or creating bad things for yourself any longer, for it's time for you now to really learn how to create happiness. You're trying to teach yourself from the higher perspective how to create happiness and trust happiness to exist, and you're trying to learn to do it by understanding to let God flow through you and let that energy flow through you and guide you wherever it will go. You know that ultimately it will lead you to happiness; and that anything that you cling to or you try to manipulate or control will lead you to unhappiness.

So, go on your spiritual journey knowing that you have chosen it from the level of your soul. Let it go and say, "I trust you, God, for I know I cannot be anywhere that I am not meant to be, for I have surrendered myself to your energy, to the flow of my higher soul, my higher purpose. My Higher Self is now my guide. When I am working with my Higher Self, everything will conspire to create my happiness and to move me into a higher, more fulfilling life and spirituality."

We suggest that you learn to operate that way, and we know that once you do and liberate yourself from what we're calling the mental ping-pong game, you're going to be a much happier person on this earth. Once you remind yourself that it's just a shift of consciousness, it's not a big deal to die, you'll be happier on the earth as well, because you won't have to fear that great monster at the end of the road. Has this assisted you?

BRENDA: Oh, yes, absolutely, most definitely.

ANGELS: Well, we were hoping we could work with these issues because we feel very strongly that it's time for your happiness, as we believe you do as well, yes?

BRENDA: Yes.

ANGELS: You realize that you need to go to the next level, yes?

BRENDA: Yes.

ANGELS: Yet you haven't quite known what it was and still had the ingrained, old patterning from your previous lives that you still were operating from. Let's just help you. Why don't you imagine, on your right side of your body are all your past lives. Just see them to the right side of you. Kind of bless them, know they taught you well, you gained wisdom there, but you're not a baby soul anymore, you know? You're not that young soul anymore. Push them to the side a little bit. Say, "I honor you, you've given me my wisdom, but I no longer will be operating from those fears."

Then to your left side, see an open, bright light, an open horizon of possibility, and start to envision yourself walking into that light of possibilities, infinite possibilities, because you're stepping into fifth dimensional consciousness. You're hoping to move into that, where everything that you desire will be fulfilled because you will desire as God desires for you, as your Highest Self desires for you. The flow is flowing you into happiness, flowing you into infinite possibility and flowing you into joy.

Feel, yes, those lives: "I honor them but they're not my baggage anymore." I don't have to carry them on my back as I go into this Light. I carry only the wisdom but I release and let go of the pain. Keep the wisdom, let go of the pain. Each time you feel those old fears coming up, remember this exercise. Let go of that and feel like they're behind you. We do not tell you to let go of the wisdom. What makes you who you are must be honored. You can let go of the pain and maintain the wisdom and see that beautiful, glorious Light and that horizon shining out before you as you walk and you learn to live in fifth dimensional consciousness, which is a heaven consciousness, a consciousness of no polarity, no bad or good, but merely following the flow of God through you, the flow of the Source, the flow of the Chi through you, toward God-given grace gracing you at every moment, bringing you the experiences that you need to grow in peace and harmony and love and wisdom. That is our blessing and our prayer for you.

INTEGRATING THE SPIRITUAL JOURNEY

BRENDA W.

#3

ANGELS: It is with great gratitude, as always, that we have this opportunity to speak with you and to work with you in this way. This is the Archangel Ariel who is speaking with you, and Gabriel and Michael are also in attendance. We are delighted to work with you and to share with you your transformation, as you are aware that you have experienced. But the transformation you have experienced is even greater than you are consciously aware of. In your transformation, you have also—we're going to just begin it this way—added some tasks. You have given yourself some added tasks or gifts. Perhaps gifts is a better word to describe what you have given yourself.

These gifts of awakening and awareness contribute energetically to Mother Earth and her ascension and the awakening of humankind; and you have found yourself aware that your own abilities, your own willingness to confront your fears, particularly your feelings of unworthiness and your feelings of trusting, are a part of these gifts. You understand that once you know that you deserve to be cared for, once you know that you deserve to be held in the energetic field or consciousness of God—then you can relax. It is then that surrender is not frightening but comforting.

So, the transformation of fear with the concept of surrender to comfort has been a major accomplishment for you and is also the first step for the next accomplishments that will come. In other words, we tell you that without the transformation that surrender means comfort rather than fear, the rest of the gifts could not awaken. You understand this, yes?

BRENDA: Yes.

ANGELS: We are pleased to see that you are awakening the rest of your gifts. You understand that where you had thought that something happens "to you," you are now beginning to understand that something happens "with you." It is actually happening to support you and to give you what it is that you most desire and require.

We are delighted to see that you are willing, from our perspective, to take your first steps to accepting the gifts without fear that God/Goddess offers you; that the Universe, the Source has to offer. Once you decided to accept those gifts you start to get on what some feel is a fast train. Sometimes it feels a bit overwhelming and the gifts come fast and furious, and the challenges come fast and furious. Sometimes the human desires to just "crawl into a hole." You might think, Wow, this is a lot for me to handle. But you understand now that nothing would be given to you that wasn't appropriate or exactly what you need for your soul's growth, and so you can let go and not feel so fearful.

So, a new relationship has been created in your consciousness—between you and God. It is because of this that you feel more peace and ready to accept the gifts that will be flowing your way. We congratulate you for that transformation. Would you like at this time to make some comment about our opening statement?

BRENDA: I'm ready. I felt that there was a great shift as well for me. I'm beginning to look past what I have always thought of as who I was and what I could do and usually limiting myself, for whatever the reason was. I just really tried, during this time, to be open to receive whatever it was that I was meant to receive, and to not push away, as I have been known to do, or let fear keep me frozen. So, I'm very excited by what you're sharing with me, as I was incredibly excited and grateful when I was in Teotihuacán.

ANGELS: Let us talk specifically about what these gifts are that you have received, and we're going to tell you that you have received gifts from the Ascended Masters. You have also received gifts from what some humans would call the Space Brotherhood. And you have received gifts, as you are well aware, from some of what humans call the Earth Deities. And some of your abilities to create links between these different realms have been awoken. What you are beginning to understand is that you can serve, in a sense, as an anchor, if you will, for some of these energies, some of these wisdoms. There are many gifts that will begin awakening as you fulfill your destiny.

We want to ask you what you think you have received from the Ascended Masters, to begin, and we will tell you how we view the gift you received from them.

BRENDA: I think the gift—one of the gifts that I have received from the Ascended Masters, I felt was that I had a sense of knowing. Actually, one of the teachers on this journey said to me that I was a healer, no question, no doubt. Even though I didn't know what that meant, I just kind of was able to not be afraid of that. There was a part of me that realized that there were many things I really have always done from the heart. And for whatever the reason, I've been ashamed of it or embarrassed of it or felt, I don't know—but I felt a very strong connection with—at the place of the Ascended Masters, with a Native American.

There was a love energy that had kind of kicked in there and I wasn't sure who that was or what that was, but I could feel it. I just felt it. That was all I needed. I didn't really know necessarily what anything was or what it meant. For me, that was a gift, to just be able to say, I feel that and it will come to me when it's supposed to come to me, rather than creating a story over it or—so I'm not sure that I know. I just know that I know. I know that something will—I know in my heart and in my soul, I know that it will come to me, and that's all I know.

ANGELS: Well, what word we were going to use was the word familiarity, the sense of what awakened inside of you was what's called familiarity. You know that in a way, the word familiarity has, as part of it, the word family, yes?

BRENDA: Absolutely, yes.

ANGELS: Yes. What we wanted you to understand was the gift that was given to you there was the remembrance of your own association with those Ascended Masters or those Beings; you were actually familiar with their energy or knew their energy better than your human thought you did. What happened was, rather than it being something outside of you, like, oh, here's some great teachers but they don't connect with me or touch me, they're too distant, they're too profound to know me—you know that feeling?

BRENDA: Yes.

ANGELS: They became a part of you. That familiarity was the remembrance that you have known them and worked with them, and it was as if you allowed yourself to remember the connection that was already there. They were like a family to you, instead of something out there that other people have access to but you couldn't possibly, because you're not there yet. You see what we're saying, how you would have viewed it before, from the outside?

BRENDA: Yes, yes.

ANGELS: Now you're a member of the family, in a sense. Do you understand that? That's what happened. That was the gift: inviting you to remember or inviting you in as a member of the family, of this family. That's what you call the love energy. That was the familiarity of my home, my family. Do you see what we're saying?

BRENDA: Yes.

ANGELS: Okay. So, you begin to understand that there is a process that a soul goes through on some level, dimensional level of existence, where the soul comes to a place where they choose their path of study, to make it simple in human words. They ask to be allowed to apprentice with a particular group or particular beings. And one of those passageways, one of those desires to apprentice is with what is called the Ascended Master realm. It's a certain teaching, a way of learning, a way of moving into what humans call a more enlightened state.

It was, for you, a welcoming in by that family: We are accepting you in to our family as an apprentice. You felt it in your heart. And once you are capable of feeling the presence of that energy that humans call the Ascended Masters you knew that you had been initiated into, or accepted or awoken to, or reminded of, that family. That was the gift that they gave you, which was a profound gift. It's because you were willing to go there with humility and an open heart, and you made your appeal to them, whether you're aware of it or not, to allow you to join your frequencies, your energies, your loving energy, and to study with these Great Masters. And that was enough for them to be willing to let you feel the energy within you, so that you would be initiated by it. Do you understand what we're saying?

BRENDA: I think so.

ANGELS: It's much as we said, perhaps even bigger than you realized, that you had been touched by energies and welcomed them into your life. You agreed to apprentice and study with those, and they have agreed to take you on. That is the gift that was given. So, now you are, in a sense, a member of that tribe. A student in that school.

Now, that gift was a profound one which will unfold. You are well aware that it is not an easy path. You are well aware that it is a path that only some are willing to take up. Not all, in a sense, to use a human term, would be chosen. There would be some work, some initiations that would be done. But you will realize that on some level, your "family" has increased to include those Great Beings.

On to the other gift you were given—there were a number of them. The Space Brotherhood has begun to also work with you and remind you of your origins in that realm, where you have galactic tie-ups, galactic frequencies, frequencies of a higher level, and how the grid lines that run through you into the earth are being anchored. That is another task that you are beginning to understand a little bit more about. The Earth Deities actually agreed to a crystal implant within you, inside of your body. So you have been implanted with a crystal, which will assist you to access frequencies and energies that will assist Mother Earth and are utilized by the Space Brotherhood as well as the Ascended Masters and others, to beam energy through these grid lines, through these crystals. You agreed to be a conduit, if you will, for these energies as they come on to the earth. And they are coming faster and faster.

One of the things that human beings are having great trouble with at this time is anger at all these new frequencies. As you can see there is so much turmoil and difficulty that it is needed that beings, such as yourself, who are willing to serve as anchors of frequency are supported and thanked for their willingness to serve as Anchors of Light. We are here to thank you for that as well. It was as if you took up that calling as well. It's not something that you are going to be always conscious of, but you're going to notice at times almost a buzzing of different energies in your body.

Have you noticed this already?

BRENDA: A little bit. I have a little bit, yeah.

ANGELS: That's the new task, okay? It's the idea that these frequencies are now going to be moving through you as you anchor them, and you might find you do get certain sensations at times. But if you understand what it is, this buzzing or whatever, it will help you to feel okay with it. We would ask if you had a question about that. Because it is a little odd, we understand, but we think that you have a capability of grasping it.

BRENDA: Okay.

ANGELS: It's just a way of your serving the Earth Herself, and being able to, as you might think, bring heaven and earth together and anchor those energies a little more. So, you'll find it kind of fun at times because your dreams might change a bit and your feelings in your body might change a bit, and you'll start to feel very connected to both the earth plane herself as well as some of the galactic frequencies that are coming in. That was the other gift you received while you were in Teotihuacan. You received many, many, many gifts that are going to be a bit of processing for you, as you understand that you've taken a huge step forward in your spiritual evolutionary process. You feel that, yes?

BRENDA: Yes.

ANGELS: It's kind of like—we're going to put it this way: You've been waiting in the sidelines or on the wings of the stage, and now you're on the stage. You stepped out of the wings.

BRENDA: Yes.

ANGELS: Now we, in this realm, applaud you on the stage. It is the beginning of the path to ending the illusion of the third dimensional separation. It is the beginning of releasing one's self from third dimensional consciousness. It is a tough goal but you understand what we're saying, yes? The things that you thought were real are going to not seem so real or important as they did because prior to that, you were so anchored in third dimensional thought. Do you understand that?

BRENDA: No. Can you explain that just a little bit?

ANGELS: Yes. Do you know what third dimensional thought is?

BRENDA: No.

ANGELS: That is traditional human consciousness, where you have believed, as a human that you are a physical body. You believe that for the most part it is unsafe to be in a physical body. You believe that your physical body and the physical body sitting next to you is separate from yours, that matter is solid, and that one is separate from God and so forth. Those are the typical ways that humans think of their world.

BRENDA: Yes.

ANGELS: And what's going to happen now is that that is no longer going to be true for you, none of those things. You will not feel separate from anyone else. You will not believe in the illusion of the third dimensional plane. You will understand the connectedness of All That Is. All those things that before were your reality will drop away, and in its place, the reality of unity consciousness or wholeness and oneness, of understanding that you're connected to things far out in the galaxies and you're connected to things deep into the center of the earth, that you are merely to surrender to God, so that you can be one with All That Is. That is the shift. It's a tough shift because what used to be is no longer; but what used to be did not serve you, did it?

BRENDA: No, and I've already felt that little bit of a shift there. Now I understand.

ANGELS: It did not serve you, so it is time to let it go. Right now is a period of great cleansing for all, and those things which do not serve you are being let go. It's okay but it isn't easy, but you will be fine as you make this transition, for it is going to feel much happier for you. You'll be so overjoyed. You will feel less alone and that will really help you to open your heart and keep it open.

We would ask if you have any questions at this time. It's funny, when you get into Unity Consciousness, how the questions drop away. You know what we're saying? When you're in third dimensional, separation consciousness, everything is a question: "What should I do here? What should I do here? What's this, what's that? I don't know, I don't understand." But when you flow into the Unity of Oneness, suddenly, you just know. And it is a great shift, is it not?

BRENDA: There was a point in time where I was in that, even in Teotihuacan I remember specifically walking up the Pyramid of the Sun and having that kind of thinking going on. Then once I had gotten there, again, it was that—it was just that breathing or that mind there, that looking up and that feeling that then came over me and said exactly that. I mean, there is no question; you know. It's just bigger. I didn't need to ask, what am I feeling, what does it mean? It was there, it was right, it was…

ANGELS: It was truth for you.

BRENDA: It was truth for me. And I think being able to allow myself to be in such emotion and to be in such love and such gratitude, without any of the opinions or creations or roles that other people have laid on me throughout my life, to just be there with that moment, that moment that lasted the whole time I was there, and this gratitude—and the tears were there all the time. I have never experienced that before, that beauty and that feeling connected, truly feeling connected. I didn't have to run out and share it or explain it or talk about it or describe it or write it down or draw it or anything. It just needed to be with me and that was enough. That was a tremendous change for me. I always have to write things down because I'm afraid I'm going to forget them or have to make that moment, and it always takes me out of there—but this time I was just "in there." That knowing—I don't need to write it down, I'll know it, I'll remember it, and I'll feel it.

ANGELS: And you almost felt that you could disappear at that moment; that the whole illusion just falls away, that you disappear into the light of God. That is really what happened. Do you understand what we mean?

BRENDA: I do.

ANGELS: The separation goes away. And once the separation goes away, you remember the peace that you feel when you're spirit. But here you are, in human body, feeling that. That is what the human race is shooting for. The human race is trying to work its way up, so that it can be an embodied version of what you experienced, and you found out that it can happen. You see what we're saying?

BRENDA: Yes.

ANGELS: You do know. Prior to that, it was always that you would die, and then in your death, you would feel that, you see? But you felt that while alive, and that's why it was so precious to you because it let you know that it could be achieved. One does not need to die to feel that kind of unity.

BRENDA: Yes.

ANGELS: That is what many are striving for. Now let us just ask you: What would it be that would have taken you out of that sense of unity? At that moment, you're in that unity, you're feeling good. What would have taken you out of it?

BRENDA: Fear.

ANGELS: And what would the fear have been?

BRENDA: Of not knowing, of worrying about, was I doing everything right? Was I—you, know old stories, old self-loathing would have taken me out of that.

ANGELS: You can see how challenging it is then to keep that unity consciousness alive, now that you are back in the "real world," you see, because the real world keeps challenging and poking and prodding you into separation consciousness. The trick that every Ascended Master has tried to show is how to be in the world, as they say, but not of it. Do you understand what they mean?

BRENDA: I do.

ANGELS: Prior to this experience, you did not understand that so well. You thought it was sort of like not to be in the material world and not to want things, in a sense: be in it but don't be of it in terms of contributing to the bad things of the world and that kind of thing. But you didn't understand the State of Beingness, you see, the Beingness that takes you out of the third dimensional world. So, when the master says, "Be in the world, in a sense, but don't be of it;" walk in the world but do not buy into the consciousness of the world. That is what they're saying. Be in your unity consciousness even though you are still in the world at large. That is, as human beings say, the trick, you know, because what is going to come at you is going to start now the challenges.

Because if you're on the Ascended Master Path, you don't think it's going to just be a breezeway, do you?

BRENDA: Not at all.

ANGELS: To be a bodhisattva is a high calling, right?

BRENDA: Right.

ANGELS: You understand that.

BRENDA: I do.

ANGELS: What that means is that you're going to get a little challenged; now can you hold that unity consciousness now? Now can you hold that unity consciousness now? And each time you hold it, you might get another level up, you see?

BRENDA: Okay.

ANGELS: Do you understand what we're saying?

BRENDA: I do understand. I do.

ANGELS: Okay. We want you to understand and it was important that you truly understood the gift the Ascended Masters gave you by allowing you to feel their energy. And what they're trying to say to you is that now you've felt it, your job is to be able to "*re-find it*" over and over and over again; and eventually hold it, even when the world around you is beating you up a little bit.

BRENDA: Okay.

ANGELS: That's going to be your challenge. Now, you have to have some guides to help you do that, okay?

BRENDA: Okay.

ANGELS: You need your spiritual mentors to do that. There are a number of energies that are happy to help you. So, before we mention to you or say to you, here, here, here, what we want you to do is think for a moment what energies you want to invite to you, to assist you on this path. Who do you want to choose as your main teachers at this time?

BRENDA: I don't know that I can answer that.

ANGELS: Think of all those that you would consider to be Masters; and you might investigate even more. But you understand, for example, you could call Mary Magdalene to you as a teacher. If you desire to learn what she has to offer. There are many who are there.

BRENDA: There is so much I want to learn.

ANGELS: Your job is to think about those teachers that you revere, and you can take them from any tradition.

BRENDA: I know I have such a strong feeling within what I, on probably such a small level, though, feel regarding a Native American or a...

ANGELS: Well, you have one who has been bugging us, by the way, and hitting us over and over and over again, over the head, to announce his name. But we haven't yet because we wanted you not to just get stuck there.

BRENDA: Okay.

ANGELS: We wanted you to understand that you've called forth the entire Ascended Master realm, okay? All are available to you. So, we didn't want you just to get stuck with Cochise. Cochise is his name, okay?

BRENDA: Okay.

ANGELS: Cochise is over and over and over again, from the very beginning, saying, "Would you just tell her I'm here?" But we felt you would get stuck too much in that, and we wish you to really understand, to look through lots of traditions, to really choose whom you want to be your teachers, you see? You have far more choices than perhaps you thought you did.

BRENDA: Okay.

ANGELS: Cochise says that his job is to toughen you up, is what he's saying. His job is to help you stay strong in the face of adversity. That is what he just said. He feels that you are too sensitive; you collapse and crumble too easily. Do you understand why he would say that?

BRENDA: I do.

ANGELS: Okay. What he's saying is that his job is to help you get your warrior spirit in place; you have not kept up your boundaries correctly. Your biggest problem is you do not understand how to correctly utilize boundaries. Boundaries between yourself and others. In other words, first of all, you allow other people to hurt you too much and then you make too big a wall. The flow of boundaries—he said, energies should be flowing in and out but it should not be out of balance. He is saying that you often want to let too much out and not enough in; or too much in and not enough out. That you have to understand that in your interactions, you have to keep the wall up, but it should be porous is what he's saying.

BRENDA: Okay.

ANGELS: In other words, you let the wall down, you let too much in, you get hurt, and then you put the wall up too thick. You see what…

BRENDA: I do, I absolutely do.

ANGELS: Okay, that's what he's saying. Instead, you need to find a way to keep and maintain a steady boundary system that works for you. It's not about taking the wall down, getting hurt and putting the wall back up, it's about having a boundary system that allows the even flow through that will provide protection but without walling you off.

BRENDA: Okay.

ANGELS: That is his message to you.

BRENDA: Okay.

ANGELS: He asks if you can understand that.

BRENDA: Yes, I understand, absolutely.

ANGELS: He will be your guide in assisting you. Call on him to establish a correct boundary system for yourself. He is saying, in your lesson plans, as now a student of the masters: "Step one, lesson one—boundaries."

BRENDA: Right.

ANGELS: "Student," he says, "you have your first assignment." How well you do with each assignment will determine how quickly the next teachers arrive.

BRENDA: Okay.

ANGELS: The first one is boundaries and your warrior spirit, feeling that you can defend yourself but without pain to yourself or others. In other words, holding space strongly, planting your feet firmly, without it being a battle, is what he's saying.

BRENDA: Okay.

ANGELS: You're going to find you're going to be given some opportunities to experience these kinds of lessons over the next few weeks. You'll find that perhaps you will need to establish your boundaries correctly and so forth. As you learn to do this without reverting back to your old patterning—in other words, holding Unity Consciousness and Higher Consciousness. Be aware that these are being given to you as teaching tools. That awareness will help you to meet the challenge of them. So, your first guide on your path is Cochise.

BRENDA: Okay.

ANGELS: Then you will be taken, bit by bit, and each time a lesson has been learned, that guide will step away and then the next Ascended Master will step forward. They're saying, "Learn to recognize when you have learned the lesson and when the next one has stepped forward for you, to take your hand." Okay?

BRENDA: Okay.

ANGELS: Now at any time, all are available, and you can call. What they're suggesting is that you call on or ask for one that would be your constant guide, not a lesson teacher, but that will be with you always, through all the lessons, as your guide. That particular Ascended Master is the one you will select. As they come to you lesson by lesson, they are chosen for you. Do you understand the difference?

BRENDA: I understand the difference.

ANGELS: Okay. So, it is up to you to feel and think and discover which great teacher you wish to now be your permanent guide through this school, if you will.

BRENDA: Okay. Is that something I will take time to find and then...

ANGELS: Well, they're saying "Likely, that you will do it in the astral plane, if you will, during dream time or that sort of thing."

BRENDA: Okay.

ANGELS: Then it will be made known to you consciously. You will think you made it with your conscious mind but you will have actually made it with your Higher Mind, in another plane of existence. It will filter down to your conscious mind and you'll suddenly go, "Oh!" You'll see a picture of the right person or thing, you see?

BRENDA: Okay.

ANGELS: But we are not going to place this upon you, for that would not be appropriate.

BRENDA: Okay.

ANGELS: You are on a noble path and a revered one; and one which they wish you to understand that many apply for and not all are chosen. Understand that it is an honor. You should feel the beauty of that.

BRENDA: I do. Now for my human teacher, if that's—I want to say my human teacher but my—in the work that I'm working with now, can I still do that work? Can I still be connected with my teacher here?

ANGELS: Your teacher is also on the same path, so there is no coincidence, for she is further along on the path. She chose longer ago, in human terms, to study with the Ascended Masters. So, she is herself a student and working with them, but has completed more lessons, if you will, than you have.

BRENDA: Absolutely, without a doubt, absolutely.

ANGELS: She can be your guide and teacher in that way. But you could explain to her that you have been instructed or explained that you were initiated or agreed to be taken on as a student of the Ascended Masters during the Teo journey. She will understand. And that you are on your first lesson with your guide, Cochise. She will understand that it is a path that she also herself is on and that she is the perfect teacher for you at this time.

This is a lot, we understand. You do not have to go any further than this. We understand to be told this is quite a lot, but we also know that you feel it, you own it, if you will, correct?

BRENDA: I do, and I also feel home, I feel finally that I'm not searching and flailing and I'm just—for whatever is to come is fine but for right now, I just feel very much at peace. I feel that I'm on a path.

ANGELS: You have finally stepped on to your path, yes.

BRENDA: That's exactly it, thank you.

ANGELS: And that is the familiarity that we've talked about.

BRENDA: I'm so grateful and I am so honored, and my intent will be strong and my efforts will be as well.

ANGELS: We caution you that there is one problem we see; that you will beat yourself up emotionally for every time you feel you've failed too much, which will in fact impede your progress. You need to let yourself learn as you learn and not judge yourself as you're learning, because that will be a big problem for you, because that kicks up the old unworthiness.

BRENDA: And that is very much…

ANGELS: A problem, yes.

BRENDA: Okay.

ANGELS: That is why you have not stepped on this path earlier, because you have felt unworthy, as we said, looking from the wings, as if you were the understudy, you see?

BRENDA: Yes.

ANGELS: And now you feel, "Okay, it's time for me to be on the stage." And don't let your unworthiness send you back into the wings.

BRENDA: Okay. You're right, that will definitely be my challenge but I feel much different about that challenge now. I'll have to be aware. I'll just have to keep myself aware and remain open.

ANGELS: For yourself.

BRENDA: For myself.

ANGELS: They are all standing and applauding right now. They thought that would be a funny image to project through this conduit because they knew it went along with the image of your being on stage. They say just to show that they stand and applaud your choice.

BRENDA: Right. Thank you.

ANGELS: They say, "Remember that a part of you is already there, that a part of you is already aware and knows, as you know, all this truth that you need to know." The trick is just integrating it into all parts of the Self, that's all. That's all it's about. It's about taking that truth you already know and finding a place for it in all parts of yourself, if you understand that. They do understand how hard it is to be human at this time, and they do understand the challenges of it, and they are here to help you in whatever way. But you are ultimately responsible for your own path. They can only help you as guides and assistants and with your requests and so forth. There will be times when you'll want them to just take over, but that's not really their role. Keep your sense of humor. Cochise is not the one to keep sense of humor so much.

BRENDA: Okay.

ANGELS: But there are others who have a better sense of humor and find it very, very funny, and you can ask for a little lightening. The Buddha energy has a little more humor available. Cochise likes to take things a little seriously. But, you need that right now for your Step One: How to strengthen yourself.

BRENDA: Yes.

ANGELS: So, would you have any more questions at this time or require any more assistance from this realm at this time? You may ask anything you wish.

BRENDA: The minute I think I have questions and then...

ANGELS: Well, just to know in terms of body, would this be okay for our last message to you about body then?

BRENDA: Yes.

ANGELS: You're going to feel, as we said, some bodily changes. More sensations are going to be happening for you as you begin to shed the density consciousness. You're going to feel a lot more tingling and things will shift in that regard because you are shifting, as we said, internally, in a sense. So you're going to feel these implants, that crystal, the higher frequencies. So, anything that you're feeling or sensing—be aware that it's part of your new journey. Be conscious of it and not so concerned.

BRENDA: Okay, thank you.

ANGELS: You might want to do some different kinds of healing works and so forth, but you'll discover what it is you're feeling or guided to do, to help you integrate some of these new frequencies.

BRENDA: Okay.

ANGELS: And keep breathing, too. Breathe and don't stop breathing. Allow yourself to breathe because the breath actually moves the energy through the body and helps to ground the frequencies as well. So, if you breathe, you can help yourself as well.

BRENDA: Okay. Thank you.

ANGELS: We will release her if you have no more questions today.

BRENDA: You may release her. Thank you.

CHAPTER FOUR

FAMILY KARMA

JODY R.

JODY: I'm going through some emotional issues since my father has passed, especially with my stepmother—family dynamics going on. I need to make a decision on something and I'm feeling very torn between what to do.

ANGELS: Well, what is it that you feel torn about? Exactly what are the tearing parts for you?

JODY: That's the part that I'm confused about. I'm not sure what it is but I just have this pain in my heart about the whole situation.

ANGELS: The loyalties, yes, feeling loyalties?

JODY: Maybe that's what it is. I haven't been able to define exactly what it is.

ANGELS: Because it's coming from, as you are probably well aware, this idea of "old story" that's causing the pain; the idea of a family torn asunder.

JODY: Uh-huh.

ANGELS: And the instability of it, and that feeling of—well, we're going to start here with you, so that you understand. We sense or feel that to you, the energy of loyalty is very important. Would you agree with that? Do you understand that?

JODY: Yes.

ANGELS: Loyalty drives you a lot, and it's a sense that once you make a commitment to something or make a commitment to someone you're solid in that foundation and you're solid in that commitment. What's difficult for you is when you sense that human energies or people are getting torn apart or are in disagreement, it is hard for you because it tears at your heart center—let's put it this way: You always want to be loyal to everyone. Do you understand what we mean by that?

JODY: Yes.

ANGELS: You want to be loyal and helpful to everyone. When a situation comes up where you find it difficult for you to do that, where you feel torn or you feel upset, it really bothers you. It hurts you because you feel that one of the strongest and most important things for human beings to do is to have a loyalty. We can talk about past life situations of feeling betrayed by family members, of feeling that things were torn apart in a family betrayal, what you would call back-stabbing, that kind of thing. And this sense that "we owe it to our family", we owe it to ourselves to be loyal, to stick together. That's the old story. That's the old karma, what humans call karma. When that gets stirred up, it brings up an old and ugly story.

We're going to pause here and ask for your comment and how you feel about what we're telling you.

JODY: It makes sense. Maybe that's why I feel so torn about making a decision that I need to make. It's just that our family involved—and it's just, I don't know if there's a fairness on the other side of the family part of the issue.

ANGELS: You sense the karma.

JODY: Where does the loyalty come into questioning? That's what my question is. The loyalty part is being questioned and I don't know whether to trust what is happening, to trust my feelings with it. I'm so unbalanced that I don't even know whether to trust my feeling or trust what I feel about the whole thing.

ANGELS: Well, what we want you to understand, and we'll help you a little bit, is that it is very old and very dense, as you can feel, and deep karma. We're just going to make sure you understand what we mean when we say karma. Do you understand that word?

JODY: Yes.

ANGELS: You really understand that these energy chords that are pulling at everyone to act out old story or drama get stirred up. It's almost as if, without even knowing it, the past and the present get tangled, become one, and it's hard for people to feel differently. They don't even know why they're reacting the way that they are. They act irrationally, even sometimes creating acts of violence that surprise even them or saying things that are quite out of character at times.

What we want you to understand and realize is that you will not be disloyal by stepping out of it, by stepping above it. It's not a disloyal act to disentangle yourself as much as you can. That is what sometimes is hard for you. You believe that if you don't do something, then it seems like you don't care or that you're disloyal. But we suggest that as much as you can step out of the frame and let go of your part of the karmic chords, you'll feel better. Do you think you could do that?

JODY: Well, I'll try.

ANGELS: Can you see why it would trigger feelings of disloyalty in you? I should be doing something or I should be...

JODY: I just have to come to a decision and I'm having a hard time, which is very unusual for me, to come to a decision. I have to come to terms with all of the disturbed feeling in myself.

ANGELS: If you can simplify your decision, simplify it for us. Speak it out loud.

JODY: I need to send money to my stepmother in Puerto Rico and I'm hearing all these strange stories coming back of her disloyalty, and that's where I'm at a crossroads of do I send her the money or do I keep it because she has not been completely truthful?

ANGELS: What you have to do is you have to step out of all of this old karma, you have to get out of it; you have to step away from it. You have to step away from everyone for a while, listen to yourself and listen to your own heart and try to ask yourself in this case...Let's imagine—if you sit for a moment and don't listen to anyone else, don't listen to anyone else's words. For a moment, first of all, connect your heart to the woman in Puerto Rico. Connect to that energy. Connect for a moment with the heart, with the energy of the heart. Do you sense her energy? You can feel it; and it's not very clear. Clean—that is the word we mean, her energy is not very clean. You sense she's confused, you can sense that she's angry.

JODY: She's in pain.

ANGELS: Now we want you to feel what it will feel like—don't think of anyone else—if you send her the money. Energetically, how do you feel if you send her the money? Then feel energetically, what does it feel like if you don't? One of those will have a stronger "hit" for you than the other. Without letting everyone else influence you, do it energetically. Step out of the fray and just get above it and feel.

JODY: Yes.

ANGELS: Notice that if you send her the money—feel what it feels like in your heart. If you feel that you can say, "I don't even care whether she's disloyal, I don't even care whether she's a good person or a bad person, but I'm going to just trust in the universe," then you can say, "With an open heart and with complete trust and faith, regardless of whatever she does to that money or with that money or anything else, I will send the money and I will just do it and I will let go and I will let God, and I won't care what anyone says." If that can feel good to you and you can just feel that you acted with an open heart and you didn't worry—it's like when you give money to a charity and you don't worry, you just give it. It may be utilized the way you want and it may not, but you give it as an act of giving.

Then do the opposite. Feel the energy of *not* giving her anything; of what that entails. Not how anyone else feels about it, but how you feel. If that makes you feel better, if that makes you feel empowered, if that makes you feel good, if you can live with peace in your heart not doing it, then you will not do it. It should be very clear when you get rid of all the other noises, all the other voices, all the other karma and the demands. Step above the fray and feel yourself acting from your heart and how it makes you feel. You'll know what to do for yourself to feel better. Do you see what we're saying?

JODY: Yes.

ANGELS: That should help you.

CHAPTER FIVE

GOD AND FREE WILL

ELIZABETH F.

ELIZABETH: I'm trying to understand why it is that I cannot watch horror movies, scary movies, things that involve pain, torture or suspense, and also why I cannot tolerate abuse to repulsion, to an extreme. It's beyond normal.

ANGELS: Well, first of all, let us congratulate you. We don't believe that it is proper behavior, or beneficial to the human race to numb themselves so that the torturing or harming of another living being is okay. We would first want to make sure that you understand, before we speak directly to your question, that we don't believe that it is a beneficial thing that a human being can stand by and watch another human being tortured and be unaffected by it. We don't think that you want to get to that point of "unfeelingness" required to experience something to that degree.

But what you are trying to do is get to a place of greater neutrality, so that you don't have to live in constant pain. Then you can realize that there are people in the world who need to experience or believe on some level that they need to experience those things to be taught or to learn. In some cases people actually do these acts to feed themselves and feel good, because those who are unable to get energy directly from God have to get it from other humans. As they feed off other humans like vampires, they need to make more and more pain in the human, so that they themselves feed energetically off the weakening of another human being. That is what the human race has done with the sadomasochistic relationship. The sadist feeds off the masochist, in a sense, and gets energy or the sadist feeds off their victim, and the energy they receive is like a vampire who would suck the life force. That is because they are unable to receive energy from God.

Now, as we bring it to you, you can see and imagine and feel the torture that you have experienced, and it doesn't surprise you to know indeed that you were in fact tortured. You had been tortured for being a witch. It is one of the reasons that you tend to keep your wisdom hidden, and you are much wiser and much more powerful and much more astute in reading energy and understanding certain metaphysical principles than most people realize. You are frightened to be recognized because you have been tortured for your gifts; so you keep them hidden.

That's one of the things that you need to heal, so that you can come more fully into blossoming as a spiritual human on this planet. You need to get to a place where you're not so afraid of what you just described. Once you free yourself of that and neutralize it a bit, you will come into a place where you'll be more open to feel and see and express your power. The problem of course is that you have to go through the deep powerful anger. What you have thinly veiled, and close to the surface, due to the torture that you have endured, is rage. One of the things that frightens you is that there are two options: One is to go into complete terror and weakness when experiencing torture, and the other is to go into violent rage. You know both states. In previous lives, you've experienced both of them.

But when you've experienced going limp, or escaping, or going out of your mind to escape, your body still contains pent-up rage and anger from those experiences. Much of the tension you carry is directed at God because you're angry that God allows these things to happen, and you're angry that this world has gotten as screwed-up as it has where such torture and rage and anger exist. And then deeper, deeper, deeper still inside of you is the realization that that kind of rage, when turned on its opposite would be capable of creating a similar act in you. It's a hot button, a huge hot button for you.

It's so upsetting to you, it stirs up so much energy within you on so many levels that you get nauseous; you get literally sick to your stomach. You can't stand the feeling and it goes into your heart. It weakens you. It's terrifying.

One of the things you would benefit from doing is bodywork which, when the bodywork was being performed, actually allowed you to consciously go into the parts of your body where you're holding old torture scenario and express it and scream it and get it out, free the energy more and not just compress it or temporarily release it. You're like a volcano that way, that if it blew, it would then neutralize everything quite a bit and you'd feel safer on the earth and not so angry at those who harmed you.

Now, you have experienced many lives of also being at war. You have seen war. You have not only experienced bloodshed and physical pain in a situation as we're talking about, the torturing of witches, for example, but you have also seen and witnessed physical pain in a situation of war. That is also a great deal of upset for you. What you need to do or work on for yourself is summarized in one word, and that word is forgiveness. In your case, it's almost a broad forgiveness, just forgiving the human race in general for all its expressions of darkness, and then extending that and forgiving God for being a God of allowing. Because this is a free-will universe and this is a God of allowing. You have to forgive God for being a God of allowing.

Then you have to go a little further and say, "God, I understand that your wisdom knows that somehow, in this great, horrifying allowing, in all these things I've witnessed, the war, the suffering, the pain, the childbirth, where you died in childbirth, the things that I have experienced and suffered, that I know somehow you understand that they have made me more wise, more powerful, more clear and ultimately, when I transform them, so much more loving than I would have been had I not had those experiences of darkness. The transforming of my darkness and the darkness I've experienced can call to it Greater Light."

That somehow God knows and understands that once humans return to the Source, with all this information having been transmuted, forgiven and brought to God, there is a greatness and a wisdom that this allowing created. So, forgive God and say, "God, it's okay, I forgive you for allowing this stuff to happen, for allowing human beings to have such a wide expression." Then you'll find more peace in your heart.

Then it's not that you will condone these experiences but you will understand at a powerful and deeper level that, as you had to experience them somehow to grow and transmute and become greater and lighter, that others somehow must be having to do the same thing in this allowing universe and you realize that they, too, will one day transform all their darkness to Light, and you realize that there is in the end only Love. There is only this one energy which when it shines forth and becomes this web of energy can be creative—and that in the allowing, ultimately, much is learned and eventually, all is brought back to the Light and transformed and transmuted but made greater because of the experience.

Then once you can do that, you can at least somehow, somewhere in yourself not only forgive all the experiences you have had that people have done to you and the things you've done to others, but then you can forgive somehow those who are currently doing it today. You can say, "I will not have to participate. I've done it, been there, don't need it, and I want now only to transform the pain to Love. But I understand that other people must need it for some reason."

Then you understand, in a co-creative universe, you don't need to call those experiences to you, that you can manifest light and love around you and leave the darkness somewhere else. You don't need to bring it to you.

It's a long answer and a little complex, and perhaps it will help you to listen back to the tape recording of it. But we think that you're getting it to some extent. We'll pause here and ask for your comment.

ELIZABETH: I understand what you're saying.

ANGELS: It's a lot, we understand. Do you believe that you might be able to do some of the transformation inside of yourself so it's not such a hot button for you?

ELIZABETH: No.

ANGELS: You don't think you can get to that state of forgiveness? There's too much anger?

ELIZABETH: If you ignore the anger, the rational part of me isn't satisfied either.

ANGELS: What would be needed for the rational part to be satisfied?

ELIZABETH: Well, when you said there is only the loving God and there is only the goodness, I say to you then we wouldn't be having this conversation. No, I don't agree with that. I don't see it.

ANGELS: We're not saying that on this earth or out of that energy can't be created darkness. We agree with you there. We're not trying to convince you that there are not bad things around you on the earth. Did you think we were trying to convince you of that? We're agreeing with you that there are bad things. But where do you think the badness comes from? Where is the origin of the badness?

ELIZABETH: God forgive me but God.

ANGELS: You believe that God is bad?

ELIZABETH: I think that for every action, there is an equal and opposite reaction; and I think that there's a negative side to—I don't think that God is just a benign source, no.

ANGELS: At the energy, at the Source, the Creative Force, the orgasmic force called God, that energy is sent out, sent forth, and it is a purely creative energy and it is a creative energy of expansion and Love. When you are closer dimensionally, consciously, in consciousness, you are vibrating closer to that Love and closer to that Consciousness then, in fact, you do experience only love. When you shed human body and you die and you release or leave your fear and anger and resentment behind in the third or fourth dimension and you allow your soul or the part that can vibrate higher to go higher, you get rid of those lower vibrational densities. Then you begin to remember and know, as so many who have had experiences on the other side will tell you, to just feel the peace. What envelops them is a sense of love, is a sense of peace, a sense of wholeness and a sense of unity, and that is true.

But as the energy of God is disbursed, as it "spreads out" and it creates these dimensional levels, these different vibrational levels, the further, the slower, the more dense the creation or level of creation, the further one gets from the higher vibration, the faster the fear comes in. God has given this conduit a beautiful analogy to explain what fear is. God had said to this conduit when she was asking about fear: "Do you remember when you have laid on your back in the sun and you have lifted your hand and you have blocked out the entire sun with your small hand? While on the earth, your little hand is capable of completely blocking out the light of the sun. Well, fear is like your hand. Fear blocks the light of God and makes you believe that that energy of God is not reaching you. But the fear is infinitesimal compared to the light and the power of God; just as your hand is infinitesimal compared to the sun. So, step back a little bit and look with a higher vision or a greater vision, and you can see your fear in proportion, just as you can see your hand in proportion to the sun."

You realize it is only your human consciousness, your human fear that is blocking out all the Light, and it is because you believe more in your fear than you believe in the Light.

That is okay because God allows it.

If God was not a God of allowance, God would have to be a God of punishment, and you would not want God to be a God of punishment, or He/She would have had to punish you for things you've done. Where is She/He going to choose who She's going to punish? How are you to judge, when you see someone doing something bad? When you see someone hurting a child? Well, how do you know that their own rage from having been hurt as a child isn't what propels them, and then where does the hurt stop and where does the harm stop and where does God start punishing? God teaches through infinite patience.

God decided to say, "I will not punish but I will set up laws and I will teach all beings, no matter where they vibrate, that as you sow, you reap. You will become responsible Masters and eventually, you will make your way back to Me. If you choose and wish to do it by experiencing greater darkness and fear in order to learn, I will not stop you. Your experiences will ultimately lead you back to Me. In the process, you will have to do what is called karma: As you sow, you will reap, and it will teach you that you cannot do to another and not have it done to yourself because you are all One."

You are the same as the person sitting next to you and they are the same as the person sitting next to them and so forth, in that all of you are part of this body that is the energy of God, expressing it as you will, by an allowing God, with universal laws which do guide you and require you to have responsibility, that makes it all "fair" in the end. Once you have cleared your karma and you have remembered the Love, you do not have to come back to the earth anymore because the energy is neutralized.

We don't know if that has helped you but it's just another way to look at it. Until you are done being angry at God, it will be hard for you to resolve some of those angers, and that's essentially what we feel is your journey. We don't judge it and we understand it's the same as everyone else's journey. From our perspective, it's our journey as well because we believe that we and you are one, as we believe all is in unity, just vibrating at a different place, a different space, a different time, in a different way. But it doesn't mean that we are something separate.

CHAPTER SIX

ACCESSING DIFFERENT REALMS

SARA L.

SARA L: I have a question—I guess accessing the different realms. I've read some books. I guess the fear is, number one, trying to go into an altered state by yourself and believing who's there, what's there, because I don't know if I've read negative energies can imitate or act like they're a good energy when they're really not. So how do you—I guess that would be my fear of who to listen to and know that it's someone legitimate.

ANGELS: Well, it's a complex question and we are absolutely happy to answer it and we will. It's going to be kind of a long answer. It's important so we thank you for it because it's certainly a very valid question. Of course, the simple answer is that you feel it—you feel it. Energies that are darker; they feed off you. In their most extreme, they literally can make your body weak. They can make you shake and they send you to places that weaken you so that they can feed off you.

Negative energy, or evil as you call it, exists on the third and the fourth dimensional level. It's real to your world. We do not deny this. However, if you are working above the third and fourth dimensional level you will be in a different frequency. The trick is to clear the human issues so you can hold the higher frequency. The most important thing you ask yourself is: do you feel good? Absolutely important. One way that a dark energy can mask itself as a light energy to the uninitiated is because ego, the human ego, has gotten in the way. One of the ways that it gets in the way is that somebody believes that they're so superior and needs to believe that they're so superior that they can't possibly imagine in any way that they could do anything but the best good. When arrogance starts to come and rear its ugly head, you can be sure that you're going to be good fodder for a dark energy to be able to utilize you.

Here is the simple answer: When you connect and when you meditate, call in the Christed Light, call in the Ascended Masters, call in the Highest Angels, call in the God energies, whatever makes you feel comfortable. Just call in the highest, brightest energies you can find. When they enter your body, when you feel that they are warming you, you feel peaceful, you feel more loving, and then you know you're on the right track, okay? That's simple, that's good.

If you find yourself getting into this position where you're feeling that you're getting a little arrogant and that you feel that you're starting to tell everybody else what to believe, what to do, what to think, and you're judging them all the time, you might think, "Okay, I'm acting out of my lower self" and your lower self is not going to be that different than the lower energies. You're going to be attracting lower energies if you are acting from your lower self. There's a match and it works. So, be sure you're acting from your Higher Self and call in the higher energies, and you should not experience or feel any fear whatsoever, and it shouldn't stop you whatsoever from doing energy work.

That being said, you have probably heard that there are many energy workers, Lightworkers, who speak quite often about experiencing psychic attack, and that is something a little different. If you are interested in that, it is a different conversation, and we will also explore that. So, before we do that, let's ask if you have understood our first message about just calling in the light.

SARA L: Yes. So, my question would be if you're sincere in calling and meditating, there really shouldn't be any issue with negative energies or someone...

ANGELS: Absolutely not.

SARA L: Okay.

ANGELS: When you connect—whatever angelic energy or higher energy, whatever it is for you for the divine feminine energies, particularly wonderful for you with Kuan Yin and the other manifestations of the divine feminine in any tradition are fine. As you call in Kuan Yin, you call in the Mother Mary, the Magdalene energies, those are very gentle and those are very calming, those are very nurturing, and those will always lead you to a place of feeling nurtured and loved, and there is never any fear of those gentle energies. So, that should be just fine for you.

Now sometimes, as we said, Lightworkers who are doing very powerful work and bringing in very powerful energies start to have experiences they call psychic attack. The only reason that that is ever done and they draw those—and they can be quite powerful and quite profound and they can be quite frightening. But if you are truly working with your Spiritual Guides you are never given as a Lightworker more experiences with dark energy than you can handle.

The reason that it's done is because you have to learn, you have to understand deeply the weakness of the dark energies. You have to understand if you cannot hold the Light of God and if you believe in the dark energies, then you need to clear those places where you're holding that fear, or believing more in your fear than the Light of God. You will be given the opportunity by your Higher Self to meet your fears and meet your darkness and transform it and transmute it so you can hold more Light.

Say to the dark energy if it ever decides to try to fight you, "Thank you so much for coming to me, thank you so much because you have shown me where I still believe in fear and darkness. Otherwise I would not see you." Then it weakens the dark energy because the dark energy wanted to put you in a fear state.

The dark energy wanted you to believe in darkness. Saying, "Thank you," tells the energy that every time you attack me, you push me closer to God, you make me reach higher and you make me transform those places that are still fear-based so I can reach higher. You do me a service. This weakens the energy. Don't fight the dark energy. Don't see it as enemy, do not go to war. Weaken it by treating it as a gift

SARA L: Yes.

ANGELS: That is the best way, if you ever experience what you might feel is a psychic attack or some of your own fear coming to frighten you, which is really what it is because nothing can frighten you that doesn't somewhere exist in you. You have the hole and it has the perfect piece to fill it in a sense. It's a vibrational match. So, it's showing you where you still have fear and you say, "Oh, thank you, I know I need to look there. I'll go do my work and then the next time you come around, that place in me will be healed and it won't be a vibrational match and you won't be able to attach to me." That is the best way to treat it, as a great teacher and as something which can help push you closer to God, rather than farther away, and then you won't be so afraid of it, okay?

SARA L: Yes.

ANGELS: Did that help you?

SARA L: Very much.

CHAPTER SEVEN

A SOUL'S JOURNEY – MOTHER EARTH AND THE HUMAN CONSCIOUSNESS

LEA S.

ANGELS: We are most delighted to have this opportunity to speak with you and to work with you today in this way. As always the Archangel Ariel is speaking with you and is joined with Gabriel and Michael.

We wish to begin today by letting you know that the angel who is with you or above your head, as it were, is the Angel Kaeylarae, the Angel of Peace. And you will see as we begin to speak with you why it is that you are working with or carrying this Angel's energy with you, and why this Angel's energy is so important to you.

We wish to begin by illuminating for you a little bit of what you might call your soul's journey through time, what appears to be from the human perspective and the linear time sequence, the idea of a journey of the soul through time or what humans traditionally call past lives or the many lives of the earth plane.

One of the things that we see and feel about you, as we summarize what is indeed a long journey, is that the greatest need for you has been to make order out of chaos. What you have needed or desired to do, for both yourself and the world, is to find a way to take that which is overwhelming, that which has overwhelmed you and which has seemed chaotic and confusing and to bring some order to it, so that it can be held, understood and coped with. It is for that reason that at your heart, the angel known as the Angel of Peace is the one that you call to you or gravitates toward you, because it is your desire to find a way to create peaceful solutions or peaceful environments or ways for human beings to be together or live together in understanding and peace and harmony.

For you, it comes from this need to take that which you felt was so chaotic and too overwhelming and to make it into a tangible form, in a way that human beings can hold, can utilize and can use to find a way to bring greater peace into their lives. It has been your soul's purpose in various ways to do such a thing, to find a way to greater harmony on this planet, in whatever way you choose to do it.

As a child, in previous lives, you were often overwhelmed by the world and the chaos of the world. You were deeply imprinted in your childhoods from your other lives at witnessing the world gone to chaos; what had been peaceful for you early on was tossed up into chaos in ideas of war or death, death of a family member, death of those you loved, death of siblings, death of those around you, sweepings in even of weather, sweepings in of events that turned your world upside down.

And it came to you, in order to cope with these experiences that happened in your earlier soul lives, soul ages, to decide that there had to be a way to be on this planet, to live on this planet, and to do it in a way so that you did not feel lost, confused or chaotic. Your idea was to then bring to others, environments and places where they, too, could feel peace or connection.

You did it in many ways for many lifetimes, through what are called more earthly ways. You tried to serve in the form of a statesman or politician, tried to figure out how to order government, order world, order people. That was one attempt in one lifetime to bring order to chaos. You tried in another life to figure out how to do it as a nun in a religious order; you wanted to be in a religious order. You asked yourself, "How could I find some way of getting some peace there?"

So, it has been your need to order the world, to create some kind of harmony that has drawn you to many attempts, in different ways to try to make that which seems random and chaotic, understandable and harmonious. In this life, the idea that comes through very strongly for us that would be an example of how you would utilize these ideas to make things flow is the idea that humans call Feng Shui. Making the environment around you flow, so that it seems to radiate some kind of peace. The ability to alter or manipulate the environment to give others a greater and deeper sense of peace within their home and so forth, is something that we sense you are intensely drawn to, and that would fulfill your soul in many ways.

We're going to pause here and see if you understand our opening message and how it resonates for you.

LEA: I understand it completely. Everything makes sense.

ANGELS: So, you can feel still to some extent how you don't like confusion.

LEA: Yes.

ANGELS: For some, it is exciting, but for you, it tends to be something that you'd rather not experience. It's a little bit too unnerving, if you will.

LEA: Right.

ANGELS: What we're going to help you with today is how to come into an even greater sense of peace. In other words, to be able to transcend the confusion of the world with alignment of the soul, the mind, the heart and the spiritual with your Higher Self; with the Divine Realms. It is only in that alignment that really any human ever finds true peace. You've glimpsed it or understood it but it still eludes you. As a result, you are still subject to the chaotic effects of the world around you. Yes?

LEA: Yes.

ANGELS: So, we're going to ask how we can help to bring you into greater alignment or to help you smooth out the rough edges?

LEA: I don't know, just by listening. I think I'm just here to listen. I really do. I really do.

ANGELS: You are ready to receive, you say?

LEA: Yes.

ANGELS: What we want you to understand, first of all, is for you to get in touch with the Greater Self. The first thing that's absolutely essential to your sense of peace is the understanding of what you are a part of; that you are not alone and you are not separate. That is the illusion that you carry, as all humans or most humans carry, the idea that they are in some way separate from all other humans and all other life around them. That is what allows the discomfort to be created.

In other words, when a human being is in alignment with the forces of All That Is, and with the understanding that one is a part of All of That, that is when the human is not only at peace with the Self but is creating peace for others around them. It is because that alignment became disrupted in the human race that the chaos that so disturbed you was created. That is also true as to why the Earth herself is often chaotic.

The first thing that is important for human beings to understand is that there is no peace without alignment to the Divine Mother Earth. The Divine Mother Earth and the human race are one. There is no separation. They reflect back at one another the states of consciousness. So the Divine Mother Earth, the Earth Mother, is a direct reflection of the human race and the human race's consciousness. The human race is also responsible to a great extent for how the Earth Mother reacts.

Humans don't understand this and when Divine Earth Mother reacts with her tornados, and so forth, they feel that she is part of a chaotic creative Force over which there is no control, or that they are being punished by God. What human beings rarely realize is that the energy that they exude and the collective consciousness that they exude is impacting the Mother Earth.

Now, the reason for this is because, at the very heart, the Mother Earth is a live being. She lives, thinks, breathes and exists very much like a human does; there is very little difference, actually, and humans need to understand this. What happens is that as humans breathe in and breathe out and they exchange their energy fields with the Earth and their fluids with the Earth—and they're mostly water, of course—they are in complete and constant almost what you might call electrical communication, that the very electrical charges in the cells of a human also impact the Earth, and the very electrical charges in the Earth impact the human. This is why sensitive humans and animals almost feel in their body the electricity or the charges before the Earth herself can erupt. They can feel it because there is a connection; there is no separation.

If human beings were at peace with one another and at peace with their heart, the Earth herself would be much more peaceful and a much more regulated place to live. So, the first thing to understand is that humans are not victims. Humans are not victims, humans are creators.

Humans don't understand that they are wedded to victim mentality. They have become so divided and separate that they can only see themselves as helpless victims. Their helpless victim mentality is the energy which is being utilized to create victim/perpetrator consciousness, which then creates disharmony upon the Earth.

The first path that you must take in order to come into greater harmony is to shed, as we believe you are trying to, all the places that you feel yourself to be a victim. That includes any illnesses that you might have or anything that's ever happened to you. To understand that on some level, somehow, somewhere, it was of your own creation. You may not have been conscious of it, and it can often be your fear that you unconsciously carry that is drawing to you certain things and certain experiences, which can be transmuted only by you, and it is not up to another human to transmute that which is yours. That is both frightening to human beings because it means they have ultimate responsibility for themselves, but also can be greatly liberating because it means they have ultimate responsibility and they are no longer slaves. They are not enslaved. Once a soul begins to understand and feel itself liberated from enslavement, usually there is a huge rush of excitement, a huge rush of vitality, because it's the enslavement consciousness that keeps the human from feeling energetic or vital. It keeps a person feeling that it's useless, it's pointless, and it's hopeless. And those kinds of scripts which run through the human consciousness over and over and over again weaken it, weaken it and continue to weaken it, until it no longer feels that it is in control of anything.

So, the first thing you must do is begin to walk a path of self-mastery, realizing that your thoughts and your ideas and your feelings and your beliefs, whether created in this lifetime or thousands and thousands of years ago and carried forth into this lifetime from other lifetimes, are what are creating your reality. Those karmas are coming back to you because of an energetic tie of a consciousness, karmas which were created, lessons which were created, thoughts which were created. In your Highest Self, all is one and all is now. There is no past and there is no future. There is only this thing now, which is a moment in time which is a composite of all other moments in time.

You can't separate yourself from your past lives, it's impossible to do that. Humans don't want to either look at their past lives because they fear their own shadow, they fear their pain, they fear what they created, or they want to get too high and mighty about their metaphysical belief systems, which say there is only the now, so the past isn't important. But the past is important because it's held in your cellular body, in your wisdom storehouse. It is part of who you are. It is not that you live in the past and it is not that you deny the past; it is just that you recognize it. If it seems to be blocking you, you then look at it, deal with it and release it, so you can go forward. And that is all we mean by the past lives.

You must rid yourself of your victim consciousness, which is deeply wedded to victimization from these lives of chaos and witnessing events such as natural disasters or other such manmade events or disease. It is through that victimhood that other lives of victimhood become attached to you. The victim consciousness creates more and more victim lives, until it deepens its path so much that it's very hard for a human soul to then dig its way out. The soul keeps repeating the same path.

Coming into self-mastery is the realization that you have created all those lives and those experiences and that you are creating today, and that you can change whatever it is you want to create today by coming into a Higher Consciousness. The consciousness cannot be changed while still operating in third dimensional, human consciousness, and that's where people get mistaken. They sit in their third dimensional consciousness and they say, "I want a new job, I want a Cadillac, I want this, I want, I want, I want." And they're creating from their third dimensional consciousness, which will not create a reality that they desire. They're still too dense, they're still wedded in fear, and that is what's holding back the frequency of creation.

If you wish to be a master and be in the frequency of creation, it is essential that you learn how to communicate with your Higher Self. If you wish to call it your Angel, it is absolutely fine. If you wish to call it God/Goddess, that is absolutely fine. If you wish to call it your Higher Self, this is absolutely fine. But it is the part of you that can understand and recognize consciousness of a higher and a highest level.

So, we ask you at this point, from this moment forward, to begin every day very seriously on a path of what humans call meditation and what we like to call connection. Every day, you will be visualizing, however you need to, some being of Divine Light, which is, in fact, you, because All is One, so you can see that you are one with this realm. It is not that this realm pushes you away; it is not that this realm does not believe you are worthy to join it; it's that you have not believed that you were a divine being. Until you see and understand the Angel in you, you cannot reach the Angels who are around you. So, it is time for you to see and know and understand the Angel in you.

Angels are interesting. Angels are far more complex than humans have been told, and Angels are far more wedded to the human race than you have been told. So the next thing that you need to do to create the mastery, is to understand that you are a divine being who has the potential and the ability to create for yourself all that you can envision, to realize that much of what you have been taught and told is wrong—it has not been true. Perhaps it has been truth for the human race up to this point but it has been a truth which has enslaved the human race. It is time to stretch the consciousness. It is time to allow your consciousness to go places which previously, it might have rebelled against.

That means that once you agree and make a contract agreement to free your consciousness, you're going to find that events and situations which push you to free your consciousness will be drawn to you. You're going to be challenged, and it won't always be easy. But each one you will know has been sent to you by God/Goddess for you to liberate yourself and come into wholeness and you are going to welcome it as a great teacher and a way for you to step into your Angelic or Highest Self.

These kinds of events come with the shedding of the victim and the realization of your own mastery. It sounds lofty and it sounds impossible. But in your heart, that is who you are. All these other lives that you have lived or you are living today are only a tiny little fragment or a little piece of the truth of who you really are and what you're capable of. We see that from this moment forth, this next journey for you is about learning what you might call the power of creation, the power of self-mastery, and stepping into a sense of being in peace and stepping out of confusion.

Now how does that happen? The peace comes because you realize that everything that's being given to you is according to a Divine plan. Once you realize that and you truly integrate it, all confusion disappears. There's no question why something happened. Why did this happen? You don't wonder, you know, because you know that it has been called to you because you have called it to you, to assist your growth to your Highest Self, in alignment with God and the Angelic Heart, and so there is no confusion anymore. If you try to analyze it with your mind, if you try to look at it from victim consciousness, you will always be confused.

We will stop here and ask if you understand or have a comment about this lengthy message we have given you.

LEA: I completely understand everything. Very clear. Everything is just very clear.

ANGELS: And it feels like something you feel you are able to achieve or are looking forward to achieving?

LEA: Absolutely, absolutely.

ANGELS: Okay. We want to get back to something which is more earthbound. We want you to understand and study the ideas known as Feng Shui, and we don't want you to stop there. It's because this study is going to lead you into a greater teaching. By beginning to understand this idea that things have a flow, that things are created along flow lines, and beginning to understand that there are these flow lines in the earth, these gridding lines in the earth, these energy lines in the earth, it is going to begin to awaken for you a much, much larger and greater part of who you are. And that energy is going to be a very comforting one for you.

Do you understand why we are saying this?

LEA: Yes, I do.

ANGELS: Now, the idea of Feng Shui as it has been taught is often quite limited, and many of the secrets of Feng Shui have been hidden. It's kind of the idea of appealing to the material realm and forgoing the spiritual understanding of the work. People are taught, "Put this here in that corner, put this here," but it's all based on superstition, just like the idea of putting a saint in a certain corner is going to make this happen or that happen. Much of that is based on fear consciousness because a human feels, if I don't do that, something bad will happen. Again, when one is in fear consciousness, one is separated from one's Higher Self. To the Angels, there is no fear because there is no separation. So, that consciousness of Feng Shui with the fear part has no place in it, okay? When you teach Feng Shui, when you use Feng Shui, we ask you to step out of the old ideas of fear consciousness; "Boy, I'd better place that gold coin there or I'll be poor."

Do you understand what we're saying?

LEA: Yes.

ANGELS: Instead, what we want you to understand is the idea of working around the Ley lines and the flow lines of the earth. This is going to be done with your heart. You have this ability and actually, you learned this ability in a life that you had in Atlantis. In that life you were able to read the flow of grid lines or understand that there was some kind of energy that flowed through the earth, around the earth and that impacted all of the earth.

As a result of that, if you start to open your heart and awaken what you're going to literally feel—it's almost like what humans might say that your heart is a dowsing rod but also, the soles of your feet and your bare feet will be a dowsing rod. You will begin to understand why it is that when things are placed or designed or built in certain energy pathways, they have strength, they have power, and they have flow. You won't be doing it because you have learned it from a book or that some other person has taught you—you'd better put a golden coin there or a crystal there. It will be because there's something intuitive inside of you, guiding you and leading you along to create and to draw and to place and to put and to know and to feel and to sense where things belong to be harmonious on the earth.

Do you understand what we're saying?

LEA: Yes, I do.

ANGELS: And you do have this ability. It is a strength in you but it hasn't been fully developed by you. Do you know this?

LEA: Yes.

ANGELS: But you sense it could be?

LEA: Yes.

ANGELS: Now, the other thing that you have an ability to do is to be a greater conduit than you are, and your ability to be a greater conduit will come for you through this work. In other words, you're not going to be the kind of person that's going to conduit in the same way that the one who we are speaking through is. It's more that you are going to be, as we said, like a "sensor." It's almost like you yourself become a sensory organ for the earth and sky. In other words, as you walk, you can sense where the wind would blow, you could sense where the sun would shine, you can sense where the earth, the grass would grow.

Ideally, if you choose this path, it could be very useful in designing communities or places where there's a harmonious energy flow between Mother Earth and the inhabitants of those places. And it could even be that you construct small altars, temples or outdoor garden spaces that serve as little altars, where someone might pass by and as they pass by, they sense something or feel something of reverence. They feel a peace, a joy. In your ability also to work with these energies, you understand that you will begin to harness the nature spirits. You will begin to harness Mother Earth herself, the light, the wind, the elements, you'll begin to understand what we believe is what Feng Shui truly is. Feng Shui has been misunderstood because of the way many people treat the earth today. They don't see it, as we said, as a great and glorious interplay between the earth and sky forces. Do you see what we're saying?

LEA: Yes.

ANGELS: And this is what you could assist with. Now, you could see why that would be something which would help you to alleviate the chaos in your heart. You can see.

LEA: Absolutely.

ANGELS: Already, you feel more peaceful when you think about yourself being among one of those creations.

LEA: Yes.

ANGELS: Wow, everything flows really nice here. There can be peace on the earth. And this ties into your Angel Kaeylarae, the Angel of Peace, the desire to make peaceful places, harmonious places. The places of greater comfort and alignment would be under the charge of the Angel Kaeylarae or the Angel of Peace.

CHAPTER EIGHT

WORKING WITH THE DIVINE FEMININE

SONDRA F.

ANGELS: It is with great pleasure that we have this opportunity today to speak with you. We'd like to begin, as always, to explain to you that the Archangels Ariel, Michael and Gabriel are always with this conduit and join their energies to speak with you. Speaking with you primarily today is the Archangel Ariel, and you will soon see why this is.

We wish to begin today by welcoming you and thanking you for opening your heart to us, to this realm, and to understanding that this realm that humans call angelic or spiritual realm is a realm of your higher frequency or understanding. When you ask to join and communicate with this realm, you are in a sense calling forth your own Higher Self or inner wisdom. If human beings learn how to connect with joy, patience and love to their Higher Selves and to this realm, there is the opportunity on this planet for greater harmony.

It is for this reason that we enjoy so much the opportunity to work with each individual and to help them, as we hope we can assist you, to find a more peaceful way to express yourself on this planet and a way for you to understand, from a higher perspective if you will, your soul's path or growth. We wish to first begin by giving you an understanding of how, to some extent, you have resonated on this planet in previous lifetimes and how you have arrived today at where you are.

From the beginning, your soul has felt more comfortable expressing itself as the more feminine or what humans often call the yin of the yin/yang—the feminine side. As a result of this, you have aligned yourself very many times with groups of women, with goddess cults and with the idea of worshiping Mother Earth herself. It is for that reason that the Archangel Ariel is for you a primary guide, and you have welcomed her energy into your life, as Ariel is the Archangel of Mother Earth and nature.

From the beginning, you have had a desire to align with the female energies. The energies of Mother Earth have been the energies that have called to you most comfortably. You have done your time in various goddess cults, both in primitive—more primitive cultures—as well as in what humans might call the Ancient Greek and Roman expression of those energies. The Goddess Demeter is one of your guides and is a goddess with which you are very familiar; your energy is being aligned in great measure with this Great Goddess.

When you have been in these cults and when you have studied the energy of Mother Earth, it has not been what perhaps modern men and women view as a feminine expression but it has had a great power and a great wisdom of its own. This wisdom is wisdom born of the feminine nature. It is not the same as the wisdom or power of the male aspect. It has strength, it has power, and it is a strength and a power of which you are very aware.

The female side of humanity has been, as you are well aware, beaten down and abused for many thousands of years now. They have tried to weaken the feminine nature and have tried to dismiss it as being less important or powerful. Often times, because of this, it has been necessary for women to fight back, to assert themselves. But they have also found themselves in victim roles through many lifetimes.

We are not saying that you have not done male lives, for you have, but it has not been a more comfortable vibration for you. When you have done male lives, you have chosen lives also equally in respect to the earth. You have been most comfortable in your male lives where earth was respected, such as in a Native American culture. When you have done a male life which was surrounded by brutality, or fierceness or forcing of oneself upon others, it has been difficult for you and you have not found yourself at home or at peace in those lives.

In this life, from our perspective, we see you as attempting to reassert your energy or power. You want to understand the idea of how does one become powerful, be powerful, be a part of nature and be powerful in that way; but also surrender to the Divine Energy or the flow which guides all of life. So, what we see that you have come to at this time is a desire to be powerful and strong and yet also a desire to learn how to surrender to the flow of life and become one with the Divine Nature, the Divine God.

You have understood the signals of nature through your studies in these cults, these goddess rituals, and you have understood how they speak to you and you have understood that there is an inherent wisdom in the natural world. But as a human being now, trying to blend or make the world of man and the world of nature a peaceful place, there are times we feel that it is difficult for you, as it is difficult for most humans, to understand how to find a blending for those two and how to make that a reality.

Now, there are many spiritually-minded human beings on this planet who do not feel the ties to the earth that you do. With you, the earth is okay. You are not at war with the earth. You do not feel that you wish all the time to leave the earth. Some people say, "Oh, I wish to always be off the earth, I'm not happy on the earth, I do not like the earth." It may surprise you or may not, but we are telling you that there are many human beings, because their soul energy is more closely aligned to other planets and other realms, when they come to the earth, they do not feel at home here. But that is not what we sense with you. You do not feel alien or foreign to this planet or the earth. In fact, we sense a deep regard for and respect for the forces that are the earth forces. We understand that from your perspective, it is the idea of how to blend or connect heaven and earth energies, how to be powerful and yet pliant, that are perhaps at the heart of your soul's journey at this time.

We welcome you here and we will be working with you through your questions and through our perspective on where we believe you to be at this time and what we believe would benefit you the most in your motion forward in your life. So, we thank you and ask now if you have a question or comment about what we have just said that you might want to make at this time.

SONDRA: The first question would be that I've not ever explored past lives and where I've been. So, any information—and I'm not sure how I feel about all of this. There is some truth I'm hearing or that I've felt. I don't know how to put it in words. So, past lives, a brief overview if possible.

ANGELS: Are you asking us to explain a bit about why one reincarnates and what happens in the process as well?

SONDRA: Yes.

ANGELS: Well, we will begin by explaining to you that the soul's energy is not limited and energy, as you are well aware, does not die, does not end. It always exists and always is transformed from one state to another. So, from the energetic perspective, you might see it as the energy of God, the Source of All, which forms and reforms itself continually. That we believe you do understand, as you have seen this in nature itself, yes?

SONDRA: Yes.

ANGELS: You are part of nature and because you are a part of nature and a part of God and cannot be separated from that, it is also true that your soul's energy also forms and reforms. There is also a consciousness which is connected to all life, and this we believe you understand as well, yes?

SONDRA: Yes.

ANGELS: This consciousness also does not die but continues to evolve and to grow and to change with the experiences which are given to it. Because of this, when we speak of reincarnation, we speak about the path of your soul or your consciousness, and it is going to be, of course, its own unique path, different from all others.

Because of this, your consciousness chooses experiences which it believes it wants to have in order to expand itself. Ultimately it comes into what you might call Divine Consciousness, which becomes one with All That Is and sees little or no separation between itself and everything. The more separated a consciousness is, the more it believes in its unique individual identity, the more it believes that it lives and dies separate from everything else. This we would define as a lower vibrational consciousness.

As you ascend in your vibrational consciousness, you come closer to unity consciousness. So, those human beings, for example, who are living with the idea that they can kill or hurt without in any repercussion to themselves, are vibrating in a lower form of consciousness or in greater separation. Once one understands that one is a part of All that Is, the idea of what humans call karma or what you sow, you reap, becomes a natural extension of that unity consciousness, for you understand that your impact on anything is going to ultimately be your impact on the self. You cannot impact anything without impacting yourself. This idea of: As you sow, you reap; what you create, you bring back to you—comes from this concept and this understanding.

Those who kill without the idea of repercussion believe falsely that they are in some way getting away with it if they are not caught. This is because they do not know or see the connection between themselves and the one they have murdered. That would be, as we said, an example of great separation consciousness.

Now, the idea that one recreates themselves over and over and over in different forms and in different ways is the idea of reincarnation. The soul comes on to the planet and creates what you might call an infant existence, an infant soul life or lives. In some ways there is a similarity to one life, so we use the term infant soul. Like an infant, there is a connection in a vast way with a spiritual awareness, but there is little deeper consciousness of what that is. It is not formed. So, in an infant soul life, in your infant soul lives, a more primitive existence is essential, for it is not a sophisticated consciousness.

The soul moves through many lives, dying and rebirthing itself, to use the experience of earth life to grow in greater consciousness. It is one of the planets, and certainly by no means the only, where a soul can choose to incarnate a number of times and move into greater soul consciousness through the act of reincarnation. As you experience your lives and your impact on others, you create karma. Karma comes back to you and teaches you, and teaches you in one way—it is one means of teaching unity.

As a soul evolves and goes through Baby Soul stages and Young Soul stages and reaches its Mature Soul stage it begins to have enough experiences, many lives, where the veil gets thin, the unity consciousness becomes greater, and one begins to understand that one is tied to everything. You begin to see that what is returning to you is being created from your action in previous lives. That is what is called karma coming back to you.

For example, perhaps you've been in a karmic battlefield for many lifetimes with a certain individual or certain soul. Those energies are highly charged and powerful. They are going to need to be resolved before one comes into total alignment or unity consciousness. Forgiveness is the only way that these resolutions can occur; for forgiveness carries the energy to burn the karmic cords.

When you encounter someone with whom you've had many lifetimes, whether good or bad experiences, there is a heightened energy, because the energy cords between you are extremely strong, having been formed through many lives. It isn't a neutral place from which you begin your encounters, and often people will say, "I feel like I've known him for many lives," when they meet someone they have known for many lives, because the energy cords between them are quite strong.

As you move into greater awareness and you move through your Mature Soul Cycle, you clear up and clean the karma you've created in your earlier cycles. You can then free yourself in the old soul cycle to deal with what is called self-karma, to learn to love the self completely so that you can ascend and go into Transcendental Soul life, which would not require a physical body.

When you come onto this earth, as you've heard often, it is a teaching ground. You learn lessons, you experience through your physical body things which could not be experienced while in a spiritual body, things which require a separation to experience. And through that, you learn, sometimes quite harshly, how to love in a more profound and deeper love, and you experiment and you learn about God's energy by seeing it physicalized and expressing itself.

So, it is that the soul deepens and grows into wisdom through many lives and many bodies. You are poor and you are rich, you are male and you are female and so forth. You are talented and you have nothing. You have learned all the different states, until you are ready to understand something greater about the world and to join in with the Greater Oneness or consciousness which is the transcendental state.

You have been on this earth numerous times, as we have said. And for your frequency you have chosen to be more comfortable in the female body. It has resonated more comfortably for you. For you it is understanding and resolving the male energy, both within yourself and outside of yourself, that has proven to be a little more problematic because you have been dominated in many of your lives by the male frequencies. You are learning to understand how to wed the male frequency in your own body, how to bring it into a harmony, a yin/yang harmony, if you will, through the use of the male/female power and how to learn to balance that within the self so it can be balanced outside of the self.

We would be happy to speak about any of your previous lives but we do want you to understand that you have enjoyed the company of women a great deal and worked with women in these situations. You have been a caretaker of women; you have enjoyed being in a more primitive life what we would call a midwife and working to help birth life. And as we said, it does not interest all human beings. There are many human beings who feel that earth, as we said, is not their home.

But earth interests you and one of the things that you did in helping to birth children was to understand and experience life coming on to this planet. These kinds of experiences have been important to you and it's where you are strongest. When you get back to the earth energies and nature and listen with your heart and listen with your Higher Self to what the earth is saying to you, you get stronger. This is where you gain your strength, and it is important for you to utilize that if you wish to come into your more powerful divinity. For your consciousness, being linked with the earth helps you to become a Wise Woman. The tribal elder is possible for you, but only with the reverence of the earth, if you understand what we mean.

We will pause here and ask for a comment from you about what we have just said.

SONDRA: I truly understand. And I kind of got away from that. I love my horse and being outside with him. I make a point every day of going on these long walks everywhere, so he's my guide, I think.

ANGELS: We would ask you, when you go on these walks, ask and call on the Goddess Demeter. Call on her and ask her to be your guide, to walk with you, to walk next to you. You're going to find an old friend in this energy and in her; almost that she will become physicalized to you. You will feel her next to you and walking with you. She usually is on your right side, right next to you or slightly ahead of you. She will walk next to you and accompany you on your walks. She has a wisdom that will awaken for you the wisdom you've learned through all your many past lives, and you will begin to be more in touch with your previous lifetimes through awakening her energies.

You have, as we said, been in the idea of the communities where women were left alone and allowed to explore their connection to nature, to God, without the "overbearingness," if you will, of the male energy that has been on this planet for some time. When you have been male, we mentioned, there were lives where you had difficulty. Your life where you were comfortable as a male was Native American.

A life where you were very uncomfortable as a male was in what you would call the Roman times. It was very difficult for you because you were not treated well. You were quite abused because you tried to be very masculine but your energy was fairly feminine in the male body, and it did not help you in those days to have that kind of energy and it was difficult for you. You were abused.

So, for you to try to trust the male energy is not comfortable for you. We do not sense in any way that you are what humans call, a "man-hater" by any means. You are not. It is not that at all. It's not that you are angry at men.

It's that it's a little foreign for you to be that way. You might say, "I can see how these Roman soldiers put on their armor and marched and conquered. I see it, I understand it, I can see where they feel powerful; I know that power." But that boy "inside of you" would say, "But why, but why, like I get it but why would they want to do this?" That is your reaction to that brute male energy. You understand it, you acknowledge it and there's a curiosity for you, but it hasn't been your resonance on this planet as it has obviously been for many others. Your strength has come, as we said, through the female vibration.

Now, it is not that you don't have the ability to take charge, and for you, this is an important theme of course. You like to and need to take charge and are learning in this life how to be in charge, always trying to balance that idea of the male and female and to bring yourself into a harmony there; not being too overbearing in that energy and not being too weak and the victim in your female side. This is the big lesson you're trying to teach yourself in this life.

We will pause and ask for comments or additional questions at this time.

SONDRA: Everything I understand. The next question is that sometimes when I do call on you and other angels, I doubt myself hearing the messages or maybe trying too hard to look for signs. I get frustrated and then I don't know if I mistake the signs; that I'm looking so hard that I imagine I'm hearing things or imagine I'm seeing things. I don't know how to resolve that.

ANGELS: This has been a frustration for you for many lifetimes, so this is not new. Where you connect, as we said, best—let us just explain something. When you have felt and understood the signs, when you have felt yourself connected—in the life where you helped women to give birth, you felt so connected to God when you held the infant in your arms. It was simple for you. Do you understand what we're saying?

SONDRA: Yes.

ANGELS: Simple. There, you never doubted yourself. There, you felt the connection. It wasn't about the mind or thinking something, it was about the heart and feeling it, and there you knew and sensed the presence of something divine. When you have gotten in your way, it's because you have been told through other lives that it needs to be an intellectual process. You see what we're saying?

Let us go to another lifetime. You have, from our quick scanning of your lives—one that we see is a life as what humans would call cloistered with women, in what would be called a convent. It was not your first choice because it is too cold—in those places, without that energy of birth, it did not resonate for you, but you were brought there and you did live there.

Where you struggled and you got angry and frustrated for the first time deeply there was this idea that, "Wait a minute, are all these women really true in their connection or are they lying? Are they pretending to be pious, are they pretending that they know and hear God's words?" It seemed to you that everyone was just trying to pretend harder than the next. Do you understand what we're saying?

SONDRA: Yes.

ANGELS: It made you very angry. Then you started to doubt yourself. You thought, "Well, maybe when they pray they ***are*** hearing all God's words and maybe God isn't talking to me. Maybe I am not good enough or I'm not worthy." And this confusing anger between being angry at these people you thought might be phony or hoaxes, this whole institution called the church, and at the same time angry at yourself thinking perhaps it was only you. This frustration caused what we're going to call a knot in your solar plexus, in the center, in the diaphragm—knotted up and angry.

When you died in that life, you were at first a little angry and then quite relieved to see that God or the energy of the Divine did not reject you, because there was some worry at a human level that a rejection might occur; rejection because you hadn't heard the messages, you thought, as clearly as the others. You were right in that many of the others weren't hearing clearly and were false, but there were others who did have their own clear connection. So, all types of communication with God existed in your convent.

Now, in all these kinds of lives, where you had been around priestesses or others who claimed to have connections or were able to listen to or hear or channel to the Divine, there was always a frustration for you because it seemed that their connections were received through what we call upper crown chakras, upper chakras. Your connection to the Divine has always been through your heart and your hands and because this was not valued in this world—for the most part you felt your gifts were overlooked and not valued. The only place your gifts were valued was in the tents where women gathered to do their crafts and to worship the earth or in what was often called Wiccan cults, where women understood and listened to the earth. There, there was value. But often, in these other places, it felt that what you had to offer was not valued. No one would ever come to you and say, "Tell us what your hands or your heart is feeling. Tell us how it feels to birth a baby goat into the world. Tell us what it feels like to touch the brown earth and hear its messages or to speak with a butterfly."

So, after some time, through these incarnations, even in these women cults, where they seemed to be all about projecting up and outward, nobody was revering the earth in the way you felt it was supposed to be cared for or revered, and a great shut-down happened in you. And today, you are trying to reawaken or reopen and find value in your means of communication.

It is not that you do not communicate, it is not that you do not hear; but your abilities arrive in a different way, on a different path, through the body itself, through the heart, through the hands, through the way that you feel and sense the energies. Do not worry so much about the words but allow the feelings to arise, and you will get back to your strength and you will begin to understand that you do have a purpose on this earth and you are needed on this earth. And if anything, this cult, this true Goddess cult, the cult of Mother Earth, the cult of bridging the Divine with the earth is needed more than ever and it is the gift that you have to give, as you feel and sense what Mother Earth needs and you understand how to listen and respond to her.

It was the frustration set up from those previous lives and the lack of support for your gifts on the earth in general that caused the frustration and that tightness that you carry even today in your heart and your solar plexus. We will pause and ask if you understand what we are saying?

SONDRA: Yes.

ANGELS: It must make you feel good to know that it is not that you are not receiving but perhaps trying to force a way of receiving that it not your natural state. Do you see what we're saying?

SONDRA: Yes.

ANGELS: Do not think that the messages you get or the way you receive in your body is any less valid or important, and don't worry about hearing but go ahead and feel it. When you are receiving messages that the situation is not right for you or the situation that is upcoming is not a pleasant one or something to be wary of, you feel it in your body, yes? You know that feeling where something gets tight, that it's restricted, yes?

SONDRA: Yes.

ANGELS: That is what we're talking about. Your body is quite a good receptor. And when you feel, as you say, that you're walking in comfort, your body begins to expand and you begin to know and understand. So, the first way for you to connect to your guides is through these senses, the kinesthetic senses. Also, begin by opening in greater measure both your third and fourth chakras. Allow your heart and solar plexus to relax a little more and to open, because they're a little bit afraid of being wounded. And the fear that you might get wounded has caused you to put up a little bit of a guard there. Do you understand what we're saying?

SONDRA: Yes.

ANGELS: It's blocking some of your greater abilities, creative abilities, and your ability to receive for fear you're going to get hurt. There is the tie-in, if you will, to this issue we raised earlier, which is about getting powerful and being in your power, because it's going to be necessary for you to open those centers to be in your power, because your power is receiving messages through there. But at the same time, it frightens you because that's where you get hurt. So this is why you're having a little trouble and you're at odds. Do you understand?

SONDRA: I do.

ANGELS: Let us ask you, what does it feel like in that place at the base of the sternum? You know what we're talking about there, by the upper ribs.

SONDRA: Yes.

ANGELS: What does that feel like to you? If you close your eyes and go into that area, what does that feel like to you?

SONDRA: Right now, it's comfortable, but I sense a tightening when I'm uncomfortable or I fear something.

ANGELS: To protect yourself. That is the relationship center, as you are well aware, and the heart is self-explanatory. Then, too, you can feel somewhat of a connection there, yes, for you?

SONDRA: Yes.

ANGELS: Now we're going to ask you to take that third chakra, the solar plexus and the heart energy and connect it now to your second chakra. Let's feel the abdomen energy flowing up through the solar plexus into the heart, and allow then the root chakra to flow up into the solar plexus and the heart. Those connections for you are relatively easy. Once you are in a place of safety, such as you say on your walks or out in nature, what we sense is those four chakras start to relax and communicate, yes?

SONDRA: Yes.

ANGELS: But now we're going to go higher than that and here's where you're getting stuck, yes? In the upper ones. You can see that. Let's spend a moment in a couple of those chakras. You can feel the energy flowing from your heart to the center of your body to your abdomen to your root chakra and down into your legs and into the earth. How peaceful that feels. For you, there can be safety on the earth. You sense that and you feel that. Again, although you may think this is true for all humans, it is not at all true. Some humans are not feeling what you feel, and your gift is to feel this. But other humans are comfortable and feel safe in the upper place that you are resisting.

Let us go to that upper part, the upper third of the body: the head, the crown chakra and the third eye and the throat. Those colors are the ones that are the blues and the indigos and the violets. Those frequencies feel a little, how do we say it—a little nervous energy for you. Do you understand what we're saying?

SONDRA: Yes.

ANGELS: Like a nervous energy. When you get there, it's sort of like you say, that's too much nervous energy, send me back into my comfort zones down there, where I can feel comfortable. Let us help you, because once you can feel comfortable in the higher frequencies and connect them to the other chakras, you will feel those knowing centers open a bit more through the consciousness, the higher consciousness, and you won't feel so unhappy, as if somehow it's been denied you.

There is a way of receiving that is called the "knowing," and that is the crown chakra. That is the way the "lightbulb" goes off and you feel that you know truth for you. "I don't know why I know but I just know. I know. I just understand something. I know I've been here before," for example. The third eye is where you see your past lives. That's where you see them. The throat of course is where you can communicate and speak what you see.

So, let us go in through your third eye and we're going to ask you to envision—don't worry about whether you're making it up. Envision the life where you helped women to birth their children. Envision a life there, where you were giving a helping hand. What would that look like? Then describe it to us. It doesn't matter that you might be believing you're incorrect; anything you say is okay. What would that look like, that life?

SONDRA: It comes right up through my hands.

ANGELS: This is what we said to you, yes?

SONDRA: Yes.

ANGELS: That's okay. Then do it this way. Do it through your hands. That's okay.

SONDRA: It's just a tingling sensation. I feel a strong sensation. But I don't see things.

ANGELS: Yes, you are correct. Well, you experienced enough pain and you're not someone who is fond of pain, so you have blocked this, yes?

SONDRA: Yes. I don't see things.

ANGELS: Yes, because some of what's happened to you has not been good, okay, and that's why. You're afraid of torture. You can feel you can get emotional, don't you, when we said that word, torture? You can feel it. What do your hands feel like when we say that word?

SONDRA: They feel numb.

ANGELS: Yes, that's exactly what you do.

SONDRA: I don't know if it's spiritual, or maybe that's just interpreting it that way.

ANGELS: You are afraid of all the things that—you are afraid of what we could call the darkness, you see?

SONDRA: Yes.

ANGELS: That's what we're going to call it then. And whether it is being embodied through humans or whether you fear it in the astral realm, it's that idea that there is something—let me go to where I'm comfortable, where Mother Earth can cradle me and I can be in the light. But the darkness is what you have shut down, and we understand this and we understand why human beings do this. But we're going to ask you to understand and think about—we don't expect you to completely get it at this point, but the journey to greater light always has to go through darkness because you cannot find the greater light while you still feel dark and fear. It needs to be faced and looked at and understood, so that it never has sway over you again. When it is pushed into a closet or aside or it is pushed away, it becomes extremely powerful. The more you push away something, the more power it gains. Do you know that?

SONDRA: Yes.

ANGELS: We will explain to you that this conduit who sits across from you has had to journey, in this life as well as in some other lifetimes—we'll just speak of this life—has had to journey in this lifetime through some very dark experiences with energy that was disembodied. We did not rescue her, if you will, right away because she needed to face it herself. She needed to know that even when something dark was confronting her, she could find the Light and it could not consume her. If we rescued her right away, it would not empower her fully. Do you understand what we're saying?

SONDRA: Yes.

ANGELS: So, it is that every human being must do their own journey through the shadow into the Light, and it will be the only way that a human being becomes free. As long as you push away the parts of the self that are in shadow, the parts outside of the self that are in shadow, that which one fears, you can never fully empower yourself. And if you are not fully empowered, you cannot be fully open to receive. We think you understand but we know that you will listen again to our words and that they will deepen for you as you begin your own soul's journey.

Your Higher Self will never push you faster than you can go. Your ego will. But if you are given an event to face by your Higher Self, it is because your Higher Self believes that you are ready to face it. And even if it does not resolve immediately, your Higher Self knows that it is essential for you to understand and to see it for you to begin the journey to wholeness or empowerment.

When you were in one of the lives that we talked about with a group of women, you were all tortured as witches. You have witnessed those you love and yourself being tortured. This is one of the experiences you have had which you do not wish to see with your third eye or feel with your hands. It was extremely painful for you. The deaths were long and torturous, and it was a senseless slaughter. It was of course done out of fear and out of misunderstanding and out of a desire to destroy the earth energies. You were not evil, you were not deserving of this punishment, and it was something which happened to many, many, many thousands of people.

But it is a painful experience for you and you do not enjoy looking at these kinds of issues, at the pain and the disease and the suffering which has gone on here on the earth. Your way of comforting yourself is different than others. Your way of comforting, as we said, is to connect to the Earth Mother. Others have found greater comfort in escape. So those who receive messages through their crown and their third eye are often those who also experienced what you experienced but who chose to disappear through their upper chakras and learned how to communicate and disappear that way. They felt that it was not comfortable for them to be on the earth.

In your case, you feel it is uncomfortable to open because then you'll have to see or re-experience some of the pain and horror that your soul has known. This is also why you have shut out your past life remembrances, in the desire to keep yourself separate from that pain. When you are ready to begin to acknowledge the full journey of your soul, you will begin to open this up and begin to have glimpses of previous lives in your third eye.

The idea that you need to force, this is not so, but you could sit with some idea of creating visions, a little bit here and there, beginning to see if you can make a vision of giving birth in a previous life or helping a woman give birth in a previous life, rather than just feeling it with your hands. As you begin to make pictures, then it will awaken your third eye and you will begin to understand how to see more from that spiritual point of view.

Before your soul can transcend the earthly plane, it will need to pull all the pieces or parts of the self to it; the integrating of the self. The parts that you do not want to see—this is true for all humans, not just you, they need to be brought back to you so they can be fully integrated and healed. The wounded parts need to be brought back to be healed, and that is what the healing is and that is what many who call themselves Lightworkers and so forth are involved in: how to bring the parts from old and previous lives to the Self and bring those together to be healed—healing the deepest wounding so that the soul can then transcend earth life and move into greater enlightenment.

It is similar to denying your childhood. In order to be truly whole in one's body, you need to be able to acknowledge your childhood. It's sort of the same for the many lives. From the soul's perspective, there's only one journey and that's the journey of your soul. It doesn't see the definitions and the divisions between lives as you do. It sees you as one energy, changing and re-changing—experiencing and then eventually integrating and bringing all those experiences up to God.

So, we will pause and ask for your comment or question at this time.

SONDRA: I understand this. My question is when I am afraid of the dark, sometimes at night, I can't get to sleep. Am I afraid of—I sense what we say is evil, something bad. Can I relate that to just not wanting to visit these past lives?

ANGELS: When one is afraid of the devil that's where it has power over you.

SONDRA: Okay.

ANGELS: Do you see what we're saying? Because also, be aware of course that it was drummed into you pretty good in that life in the convent. So be aware, you see, you've had those experiences of knowing and understanding that there's something that's not of the Light. How do we explain this to you? Those energies that are called evil, whether in human body or in fourth dimensional realm, those energies only have power when they are connected to a place in the human that's wounded, that's not whole. In other words, the same things don't scare everybody. Do you know what we're saying?

SONDRA: Yes.

ANGELS: They scare you because you have not unearthed or dug up all the wounding and that is what you fear. When you have healed those places and you have met with the darkness or the shadow, you won't be afraid anymore. Nothing will ever frighten you. Think of the idea that Christ wrestled with the devil because until he could face the darkness, he could not get all the way to the Light, you see?

SONDRA: Yes.

ANGELS: That is why you have to face it. What you're going to find, interestingly enough, is that it is not frightening at all. It is actually just horrible wounding, horrible, horrible woundedness that has been created. Pain and suffering and power and evil are just wounds that humans and other beings have done to one another. This energy, because energy never dies—it gets stuck, literally stuck in a fourth dimension, a spiritual realm which is not an ascended one, which is part of the lower astral plane. Third and fourth dimensions are the lower astral plane, where you live and where your mind can travel.

It can have consciousness attached. We're not saying that isn't true. There is at times a consciousness which can be attached to it or sometimes it can just be free-floating fear that does not have a consciousness attached. But it does not have any power anywhere over anything or anyone, unless you give it so, and you give it so by fear. It feeds off your fear. So, it's best just to face it. Your best bet would be to keep all the lights off and sit up, and when you feel the dark, fear-based energies coming to you, rather than turn the light on, just say to them, okay, what do you want to say to me? What are you about? Who are you? Let's talk, okay? Let's talk. I'm not going to be afraid of you anymore.

When you feel it they will say, "We are evil or we are hatred." You'll feel that in you and then you're just going to look at it and you're going to look at that energy. You're going to say, "I understand that you're wounded, you're the wounded parts of me and you're the wounded parts of others, and I'm not going to be afraid of you." You'll look at them and say, " I'm going to invite you back to the Light." They might not want to go and it's okay if it doesn't want to go. But you're going to find yourself feeling a little more empowered if you face it rather than if you allow it to have power over you. You understand what we're saying?

SONDRA: I do.

ANGELS: And in the end, you're going to find yourself whole or more whole by facing your demons, by facing this darkness. You'll find that your third eye will begin to open, your crown chakra will begin to open, and you'll begin to really communicate more clearly with your guides, hearing their words and knowing their thoughts, and you won't be so afraid because you will have sat there and been able to look at and see the darkness and realize that it is nothing to be afraid of. It's going to be a journey for you but you're going to be okay.

You will come out on the other side. And as we said, your Higher Self will not lead you anywhere it doesn't believe you're capable of enduring.

SONDRA: So my question is, when this has occurred and it has happened, I've called on you and my other angels and they have always been there and they've put the brakes on. Should I hold off a little earlier than calling for you and see if I can get through it myself but know that if I need to, you will be there?

ANGELS: Well, this would make you feel more empowered yourself, yes? In other words, it's okay to need us but you don't even know what it is you're fighting, do you?

SONDRA: No.

ANGELS: And how can you ever be empowered when there's always something that you have to fear because fear blocks love. There are only two states: fear and love, and fear is the illusion that love does not exist. If you do not know what it is you're fighting, you can never, ever, ever be empowered. There will always be a weakness in you. So next time, perhaps you might want to ask it, "Who are you? Who are you?" Who do you think it is? Who do you think it is that you're afraid of?

SONDRA: It's not in this third dimension. It's something—

ANGELS: What does it look like to you?

SONDRA: It feels, it doesn't look.

ANGELS: To look is too scary for you.

SONDRA: That's right. It feels threatening.

ANGELS: Like a dark coldness.

SONDRA: Yes.

ANGELS: That's what we feel it is to you; a dark coldness. Now, let us explain to you that when you were imprisoned, and you were imprisoned in another life and you were chained and that was the first time that this energy visited you. You got the energy attachment or the energy goblin, if you will, in a previous life, when you were chained in a very bad prison. It was an accumulation, if you will, of the energy of fear, not only yours but all the fear that was down in that dungeon. You can see that it is a kind of dungeon fear. Do you understand what we're saying?

SONDRA: Yes.

ANGELS: So, it's followed you. Now, if you understand that it has come from a previous life that attached to you when you died—and you died a very horrible death in that life, a slow and agonizing death, that energy, because of your slow and agonizing death and the fear of all those around you—you were in what humans would call the hell realm. You can't make a better hell realm than that, right?

SONDRA: Yes. (tearfully)

ANGELS: So, you can see you get emotional, yes?

SONDRA: Yes.

ANGELS: You can feel this. Now, you understand that when you get emotional, it's because these stories have hit a resonance in you, yes?

SONDRA: Yes.

ANGELS: Okay. Now, this hell realm that you visited is where these beings live, these dark demons. But understand for a moment—let's do something for you for a moment. What if those demons are only just the wounded energy of all those poor souls who suffered like you? What if, instead of being something else, it's the collective horror or fear of those poor wounded men that were there? Wouldn't you then feel sorry for it? Wouldn't you then have patience for it and love for it?

SONDRA: Yes.

ANGELS: Yes. So next time, when it comes to you, rather than being afraid of it, see it as the wounding it is. See it as well—a funny image. You know, in the movies that they make about the Caribbean pirates?

SONDRA: Yes.

ANGELS: They have those ghosts, those men.

SONDRA: Yes.

ANGELS: Well, in a sense, it's not dissimilar, okay? But those souls in the movie pretend that they enjoy their ghost realm and your souls do not. They are tortured, they are dark. It is really just the cries and the screams and the tortured calls of these wounded souls. Visit it again but visit it now with sympathy for yourself and for them. Say, "I know you are wounded, I understand the pain and the suffering and the wounding, but I release myself from it. I release myself from you. If you choose to release yourself from this wounding, my angels are now going to come in and they will take you and your wounding to a better place. I offer myself as a conduit for your wounding, for the darkness. Go through me to the Light, go around me to the Light;" however you feel comfortable doing it. Call on the Archangel Michael at that time and then become a helpmate for that darkness to lift it to Light.

Sometimes the darkness will fight and will not go but the wounding will go. The wounding will go, so some of that darkness will dissipate into Light because you're offering to help it instead of pushing it away. Do you see what we're saying?

SONDRA: Yes, I do.

ANGELS: This will help you and should help you be less afraid.

PART II

STARSEEDS, SEEKERS, FAIRIES, ALIENS AND WEE PEOPLE

GLOSSARY

Author Barbara Marciniack, calls them *The Family of Light*, or *Bringers of the Dawn*. Others call them Starbeings or Starseeds and Lightworkers, but from my perspective there are many people on the earth today working with higher dimensional frequencies and wisdom. They are here to assist, each in their own way, to bridge Heaven and Earth. Part II contains their stories. Although human at this time and having reincarnated on the Earth many times previously, these people have also done lives on many planets and carry the remembrances of being more than human. They have access to dimensional consciousness beyond third and fourth—they see sacred geometry, can communicate with animals, fairies, and angels; and understand the concept intuitively that we are all One.

We are alive on many dimensions and as we realize that—and remember who we've been on all planes of existence (and once again integrate the information into our human selves) we grow closer and closer to our true Avatar Mastery.

Below is a glossary of terms that you might want to know to read this second half. The channelings I chose were typical of the type done for Starseeds and Seekers. This little glossary is far from comprehensive on the subject of extraterrestrials but was designed to cover some of what you will need to understand Part II.

The Akashic Records

The Akashic Records are the "libraries" of God where everything which has been done (or will be done) is stored. These records are not stored "third dimensionally" as they would be on the earth but are stored energetically and can be accessed by lifting your consciousness to the correct frequency and asking the Archangel Metatron to release the information to you.

The Pleiadians

The Pleiadians, who herald from The Pleiades, carry a vibrational signature that is much aligned with the energies of the Divine Feminine and the Water Element and often have simultaneously incarnated into dolphins and whales. They are masters at the arts but most of all they are masters of song and sound healing. They understand intuitively how to communicate with vibration and sound. The history of the Pleiadian soul progression is interwoven into the earthly soul progression. The karma is essentially entwined.

In the Pleiades they had created a world of complete peace and harmony. They were vibrationally aligned with nature and communicated and spoke with all forms of natural life. The frequency was what humans would perceive as fifth dimensional and higher. They achieved this state of "beingness" by pushing away any negativity and essentially denying the shadow side of their natures. As the Orion Wars caused more and more beings to leave their planet of origin some of them came to the Pleiades. This contributed to the harsh "reality" of the Orion Wars entering their Eden-like existence. The energy stirred up by the Orion Wars began to lower the vibrational frequency of the Pleiades and the Draconian Reptilians who were already immersed in their conquest wars of intergalactic domination spotted them on their radar. In other words prior to that time the Pleiadians were vibrationally too high to be seen by the low vibrational Reptilians—but once the Pleiadians started to feel even the slightest tremors of their own shadow and fear they could be "seen" once again. The result was a sweeping in of the Reptilian invaders and a destruction of the Pleiades.

I have regressed and channeled for enough Pleiadians that I see the common story emerge time after time. The total and complete inability to comprehend what was happening to them at the moment of invasion—they went from what was essentially still a very much peaceful and harmonious world to suddenly being overpowered and held captive by rageful Reptilians. It took the Pleiadians a while to even comprehend the evil that was upon them as they did not have knowledge of such things. The Reptilians understood how to paralyze their opponents with frequency control and those that could not escape were immediately thrust into confusion and fear which lowered their vibrational levels: Where before the Pleiadians could teleport to escape, now their fear kept them dense and enslaved.

As time progressed and the war raged a great deal of DNA experimentation arose on both sides. The Pleiadians used the captured Reptilians to alter their DNA and attempt to merge it with Pleiadian DNA to create a more peaceful species. The Reptilians understood that the Pleiadians had gifts that they wanted and they enslaved and bred with them in an attempt to gain some of the gifts of the Pleiadians and to dominate and control them. As a result of that you will find many humans today who carry both the Pleiadian and Reptilian energy as a result of being a product of those experiments.

Those that escaped came to earth and many of them "hid" in the fourth and fifth dimensional fairy realms on earth to heal their wounded souls. But the karma followed them, as karma always does, and the Reptilians and the Pleiadians have relived their karma through their earthly human forms time and time again. Although there are many other galactic beings who have suffered due to the violence of the Orion Wars (popularized in the Star Wars series), according to the angels every war that we are aware of on earth is an extension of the Orion/Galactic Wars that were waged intergalactically with many other star systems, not just the Pleiadians. WWII for example with its DNA experimentation in the Nazi camps and the desire to breed a master race was once again an Orion Wars karma carried to earth. Today the HAARP and the GWEN towers are example of the frequency wars being waged on earth.

PERSONAL EXPERIENCE: Many of my friends are Pleiadian. One of my good friends talks dolphin in her sleep. I shared a hotel room with her and awoke in the middle of the night to hear her speaking a strange dolphin speech which went on and off most of the night. Since then I have heard a few other stories of dolphin-speakers. At night they return to their pod and communicate with the dolphins. I also know two Pleiadian Mermaids. When I have done energy healing work on them they return to their "mermaid" state and see themselves in their mermaid bodies.

The Arcturians

The Arcturians are a highly evolved species who live fifth dimensionally and higher. The human Arcturians on this planet are gifted healers, counsellors, and therapists and long for community. Most Arcturians I have known at one time or another joined a spiritual community and lived with them. They also left the communities because they realized that these communities often did not work—the idea of equality had not been firmly established and the need to control was still alive even in the spiritual communities. Human Arcturians tend to incarnate in bodies that do not "stand out" in any way. They like conformity because they believe it leads to a more harmonious way of living—on their own home turf they have evolved to all looking pretty much alike to eliminate jealousy and competition. They are truly focused on "One for All and All for One" and will lift the lowest member up to a higher place if they slip.

In order to achieve this unity on their planet they regulate reproduction very tightly. Only select ones may reproduce and the greatest honor is to raise the young. They do not fight the idea of group over individuality and welcome it. This is quite a contrast to the Pleiadians who love to be expressive and individualistic and even stand out from the crowd.

PERSONAL EXPERIENCE: My first contact with an "awake" and conscious Starseed was an Arcturian. I was at a friend's birthday party many years ago and I saw a man who appeared to me to have very high vibrational energy. I felt no inhibition to go directly up to him and say, "Hi, I'm Margaret and I was wondering: 'Are you an angel?'" He answered right away, "No, I'm Arcturian." He then proceeded to tell me to read the book, *We the Arcturians*. After that I met a man who painted pictures of his Arcturian life and hung them all over his home. He was remembering the world he had "left behind."

The Sirians

Sirius A and Sirius B Star Systems have very different types of beings and it is impossible to classify them into one group. They vary widely. I have encountered a few types of Human/Sirians from the Sirius star systems: The Cat people (who also come from Regulus) and the Elongated Head blue people who look human but with bigger heads and also what we think of as the Wee People. The Sirians are behind the building of many of the largest structures such as the pyramids—they understand astronomy and astrology and the paths of the stars and the systems and have always had a means to communicate with other Star Systems. They are behind the understanding of sacred geometry and we see their influence in many of their creations around us today. The Egyptian Ankh was a Sirian device used for frequency manipulation and communication. Most Sirians work with the beings from other star systems and are also very helpful to mankind. Although they wish to work with governments and leaders they also realize that currently on Earth their contact must be limited due to the agenda of control and manipulation which rules the governments on the planet. They are dedicated to assisting mankind in awakening from their state of "sleepwalking" but like all high spiritual beings they understand that humans have to learn their lessons on their own; so the Sirians offer help but won't interfere unless asked, or unless it is necessary for the survival of Mother Earth herself.

PERSONAL EXPERIENCE: I uncovered a life in Teotihuacan, Mexico during its height around 450 A.D. where I was a Sirian emissary and I went back and forth between the ships and the priests relaying messages of what was happening with the Galactic Federation and the Orion Wars.

The Draconian Reptilians and The Zeta Reticuli Grays

The Grays and Reptilians are two different species. The Reptilians are the shapeshifters who often host in human bodies. Many human Reptilians are like many other Starseeds who are caught in the human karmic soul drama and they—although they don't like it—are also subject to the laws of the universe such as karma. Many of their schemes turn on them as well and I believe we will be seeing more and more of this as they grow more desperate and arrogant. What they have been able to do is to manipulate the human race through implants and other experimentation and so they have kept humanity "asleep" which has served their purpose of control. The non-human Reptilians live underground and appear to be large, fierce lizards.

PERSONAL EXPERIENCE: I witnessed a human being become extremely angry and "shape-shift" into a Reptilian monster-type being. Needless to say it was frightening at the time because I didn't understand what I was seeing. When they are angry they are most susceptible to being unable to hold the human form intact.

The Grays

These are the little gray people with the big almond eyes and seem to be behind the abductions and much of the experimentation we hear about. Although I am the only one I have ever found to channel this particular piece of information about them, what I have gotten about the Grays is that they are the "rejected" Arcturians. Long ago those Arcturians who could not hold fifth dimensional or higher vibration were sent off planet (much like what we did when we sent the criminals to Australia) and they have been trying to establish an identity and community ever since. They appear to be a lot more lost than the Reptilians and although they too are behind much "bad" stuff on this planet they seem to just be serving their own ends—wanting to reproduce and maintain their species rather than actually control the Universe in the same way the Reptilians appear to want to.

The Andromedeans and Praying Mantis

Those that I am familiar with from the Andromeda Star system have a very similar energy to "Mr. Spock" on Star Trek: Scientific, unemotional, detached but with "good hearts." The Human/Andromedeans I know often suffer greatly from feeling always outside the human experience; they watch and observe with curiosity the goings-on but don't get "hooked in" in the same way as the average human. They are here to learn and understand the wisdom of the human heart and the human emotional realm and often they will put themselves into situations of "self-help" or "spiritual studies" to experience and witness the events.

The Praying Mantis Species appear to be observers and as far as I can tell they do no harm. They stand about 6-7 feet tall and will visit fourth dimensionally on occasion. They usually travel in pairs. They will observe to study and learn but will not interact with humans in any way to impact their lives.

PERSONAL EXPERIENCE: I have met a few Human/Andromedeans—sometimes they will freak you out because they seem so removed and analytical. One of my friends freaks people out because he stares at people when he first meets them—until you realize he's just collecting data and he's actually quite nice. I have also had two large praying mantis beings visit me fourth dimensionally. They just stand there and observe.

The Seekers

The Seekers are a spiritual group of "older souls." It is a group of souls who are studying with the Ascended Masters and who incarnate in many, many different guises and planets and universes to study life, and for many of them, eventually Life Creation. They do not relate to any one group as much as they relate to their Seeker Path—although you will see by the channeling I do for one Seeker that he needs to settle down and identify with a group if he is to learn the lessons of the heart.

For some of them their ultimate goal is to work with the Merlin energies of creation and become Life Creators or Life Carriers and when they "graduate" they become one of the ones who actually "seeds" life on other planets. However, many of these Wizards have misused the energy and created destruction. They have some serious karmic clean-up to do!! It is not Merlin who is "bad" it is his apprentices who have often gone astray or engaged in Wizard Wars. In my opinion the last thing you want to do is engage in a Wizard War!!

CHAPTER NINE

THE TASKS OF THE STARSEEDS

SANDY S.

ANGELS: We are most delighted to have this opportunity to speak with you. We wish to calm your heart today, to help you to be in the world, to be in it but not to be of it. We do not want you to feel every bump and every pain within your physical human. We wish you to understand that your physical human is not capable of holding all that you're feeling, and that is why you are feeling so stressed. Your human cannot hold this information that you are receiving from the Earth, from your galactic self, from all the pieces of yourself. Your human will need to die, in a sense, in order for you to be reborn.

What we are talking about today is not a death of your physical body but the death of your human consciousness, or perhaps you might feel more comfortable saying the integration of your human self with your Higher, Galactic and other Selves.

When your human heart tries to carry the weight of the world, it sinks. It cannot be successful in this endeavor. And because it sinks, because you feel the weight of it, you find yourself in what is thought of as helplessness or depression. You must begin to learn how to step out of your human heart, and to a great degree it will feel as if you've detached yourself to some extent. But the detachment should bring with it peace. The type of detachment we are speaking about is a detachment which leads to peace. The idea of being detached, as in being "zombie-like" and not feeling is not what we are speaking about, rather we are speaking of an "Over-self" that can hold the reality of what is happening but still remain attached to your Higher Self as witness.

It is the falling apart of those systems which aren't working that you are feeling and you are sensing and all humans are sensing. Those who are profoundly attached to those systems in one way or another feel the pain of their fall most profoundly, because of course, that is how many humans have defined themselves. They believe that is who they are. They truly forgot that they are anything else other than human. They've been encouraged to forget because enslavement doesn't occur with an awake being. Enslavement depends upon keeping someone locked within their human, limited consciousness.

You are different than the average human because as a Lightworker or, as you like to say, a "Bringer of the Dawn," you have access to information and knowledge and parts of yourself that most humans do not. As a result of that, you have tools that will allow you to maintain a level of detachment during difficult times, times that would bring down the average human.

Your awareness from your higher perspective helps you to understand that the very reason you're here is for the breakdown of these systems. You are here to bear witness and to assist mankind to move from the breakdown to something else. You are also aware that the breakdown is necessary in many regards, because human beings will stay far too attached to the old ways if they are not woken up profoundly.

What is interesting is that the Dark Forces are bringing about many of these collapses. They have a belief system, from their point of view, that the fear which is generated by these collapses will make them happy, will feed them. And so it does not upset them and at times, they encourage it, through war and other events, to create chaos in order to feed, as you know. You know this. But if you refuse to buy into the chaos and the breakdown and you liberate yourself despite it, you can understand that your personal journey towards enlightenment has also progressed leap years, light years, because you can hold the Light, the Truth of something Higher, when the illusion or the matrix is collapsing, because you are not plugged into the matrix of collapse, you are plugged into the matrix of creation.

It is only your ability to hold on to and plug into the matrix of creation that will allow you to transcend the experiences that are happening all around you. Detachment is extremely important, but there is a reattachment piece as well, and that is the reattachment to your Higher Self. Pure detachment from everything will not save you. Detachment from the lower, and reattachment to the Higher, will. Now, once you are truly attached to your Higher Self, even death has no hold, has no fear, because you are not living in your human, you are living somewhere else. The death of your human body doesn't upset. It has no hold.

So, your job at this time is going to be the final release from your human stories, the final release from your humanness, to fully embrace that which you are, which is something greater than your limited human has been. We are going to pause for a moment and just welcome you and see where you are with us at this point.

SANDY: I'm just taking it in. I'm just hearing what you're saying and it's all fitting where I'm at.

ANGELS: What is the big button for you that pulls you down into your human again?

SANDY: Fear.

ANGELS: Of?

SANDY: Dying.

ANGELS: Of dying.

SANDY: It's not as much death as pain. It's fear of the unknown of it. Is it going to be torturous, is it going to be brutal, am I going to suffer? Not knowing and not having control over it.

ANGELS: We will talk then for a moment about death. Now, what we want you to understand is that kind of death only occurs when someone is plugged into the third dimensional, limited matrix. You understand? That death is not possible when you are in your Higher Spiritual Self. It doesn't exist.

SANDY: Yes. And when you were speaking, I understand it. Conceptually, I understand it and energetically, I understand it. But the piece of my human that doesn't fully trust is still holding on and saying, "Yeah, right."

ANGELS: Yeah, they will come and they will get me like they have so many other times.

SANDY: Exactly.

ANGELS: And we understand. We do understand that that is a part of your creational realm. We understand that what you fear, whether you realize it or not, is yourself. You fear yourself because you're afraid that you will create that for yourself again, yes?

SANDY: Yes, absolutely.

ANGELS: And that's really true. It's interesting in your case. You are enlightened enough that you don't fear someone will do it to you; you fear you'll do it to yourself. And you fear that you're not going to be able to transcend. What you have to begin to realize is that each time you find that fear manifesting; you actually don't run from it. You sit with it, you look at it, and you notice what it is. Where is it that that is plugged into your human body? Breathe into that and call on your Higher Self and ask your Higher Self to come in, to come swooping in, and remind you that that is just the fear and the illusion of your third dimensional, human self. You have no reason to experience that kind of death. That kind of death does not serve you.

You're learning and wanting to teach others how to transcend those kinds of experiences. So, why would it suit your soul's growth to do it again? It would not, you see. You're trying to learn and to teach others how to have that fear but to liberate yourself from that fear. You have to first have the fear, and it has to be real for you, and then you step into the next piece, which is the liberation from the fear. If you did not have the fear, you could not liberate yourself and then teach others how to liberate themselves.

So, rather than see that fear as a reality, see it as your teaching tool. Oh, good, it's coming up again and I'm going to be the student now and I'm going to learn how to get rid of it by applying various tools of my own that I'm discovering. And then when I figure out what works for me, I'll be able to hold classes and teach others or talk to my friends when they're frightened and sit with them, or when I'm doing my hospice work, working with the dying, I will be able to pass these tools along to them, you see.

That is why you're even bothering to have the experience of the fear; so that you can transcend it and then teach others. Rather than locking into it as a reality of your own death, lock into it as a reality of your schoolroom. Then it becomes a thing that you're sitting at a desk, you're studying it as though a teacher was teaching you, and you're learning the tools. And it doesn't become so personal, which allows you not to have the fear so much. Do you understand?

SANDY: Yes, I do. I feel like I am doing that. There is another fear that I—as you were talking, I felt a bigger—not a bigger fear but another fear that is interfering. Can I share it?

ANGELS: Yes.

SANDY: It's a lurking fear. It comes from behind me, above the head. It's a lurking fear of my own ego, that I'm going to get too powerful, and to own my own power and to be who I am in this world, I'm going to get carried away and I'm going to be an egomaniac. I'm afraid of the power, of misusing power, of all the information that's coming in.

ANGELS: How would you misuse it? What would you do in this life, at this time?

SANDY: Become God, you know, feel god-like.

ANGELS: And what would you do with that power?

SANDY: I would…

ANGELS: Would you make others suffer?

SANDY: No, no.

ANGELS: Okay.

SANDY: But I would forget that I was a child of God. I think that I would be—

ANGELS: Think that you were the "end all and be all?"

SANDY: Yeah.

ANGELS: Does that make you laugh when you say it?

SANDY: So, it's easier for me to feel small. It's safer in a way than to feel the big grandiosity of being everything, because we all are everything. We all are pieces of it, so there's truth in it. I'm just afraid that I'll be blinded and be—I don't know if—I don't know what to say.

ANGELS: We understand. But it helps for you to actually state how you would misuse it because then you realize you really wouldn't in this life. Oh, if I am more powerful, I can make others kneel at my feet and do my bidding.

SANDY: No, it's not so much that. It would be more like they will just see how great I really am or they will—well, yeah, they will worship me. I think there's a part of me that likes being superior or likes people—I'm really just coming clean now and owning this part of me that likes to be the teacher or the wise one, the one who can help others, you know, and others—I'm not saying it's all that but there is that piece that I'm afraid of in myself. It's like dark.

ANGELS: Well, yes, if it becomes ego-driven, then only people who are resonating with that same energy become attracted to you.

SANDY: Right.

ANGELS: If you are truly in service to the Light and wanting to bring information through you of higher truth, higher reality, your job is always that you're going to try to empower others, you see. Being in service to the Light is that. Those who are in service to the Light are saying, "Oh, by the way, you're a Master too just like I am." They never say, "Oh, by the way, I'm a Master and you aren't," you see. And that's the difference. When you find yourself saying, "Oh, by the way, I'm a Master and you aren't," then oops! But if you're truly allowing the Light to flow through you, as the great Masters do, they always are saying, "You are a Master, you see. You are the master. You've forgotten perhaps, but I forgot at one point." You say, "And I still forget, right?" You say to them," I still forget all the time."

You say to others, "Let's awaken the Mastery in you, so that you and I can be Masters together and stop this fear-based enslavement that we're living in." You see? When you're working from that intention, there's no possibility of misuse. The misuse comes from the intention to be above or greater than. If that is true, then yes, you need to stop and realize. The idea is that once you have the key, you just want to run around and unlock all the prisoners, right? But you're doing it because you were in prison, too. It's like you're a prisoner who got the key first, and you run around and unlock all the prisoners. But you're not saying, "Oh, by the way, I was your jailer; bow down to me because I have your key." You say, "Oh, by the way, I happen to be a slave, too, but I just got the key and I'm letting us all go."

SANDY: Right.

ANGELS: And if you can look at it that way, it will take away any of that doubt that you have.

SANDY: Yeah, because the doubt keeps me small, you know, and I feel like that's a trick. It's a trick to keep me small, a trick in me that doesn't want to grow up or doesn't want to see—I don't know. I'm putting it out because I want to free myself from it. It's enslavement. That kind of thinking is enslavement.

ANGELS: It is enslavement and you are correct, because let's say the slave gets power after being so beaten and enslaved. Often times he will take the power and become as bad if not worse than his own master, you see. That is what has happened with you and many others throughout their many incarnations. The suffering was so great that when each of you took back your power you used it for revenge. But it's not the way to free you from karma. So, if you are here to teach others how to free themselves from karma then what you're going to want to do is you're going to assert: I freed the slave, but I don't want to be the master. I want to run around and free all the others and I want us to be in community as free beings. And where we feel that we're not free, I want us to talk openly about that, you know, and share our communications, and be equal and show each other our skills and our gifts, and try to be in loving harmony.

But you're going to be subject to—you know this world is going to be in a great deal of difficulty, so it's going to be very difficult not to buy into it, to not let it take you down into the old places and then to begin once again to feel enslaved and then wanting to come back in your power, you know, and be brutal or misuse it. Or "Look at me, I'm so powerful"—those old stories. So, you realize that's not what it's about. It's really about, at this time, anyone who wants to get on board that Mastery Train is welcome. Your job is to get on yourself and then reach your hand out and say, "Here, climb aboard." That's all. Nobody is higher or lower. Everybody is on the same train. That's an image that will help you.

It's the old template, the master/slave, you know, the king and the servants and so forth. But that's what you're all trying to move out of. So, again, you'll just know when you feel the old template, the old matrix, not the new one you want to plug into. It's not that it won't be difficult at times but at least you'll understand a little better, so you won't be buffeted and then fall into such depression that you don't know if you'll ever get out.

SANDY: How can I feel safer inside myself? How can I feel closer to my guides and to God? Meditation helps me to do that every day and night, but I feel like I want to bring that awareness every minute to my life but not be spacey either. I'm trying to figure out how to keep my feet on the ground with everything that's happening and still feel my connection to God.

ANGELS: Be a Living Master, yes. You understand the idea? A Living Master.

SANDY: Yeah, I do.

ANGELS: And that's really what the ascension is about: Living Mastery. The idea is that you hold inside of you the consciousness that you have in your meditation. And you learn to let your body literally hold the vibration. You have to allow the body—which is why the chakras are shifting and changing in so many ways; the chakras are changing to allow the body to hold the new frequencies and more—higher information. Some of you go up to your guides when you meditate and some of you try to bring your guides down to you when you meditate: meet in the middle.

Once you can hold it comfortably in your body, your body stops reacting with anxiety. It begins to calm down, and then the next level or the next layer comes in, "washes in," and the body reacts and often feels discomfort until it has integrated the information and so forth. But if you think about how much you really know at your Highest Self, and you think about how little your human has known, and you think about the fact that you're integrating how much you really know into that limited vessel, trying to get that limited vessel to plump up in a sense so it can hold all this information, all this vibration, you can imagine that there are going to be download times and integration times and download times and integration times. First you download and then you must integrate. Very occasionally, you'll give yourself a little rest. And then it's back again to another challenge.

If you can realize that it's a progression and you can realize that when you're feeling these stresses, that it's the download time, it's the pushing time, it's the moving time, and when you start to feel calmer, you realize it's the integration time. You can be prepared: "Oh, I may be getting another download time." It doesn't shock you. It doesn't freak you out. It doesn't make you feel that you've gone backwards or you're less on your spiritual path. It lets you know that you're actually moving ahead on your spiritual path because you're shaken not because you stepped back but you're shaken because you stepped forward. It will help a little bit. Do you understand, first of all, that idea?

SANDY: Yeah.

ANGELS: Okay. So, each time you shake or you're stressed, it's not that you are off your path; it's that you're on your path. But realize that you have to integrate new knowledge and new awarenesses of yourself.

You have—just one moment. We have to figure out a human way to express this, okay? It's going to be a little bit difficult because there are no human words. You have what would be thought of as a sacred geometry soul signature, vibration, or picture. Energetic stamp is perhaps the best way to put it. It is how you're recognized out of your human, and this is what it looks like. It would be like a flower. It has a circle like this, and then it has—like a child draws a flower. It has all those petals all around in those half moons around it. And that sacred geometry will integrate you.

So what you might want to do is to hold it here, which is where we see it being held, above the heart, below the throat, and hold it there. When you hold it there, it hooks you into the Higher Self, and it becomes your recognizable signature of your Higher Self. When you hold that or are able to connect with it, you are automatically sixth dimensional. It's your sixth dimensional soul signature is perhaps the best way for us to say it.

Now, integrating that information, integrating your sixth dimensional soul signature into your human body is a level of integration. When you can hold that clearly, what happens is, you begin to be able to, in your human body, communicate with others in the sixth dimension. As a result of that, they're able to recognize you very quickly—the Sixth Dimensional Beings. They would say, "Oh, yeah, we recognize that."

Now, when you've had that veiled or clouded over, the sixth dimension and those Beings have been closed to you. It's a strange way for us to talk but it's an example of how these various healings and these various integrations are occurring at this time. And you have a Seventh Dimensional Being, for example, and that has a particular soul signature, which is a tone or song.

So each of these "Beings" that you *are* awaken and then hook you up to your Higher Dimensional Beings, and you begin to communicate with your Galactic Selves, you begin to communicate with, as you say, your Higher Self, your God-Self. And ultimately, when you can detach from the human drama and feel your Higher Selves, you can still be awake to the human drama, still hold it and help to transmute it, which is what you're trying to do—but not doing it through your human self. Because as we said in the opening; your human self can't hold it. Your human self will collapse from the weight of it.

It is imperative that you awaken these Multi-dimensional Selves because they can hold it. They can see and understand, and they have life beyond Earth. Regardless of what happens, they know and feel their aliveness, you see. Do you understand?

SANDY: I do. I do. Now I feel like I understand this and because I've been afraid to see, literally to see these beings, I feel I've—I've been asking to be shown or to be given these awarenesses in ways that I can handle, so that I don't get too freaked out. Lately, I've been feeling as if I'm neither male nor female. I feel my Beingness. I feel very expanded. So, everything you're saying is validating what's happening for me, and I feel my sleeps have been very, very deep, which is very unusual for me because, again, I've asked to have deeper connections with the unseen worlds but I have been afraid to see these things. I believe it's happening in a way that I can handle, and I also think if I can allow myself to see, I would feel less handicapped in some way. I feel that being afraid to see, literally to see—I know and I understand—but to see, I feel like that would be a bigger tool for me, if I could have access to that, too. I don't know if I'm making any sense with what I'm saying right now. It's just kind of coming out.

ANGELS: Well, we understand what you're saying. What you're saying is that you are getting the information and trying to integrate it into your human slowly as you feel you can hold it. But, what have humans been taught? What have they believed? As you awaken, it seems almost absurd, correct? Can you feel the absurdity of the human condition?

SANDY: Completely. Everything is feeling more and more ridiculous.

ANGELS: So, let's just talk about some of the absurdities, if that's okay with you. What is absurd about being human or the human condition as it has been believed that it is?

SANDY: A belief?

ANGELS: Yeah. What's a human absurd belief?

SANDY: Well, one of them is we take ourselves too seriously. And I say myself too: we believe our perception, whatever that is, is THE perception.

ANGELS: And the average human is operating with two strands of DNA with a split brain, and you think you're getting "it," right?

SANDY: Right.

ANGELS: This causes your galactic Sirian Starseed Self to howl with laughter, when you think about how much your Sirian Self knows. But you've chosen to come into a human, two-strand DNA, split-brain existence, so that you can evolve from your lowest back up to your highest. Being a human tends to be like being a child, because children reach a certain point, a certain age, where they truly believe they know it all, and they don't—they can't imagine that there's actually information out there that they don't have, that matters, or that is. They just can't believe that they aren't the end all and be all, as we said. And being human is very like that, with limited understanding and limited resources, declaring one's self as God.

Interestingly enough, as that illusion dispels, the problem is you become afraid as all the ways you have defined yourself begin to crumble. If you realize that every single thing that you have thought or been told since your childhood is a lie, you're going to lose your mind. So, you have to show yourself slowly that it's a lie and integrate it slowly. Then you look back and you realize what would have completely driven you insane five years ago or a year ago or six months ago or however long ago, you can now hold comfortably, correct?

There are those who just a year ago thought past lives were insane and now understand it, or thought that being multi-dimensional as a Space Being was insane and now can hold it. And some are brave enough to declare it and not feel afraid of declaring it, because those who are here as the rebels, to pave the way, must declare their truth. Otherwise, others will never be able to have a pathway. The steps will not be laid out for them to follow.

So, you are doing what you feel you need to do to safely wake up, but the integration part is tough, and you've had to look at your human stories, your past life stories, your dark, your shadow, as you say, and the parts of you that have been believing the human story and participating in the human story quite intensely. But, you're here to liberate those and to help yourself realize that you don't need to keep playing that. You don't need to keep playing that.

Now, that doesn't mean that automatically, every single human is going to be in agreement with you and every single human is going to say, "Oh, yeah, you were right, Sandy, we are ready to ascend, we don't want to keep playing the human enslavement drama." There are going to be those who *want* to keep playing. The trick is, for those of you who *don't* want to "keep playing," to ascend despite the fact that there are going to be a lot of those who want to keep you enslaved or keep themselves enslaved, you see?

SANDY: Yeah.

ANGELS: If you can see it as separate and you can see it clearly, you won't buy into it so emotionally, and it's the emotional piece that destroys each human, every one of you. It's the emotions. It's actually not the thought. The thought comes in and triggers the emotion, which destroys you. The thought itself has no emotion attached until it's housed within you, and it's the emotion that creates the chaos. So the idea is to have the thought and the knowledge and the wisdom without the constant emotional stimulation that creates the pain and chaos. That's the trick and that's where the Mastery is really held.

The emotion, as you say, is fear, the fear of death, the fear of your misuse of power. What other things do you fear?

SANDY: Something that I think I put in the fear department; struggling with—with all these changes that are happening, all the awareness and the raising of the vibration, am I just holding onto an old notion of wanting to—I'm ambivalent about—do I want to have a relationship during all this? Is that okay? Is that an old paradigm? Am I holding myself back by—?

ANGELS: Because you want to "hook up" in a relationship in your fully realized self.

SANDY: Yes.

ANGELS: Because what you understand is that if you hook up now, it will probably break up, which will break your heart and might put you backward on the path. And so you're going to wait until you know that the hookup will be...

SANDY: At the highest level.

ANGELS: Yeah, and will stick around.

SANDY: But does that mean—I guess what I'm thinking—am I barking up the wrong tree in thinking that it's going to be in this existence? It doesn't really matter whether it's on an astral plane or here. It doesn't really matter in the greater sense. I understand that. It shouldn't matter. But there's a part of me, with all the things that are happening now, I feel like, wouldn't it be great to be in my house, rather than living alone, to have a partner to build a fire if we have to, you know, survive or if there are things we need to do, to share it with someone, to share the mission with someone and to share the consciousness with someone. Is that, you know...

ANGELS: You will find others. It does not have to be a love partner, a male/ female or female/female.

SANDY: Well, I have the others. I have that in my life.

ANGELS: That is what is going to support everyone through this, your Soul Family, those you can speak to about this stuff openly; who get it. They are the important ones because they are the ones who will stick around without the drama. The thing that you're worried about is the drama piece because any love relationship often re-stimulates old karma, old stories, old dramas, old emotions, and can often drag you down and away from your mission. You're seeing it in others. You know this. You've seen this.

Your intention is to have relationships of purity, relationships of trust and of love and of mutual support, regardless of whether they are male/female or just friendships or whatever. Because as you become more multi-dimensional, your choices for how you express love shift, and that is always true for Masters. Masters always shift. As they love greater, as they love larger, they don't always just focus on the wife or the husband or the children. Their love can go further than that and it can fill them equally.

The idea is to learn how to be filled regardless of where it's coming from and know that you have the support. You used a romantic example: "I'm in my house and I have a partner who will build a fire with me". It was a romantic image or template, which doesn't mean anything in terms of reality because that partner could have a bad back and be unable to carry wood or that partner could decide that they need to leave tomorrow, or that partner could any number of things that would not fulfill what you think should be required in a partner.

Your best bet is to keep yourself moving upward and allow that higher energy to attract to you who is it you need to have in your life at this time.

SANDY: That's what I thought.

ANGELS: And not to work on the old template. That fantasy or image that you gave us has no basis in reality, you see. It's an idea, which of course isn't supported by what may come to pass. You see what we're saying.

SANDY: And that's why it doesn't really work for me. When I got there, it seemed like make believe or almost like a cartoon. It seemed so removed. What is that, you know? It doesn't seem real.

ANGELS: Yeah, because it's not what you're here to do. And we remind many of the Lightworkers that you aren't really human. You're not really here to keep the old human template going. Oh, I'll have a family and children and have the house with the picket fence. It wasn't why you came here. There are plenty of others to do that but there aren't a lot to do what you are here to do.

SANDY: I guess the true image is having someone who's on the same mission as me, who is side-by-side, doing the same mission, in whatever way they're doing it. They get this. They just get this.

ANGELS: Yes, and that is appropriate; the idea to share the mission with someone. You can put that out to the universe and attract the energy of someone that you can trust to share the mission with, but don't tell God what it should be or who it should be or how it should be. Allow it come in any form. Often times, the neediness—this may sound strange to you, but we're going to let it sit with you—the neediness of a Lightworker is often what attracts the dark forces to be able to step in and fulfill the need. Then all of a sudden, the Lightworker goes, "Oh, my God, I thought I could trust that person and I feel so tricked and betrayed," because you had thought that this person was fulfilling this need. But then you turn around and feel in some way that the person you thought was there to love you as a partner, a life partner, and who was there to support you or help you, and you were there to support and help them, suddenly, they're not who you thought they were, you know?

So, that often happens when someone puts out their need based on the ego: "I need someone to be this tall, this short, or this intelligent." So, the neediness: "How do I deal with my neediness?"

SANDY: Well, how does it get raised to a higher vibration, because it's getting less and less and it's not a genuine need? That old way does not work for me, so I've closed it off but I feel that I don't want to pretend I don't have it or fool myself, you know, and shut it down and then it's really there. How do you really raise that to a higher vibration?

ANGELS: Well, yes, that idea of defending yourself against the need as humans have done so often. For example: The child who is in school and everyone else has a boyfriend and they say as a defense mechanism, "I don't need a boyfriend."

SANDY: Right.

ANGELS: But, of course, they want a boyfriend. The defended self can get very tough by pretending to close the heart. But, that always only comes from an empty heart. Because we're talking to you about Mastery, we're talking to you about things which are very difficult and not human, you see, so we understand that. But, you're not closing your heart; you're filling your heart. You're not operating from an empty heart. The child that needs to close her heart feels her heart empty and so has to protect it. The Master has a very open heart; always very loving and open—receiving energy. Once the heart is filled, then those who come into the surroundings or into your Light are contributing to an already filled heart.

If you are acting from Mastery then the whole vibration that you emit, that you send out is very different, because you don't need anyone, so you are not willing to accept anything but the best. Whereas the child who has a wounded heart when no one is paying attention to them, all they will need is the slightest bit of attention to put the wall down and become grasping and needy because the heart is empty. That's what leads you to be taken advantage of, just like that child. Often, a child will take attention even from a bully, a bad person or someone who is dealing drugs or so forth because, "Oh, at least they're paying attention to me, at least they want me to do drugs with them." This happens when the heart is closed due to neediness but longing to be sprung open by anyone or anything. So even on that level, you could see how the dark energies would use the weakened, wounded child to manipulate.

If someone is secure and their heart is filled, there's no need for all those things. You're in control; you're the Master. But, from an open heart; not a closed heart. You are always the determiner of whether or not the vibration coming to you is what you want to accept, and if it isn't what you accept, you turn it away knowing it isn't in your best interest. That is the Mastery you are attempting to attain so that you won't be utilized or at the whim of everyone out there that you think you need, you see?

SANDY: As you're saying this, I was just accessing how my fear of men, fear of relationship, fear of getting hurt, fear of being betrayed, has kept—I built up a very big wall against relationships from the fear of all those things. So now, I feel like I'm releasing that armor and trusting my own guidance, trusting my own Higher Self, that what will be attracted—that it's safe—I don't need the wall. I don't need the wall to protect me. Men can come close but I can still choose and say no and don't have to be afraid that I'm—to

ANGELS: Because you don't have to say, "Oh, look, he's paying attention to me, you see, and be needy for it."

SANDY: Right.

ANGELS: You don't need it.

SANDY: I don't need it.

ANGELS: Yeah. And if you don't need it, you are truly liberated from enslavement, and that is what you are trying to teach yourself. It's not an easy lesson but it's worth learning because you cannot be truly the master of your own heart unless you learn this lesson.

SANDY: The other question that is somehow connected to this is: Health wise, I feel like I've cleared a lot of stuff and my health is feeling cleaner and clearer than ever before. There's still stuff going on, second and third chakras, but it's less than it had been. But I still struggle with the herpes virus and papillomavirus, those two viruses. I've done a lot of work with healers. I'm doing a lot of stuff to clear it and yet, when I went to the gynecologist and I got my pap smear back, it tested positive again for papillomavirus. So, I'm just wondering, can this be cleared? Can it be cleared from the body or is this something that I just have to live with and adapt to?

ANGELS: Well, our belief is you could clear it from your body. Certainly, everything is possible. As you know, you've been raped many times through many lifetimes, and for you, sex is a hot button issue because of that—the wounding. And from our perspective, okay we understand it feels different from the human perspective. But from our perspective, you manifested this and have not gotten rid of it. Everyone can get it but you know how not everyone manifests it in raging bad times or it doesn't contribute to their health. It seems maybe they carry it but they never manifest it or it just disappears or they will say, "I haven't had a breakout in twenty years," you see. So, everyone has different levels of these experiences. And that's true with every disease, obviously, not just the ones we speak of.

The idea is that it is a way of protecting you, and you understand that. Not only is it a manifestation of your wounding. You have understood: I'm wounded in my sexual organs. I'm wounded there. I've been brutally raped, I've been molested, and I've been hurt through so many lives. And so it's so wounded and you understand of course the energy of that wounding has always attracted more wounding. That, you understand.

But you also have begun to understand, too, that in some way, it's also felt like a protection. In other words, when you are wounded in there, you are ill, it keeps you from wanting to be open, you know, and have sexual encounters. But also, it almost serves as a barrier in some ways for you, protection. So it's not, from our perspective, just letting go of the old past life woundings and the mutilations and the pain and the horror. The second step is the wanting to be what you would consider vulnerable in that area again. And we believe once we use that word "vulnerable" in that area, you're going to say, "No way!" and we wouldn't blame you. So, it's an expression not only of your wounding but also of your desire to keep that area closed and safe.

What we would suggest that you do is, first of all, not worry about it so much. In other words, don't focus energy on it so much because it is a strange, double-edged sword. Focusing the energy can make it feel like you're trying to open it up, which can make it want to close more. Do you see?

SANDY: I understand.

ANGELS: Better that you just love, that you just love the area. Just love it and just say, "You do what you feel you need to do; I love you." Say to your wounded parts: "If that's what you feel you need to do right now, it's okay. I'm not going to go to war with you; don't worry." It's like a child with a blanket. You don't want to grab it out of its hands. You just say, "It's okay you can hold your blanket if you need right now. We're going to work on feeling safe on all levels. And once you feel really safe, you'll be able to let go of your blanket and you'll feel safe to let go of it. Too much focus stimulates the fear, not just the healing. Let it go for a while and just send love.

SANDY: That's good but it's funny because I had that virus—it's been dormant for years and year and years. I never had had an outbreak and then last year, I had two outbreaks and I have never had any, and that was it. I've had the two. It spooked me and it made itself very known.

ANGELS: With the virus that you have you understand that it was the old stories, right? The old stories have come to the surface, and that's what happens. It happens for all humans. As their old karmic stories come to the surface, their bodies recreate the wounding in one way or another, whether it's through constipation or some kinds of terrible pain. It does not need to be herpes but it can manifest in many other kinds of pain. It can manifest as shortness of breath or headaches. The body will recreate the area of wounding for you to address it and love it and integrate and heal it. Thank it for letting you know where you had work to do, love it, and it will heal itself. But now it will be healed rather than suppressed, it will be healed by being truly released. That's why it came up.

Often, it is an age thing. If in a past life, one is wounded at a particular age, in the present life, when you hit that age, immediately, the symptoms—the other thing that often stimulates the symptoms is if you meet the person who wounded you in a previous life to heal the karma, meeting that person will recreate the karmic event in your body.

SANDY: Interesting.

ANGELS: For it to be healed. It's always for a reason, but ultimately, it is to be healed. But in your case, don't try to heal it forcefully or be angry or do more. Just say, it's okay, you're loved, you're safe. We're going to work on the safety issues, so eventually, you will be relaxed enough to let go of your wounding as well. And once the whole safety issue—you mentioned with death, I'm afraid of torture or dying a painful death. Obviously, you can see the link, yes?

SANDY: Right.

ANGELS: That pain and that wounding are due to mutilation from a previous life and rape and so forth. And the rage, of course, the rage. You're trying to figure out how to integrate much rage.

SANDY: When you said the word "rage," I thought, well, that probably explains the digestive stuff. That's a target area.

ANGELS: The rage. And you do have a lot that you're trying to work through. It's a terribly difficult thing for all humans because you have been wounded, you have been hurt, you have been destroyed, and you have been killed. And your natural reaction is to get enraged and to destroy yourself over and over and over again.

What's interesting is that once you're hurt deeply you just keep recreating it for yourself. Human beings become their own worst enemy. This healing, once again, is not done through your human lower consciousness—because it can't be. Your human will be enraged, your human will want revenge, and your human will feel the sorrow which will depress you. It must be transmuted through your Highest Self, because only through your Higher and Highest Self will you be able to access enough Love to heal that much wounding.

SANDY: I went to a meditation last night and they did a visualization to find your highest purpose, whatever it was. It was very profound. The only thing that came to me about my purpose was to love and be loved. It was that simple, you know. I mean, there's a lot more—I don't know. I guess what I'm trying to ask you right now is any specific things I can come back with that will help ease me in my journey, because I tend to work on myself a lot and it's gotten easier. I mean, I think I'm feeling better. I'm feeling better than I've ever felt. I have to say that. Something is happening in a very positive way. With everything that's going on, I'm feeling more joy. But do you have any recommendations for me, for my health, for my mind. I mean, you've been giving me a lot and coming back with a lot, but anything—

ANGELS: Well, often times, you benefit from teaching others that which you yourself need to heal. So, again, as we said, to help those who are dying to die peacefully is a great gift, not only to you but to them. Because as you assist others to transition peacefully, you heal it in you; and you see and understand how to move through life into death peacefully. You heal yourself and others simultaneously. Helping others to access forgiveness, and to move out of rage into their Higher Self of forgiveness will help you to heal as well as help others to heal.

So, the purpose, the Higher Self purpose always comes, many times anyway, from the wounded self. And because what you experience, you learn, you know, you become an expert on, so if you are an expert in this, what would happen when you are in-between lives? You would help others or assist others to pass, you see, from life to death, because you carry the gifts back and forth between your spiritual self and your human self, when you're in your soul purpose. What you learn, what you have declared as a major and what you have decided to be the bearer of in your soul group, the wisdom carrier for particular lessons in your soul group is what you become an authority in. It is there that you heal yourself and others.

Understanding what it is that you do well, which is to counsel, which is to guide, which is to assist people to transition smoothly, to meet them on the other side of the curtain, to help to guide them, to calm them down, to give them the peace that they're looking for, all of those gifts that you do on the other side of the curtain, you can do on this side of the curtain. Do you understand?

SANDY: Yes.

ANGELS: And it helps you to be more at peace because you feel like you're doing something of benefit to the world. When someone feels that they're doing something of benefit to the world, they really feel better about being on the Earth. So, that is how we would state your soul purpose. And of course, that is to love and be loved but it's more specific in a sense as well.

SANDY: Right.

ANGELS: How do you feel about what we've said with these gifts and abilities and studies, if you will?

SANDY: It feels like you really know me. I feel very validated. I feel like you're just so right on. I've been studying it. I don't even have words to—you're so right on, just exactly right.

ANGELS: You can see that that's where you feel the most empowered, and that's what your higher purpose needs to be the most empowered. Then to make this whole session today a circle, trusting yourself to be empowered with those gifts and those tasks, and to carry them out in humble service, knowing that your true worth and love is to be in service and to be in humble service. You don't need to grab any more at getting your power back because you are empowered now. Your heart is full. You don't need anything. You're completely empowered, and so you can give your gifts to the world without struggle and fear and anger, and getting over-filled with your own ego. You just do it in humble service, and then you are truly in Higher Self alignment.

SANDY: And one last question: Two friends are healers, two separate—they told me to make sure you have provisions. You know, not to be alarming and not to create fear, but just to make sure you have provisions in the house and dry foods and stuff like that. I work struggling with, how to not get into fear—I'm going to the grocery store and getting rice and just having—if nothing happens and I don't ever need it, it's fine. But yet I think I am very unnerved by those recommendations. So, I just had to put that here because there was a "pressingness" that's—

ANGELS: Well, they understand the potential for chaos. What they don't understand is the work that is being done on the other side to limit the chaos. Can we explain something to you that this conduit knows?

SANDY: Yes.

ANGELS: This Earth, as you know it at this point, if there had not been assistance from what you think of as your galactic friends, would currently be annihilated. They have done many interventions. Those who are the "good guys" don't announce it. They don't need to swoop in and be your saviors. They do what they feel they can do, to the best of their ability, and they have ways of doing it—ways that seem extremely odd. But they have—there was to be an explosion of the Yellowstone Supervolcano as well as many other volcanoes back in March 2010. A parallel Earth was created to house the event. They have done many profound interventions and they themselves are even a bit taxed at this point because they have regulations and rules based on what they can do.

But they feel their job is to stop the complete annihilation. So, they're working to try and help that. It doesn't mean that there won't be pockets of these volcanoes and these earthquakes and these storms and this chaos. They don't stop every pocket, every incident. But they are there to attempt to keep the complete annihilation, the devastation that something like the eruption of the Yellowstone Supervolcano could bring, from occurring. If it is decided that it's time to go, then they will not intercede. But in that case, your rice isn't going to help you. It's going to be beyond a bag of rice.

You are here by choice, to bear witness to this transition. It is not a bad thing to have extra provisions, just because there may come a time when there are shortages.

SANDY: That's what I was told.

ANGELS: So, it is not a bad thing to have extra provisions. But you should not live in fear, because what we want to remind you is that the ultimate decision whether to live or to die at any time, believe it or not, despite what you've been told by others, is up to you. And if it becomes a feeling that there is no more that you can do here on this Earth and you've done your best and you're ready to ascend and leave, you will exit, you will check out. You have more control of what you do and what happens to you and how you live and how you experience your life than you think.

So, don't fall into fear and victimhood that dire things will happen and you will not be cared for. But if you wish to make sure that you have some provisions or so forth, that's okay. But you may decide that if it comes to that point, you don't want to be around anyway. Do you understand?

SANDY: Yes, I do.

ANGELS: So, follow your Higher Self and you'll get where you need to go, all right?

SANDY: Okay.

ANGELS: There are a lot of people who are building underground places to be safe, but there are others who believe the biggest hell they can think of is to be in one of those underground places. And that is not any measure or idea of safety whatsoever, in their point of view. So each human makes their choices based on what they feel they want to experience.

SANDY: Okay, that's very good.

ANGELS: So we're going to release her now if that is okay.

SANDY: That's fine.

CHAPTER TEN

THE WEE PEOPLE

JULIE W.

(This is a human/Sirian with connections to the Wee People)

ANGELS: It is with great excitement that we have this opportunity to speak with you, to work with you, to converse with you and of course, to share with you from this realm and to thank you for your work and your presence on the earth at this time.

This is the Archangel Ariel who is speaking with you. And as you are familiar, the Archangel Gabriel and Michael of course are always with this conduit, and any angel is also available to you. Your guide, who is known as Samuel, is also here to share this experience and to send love to greet you as well.

We wish to begin today by, as we had said, thanking you, for it is by your presence on this earth, on this planet that you give comfort to so many. And much of the comfort that you give, you are unaware of giving. Your very presence on this planet is in many ways comforting to many of those in this realm as well as on the planet earth.

Your energy is essential, essential, at this time. It is a great sacrifice you make to be here (on the earth) and to do what you do and the work that you do at this time. In many ways—you are seen—we're going to get a giggle from this and hopefully get a giggle from you when we say this: But to so many, they view you as a hero. You are kind of like the brave hero to many. Those who see you as this are known as the Wee People or those who are not incarnate in the third dimensional human realm but are incarnate in their own consciousness and their own realm but still upon this planet.

This planet earth is housing many different types of life, and some of the life is not in the visible realm to humans. Much of the life that is housed exists outside of the range of human sensory apparatus. There's a feeling in the human—what you might call the "average" human being—who is not able or willing to accept life outside of the human sensory realm, there's a feeling that this is all "make believe," that there is not a reality to these other worlds.

But to these other worlds, to some extent, the human realm is not real to them. And many of them like it that way. The Wee People, the little people who live in their own world of their own making, which is an earthlike existence but much closer to what you might call a Garden of Eden; a world where there is peace and harmony, where life exists harmonious with nature, with one another. There is not an understanding among those who exist in that world why it is necessary to create disharmony or conflict.

The harshness of the human realm is extremely difficult for them not only to endure but even to understand. So, the planet is shared by these beings but they are illusory to most of you. In other words, they try to stay out of the way as much as possible of the typical human because they don't feel comfortable—not only would the toxins in the third dimensional world that you know be poisonous to them, but the emotional toxicity is also too much for them to bear.

Because of this, they stay in their world, which is a parallel reality to your world. What we're going to explain to you is that the reason that they see you almost as a hero is because you said one day that you were willing to venture, to help during the bridging of third and fifth dimension and to try to help the Wee People and the human race to come closer. In other words, there is a knowing among your people that the earth is going to eventually be not as vibrationally dense. As the veils lift, as the density lifts, there is an understanding that the Wee People are going to begin to be more and more visible to more and more people. Their parallel world or reality will be more accessible.

It was essential, you felt, that as the veil lifts or the density thins, that the Wee People have some kind of conduit or some kind of communicator or messenger to help in the transition. That is why so many human-fairies are also awakening. One of the jobs that those of you who associate with the fairy and the Wee People realm have is during the transition known as the Ascension or "thinning of the veils," those of you who understand the realm of these fairies and Wee people are needed to ease the transition. Once again as the "veil thins" the fairies and the Wee People and the elves who have been hiding in a parallel reality but on the same planet will be willing to be seen.

It is going to be very important that the fairy and Wee People realm achieve harmony with the earth if in fact some kind of Eden is to be created upon the earth. It couldn't be created upon the earth ignoring those parallel worlds and realities. And ultimately, they will be used—we're going to use the word harnessed—to assist in the agriculture and so forth.

So, we want to begin today by helping you to remember your people more clearly and to remember that they are real and not just fairy figments but actual worlds, actual villages, colonies if you will, of consciousness, and that these beings are reaching out to you and look to you for guidance or assistance. You let them know, whether you're aware of it or not, you communicate with them and let them know what kind of progress is being made in the third dimensional world and how this "thinning of the veils" is working, and whether or not it's happening quickly or so forth. But they feel quite in awe that you're able to tolerate the toxicity of the human earth at this time and that your consciousness doesn't fall into sadness or depression, but that you are able to keep going and endure.

Two things in your personality enable you to do this. You have an interesting mix of the practical and the whimsical that allows you to sustain even in a difficult, third dimensional earth. The whimsical allows you in some ways not to take anything too seriously and that is the nature of the Wee People and even the fairy realm to some extent. There is not a sense of heaviness or gloominess or seriousness. For how could there be when you realize that, in truth, all is right with the world? That love and joy and joviality and happiness is something which you carry deep within you and deep in your heart, and you can always draw on, and that allows you to not take things too seriously.

That is combined with an interesting practicality. Your ability to be practical and to operate in a practical manner on the earth and to accomplish and to succeed is also a strength or asset to you. And the combination of just feeling that you do what you can in a practical step-by-step fashion, and that you don't take anything quite seriously because we're going to say that deep inside, there's always a feeling that this isn't really your world anyway—this combination helps you to be successful. You see what we're saying? Do you understand?

JULIE: Yes.

ANGELS: So, why would you really take it so seriously? Because for you, it's almost like it's not the real reality, it's just the alternate one that you've stepped into temporarily. Do you understand?

JULIE: Absolutely.

ANGELS: Those are your strengths. You know how in the human realm, the humans will send out their finest and their bravest to be the explorer and set sail on the ships? You are viewed in that way by those in your natural home; what humans call the Wee People. You are considered a little bit of the hero because of that. And when you come home, there's a huge homecoming for you, like a hero's parade.

We are allowing the feelings that those people have for you to imbue this conduit so that she feels the love, and this is why she is having the tears right now on her face because we want you to understand and feel. We're allowing it to be sent through her to you, so that you know that this is real. Because without the feeling, you wouldn't know how much you are truly loved and feel the love coming from your people to you. We are allowing her to feel it a little so you can feel it. Do you understand what we're saying?

JULIE: Oh, yes! Thank you.

ANGELS: It's just a reminder because that's going to help you keep going. As long as you're reminded of your happy home, you seem to be able to endure a great deal. So we thank you in this realm we call angelic. And also, your people feel excited that we are sending their message through this conduit of great thanks, to remind you of the homecoming that's awaiting you.

JULIE: Do I have to die to have that homecoming or can I have it when I'm totally immersed in consciousness?

ANGELS: Well, you are feeling it already, yes?

JULIE: Yes, absolutely.

ANGELS: So, it's not necessary for you to die. Actually, you're not going to actually die in a typical human way anyway. What you're calling your death is just going to be a reemerging into your real world, so you don't have to worry about that. You've been able actually to stay, even in these journeys that you've done as a human, and there have been only a few—you are not in the same category or league as many other humans.

We're going to just make it simple by saying you've been able to stay relatively karmic free and that has been a great strength because you haven't wanted to get too caught up in the human wheel. In other words, you've gotten caught up just enough to learn what you need to learn, if you understand our meaning. Because you're here to learn and you're here to understand what the human realm is about, so you can be that bridge, but you're careful not to take on a karma that might take you away from your people for millennia.

It's a funny message we have for you but it's really in a sense the one that you needed most. In other words, all other messages come from that message, if you understand, and that truth about your goals and job. You're doing a very admirable job and at any time that you don't want to continue it, you are free to leave. That is what we want you to understand. But we think that you're at the point where you're feeling you want to continue and take it through. You've gone this far, in other words, yes?

JULIE: Yes, and I feel like I'm in so many ways happier and freer and less encumbered by the third dimensional world than I ever have been.

ANGELS: Well, much of the karma and the darkness have been lifted from you. You understand that?

JULIE: Yes.

ANGELS: You're now dealing with what are essentially your true self and your true mission here, and you've kind of cleared away all the cobwebs and crumbs, you know, and now it's down to business. But as we said, fortunately, you don't get so caught in your third dimension that you forget the joyfulness, so that keeps you alive.

You can see, though, in a sense, you can feel and see your world and remember it. It is very real and is not an unreal world; it's just in a different dimensional plane of existence, that's all.

JULIE: I think part of my dream has been to recreate the harmony and the beauty and the connection of that world in this world, so that there is a true bridge and that others can come and feel that.

ANGELS: Yes. That is the community that is calling to be created by all of those who have the frequencies of the fairies and Wee People of the world. The time has not been right. As you know, there has been too much toxicity on the earth. But it is the time, as you also know, of great clearing. At this time, the clearings have begun. As the density is transmuted it will get clearer and clearer, until it will be time for your world and the earth world to be more and more as one.

It's going to be essential that those of you who have this vision and dream are able to create a community and work harmoniously together: to give it space, to make space for it. Do you understand what we're saying by that, to have the space?

JULIE: I'd like to have you elaborate on that.

ANGELS: Well, in other words, let's see... If enough energies of like-minded humans gather with this frequency, they call and create a space of safety for those who live in this other fifth dimensional world to manifest. In other words, they need to feel that there's a safe place created where they can experience human life and step into your world.

JULIE: Absolutely.

ANGELS: And be safe.

JULIE: Yes.

ANGELS: What is essential is a signal is going out on the higher frequencies to bring together those who feel the energy and want to make a safe space, a sacred space that you can then call these beings to. They will set up a village literally within the space you've created, the sacred space. They will build their village. And soon, what will happen is it will become visible to all of you and you will become friends with them.

What we see in the future is literally this idea that–let's put it this way: In the space, on the land, in the place you've created, you walk out and you say, "Good morning, Samuel," you know? "Good morning, how are you this morning?" You know and you can sense and see. As the density on earth begins to lift and more of what is called the fifth dimensional consciousness can be held on this planet, they will become more visible and you'll feel—not only feel their presence but you'll literally be able to see them, until their village and your village becomes one village. Do you see?

JULIE: Absolutely.

ANGELS: That sounds like a fantasy at this point and this moment on the earth, it is. But unless you begin to create it now—do you see?

JULIE: Totally.

ANGELS: Slowly building it with like-minded people, the sacred space. The idea is that you make it ready and you create it.

JULIE: Is it time for me to ask a question?

ANGELS: Yes, you may always ask, yes.

JULIE: Because I've started looking for land. I have connected with a friend, a male friend, and he has—I'm not sure if it's an identical dream but it's a similar dream. And we're looking together because we're both ready, and we're actually going to go see a place tomorrow that's 130 acres. So I just—do you have anything --

ANGELS: What we want you to do is when you go; to make sure that the two of you are alone, have time alone on the land.

JULIE: Yes.

ANGELS: Sit and invite your Wee People to join you. Commune with them and ask them if this is the land that they feel safe on? Is this a land they feel that is sacred to them? The only thing that's going to be very important is that you don't want an answer from your human mind.

JULIE: Because then you would plant an answer just because you want it.

ANGELS: Yes. What they're actually asking us to say to you is, "Do not know in your mind but feel in your heart." They're also asking that you literally put your ear to the ground and ask Mother Earth, "Do you want us here?" Ask the spirits who reside in that area already, "Do you want us here?" Let them tell you. If you feel a warmth and a love and a harmony, you're in the right place. If you feel rejected or cold or some other feeling that doesn't feel right, respect that.

Then you need to go with all your friends who are earth deities, and after you have done this, you need to make sure that all your friends who you completely trust—it does not have to be a lot, better to have a few who are pure of heart than a lot who some are not pure, okay?

JULIE: Sure.

ANGELS: Do you understand what we're saying?

JULIE: Absolutely.

ANGELS: Walk the land asking, "Are we invited, do you want us here? Are we invited? Is this space open to us to come in?" You will be given permission if it is the correct space. Then you can invite your Wee People in and they will be glad to be there.

But not all space, as you know, is open to be inhabited, not only by humans but also by other realms such as Wee People. Sometimes Native American energies can block the human from coming because there can be the energy of mistrust that has been implanted.

JULIE: Yes.

ANGELS: So, it's not that you can't work with those who are putting the mistrust energy out there, but they will have to be convinced that you are worthy and they will have to be appeased and invite you. Once they feel appeased and have invited you, then it will be fine. So all those realms must be honored—the trees, the earthly realm, the Native American energies that walk and roam and feel to be caretakers of the earth, the spiritual energies, the fairies and Mother Earth herself. You will feel it in your body. If you only know it in your mind, we would suggest you don't trust that.

JULIE: Right.

ANGELS: It's going to be much more about what you feel. If the land is right, it will begin to awaken in you the remembrance of who you really are and your own truth of who you are, and you'll feel comfortable there. As we are calling you a Wee Person, you will feel comfortable and know that that is your home. But they're counting on you in a sense to stake out a home for them.

JULIE: Okay.

ANGELS: That is really kind of what you are doing and why you are a messenger or a bridge and why we made an analogy to you as being like the explorer, like the human Magellan and so forth, you know?

JULIE: Yes.

ANGELS: Okay, I'm going to go out into the land and I'm going to discover a good home or place. It's kind of similar. That's why you are their hero. It's funny to be thought of that way, isn't it, for you?

JULIE: Yes.

ANGELS: We are laughing because they are hopping and jumping, like dancing around and clapping and applauding and so happy to have you do this work for them. They are so happy. It's what you have all dreamed of, is what they're saying, not just what they've dreamed of but what you've all dreamed of is once again having peace on the earth and harmony once again and a place for those energies to feel safe once again. Mother Earth herself is so looking forward to having awakened beings on this planet again. It's hard for her sometimes because she feels there are so many who are still asleep and she is ready to awaken.

JULIE: Maybe that's why I like dancing and jumping around so much.

ANGELS: Yes, that is exactly—they do like a—it's hard of course to describe in words but their knees rise up toward their chest and they like to (indicating). (Laughter). That's their signature. So, you relate to that, yes?

JULIE: Absolutely.

ANGELS: Hard to be so joyful on a planet where joy is not considered to be of much value.

JULIE: Really, although there's part of the dance community where joy is paramount, and that's a really lovely thing.

ANGELS: Well, that's essential. Otherwise, it would be too difficult for you to be on this planet.

JULIE: Yes.

ANGELS: The vibrations would have taken you down without those outlets.

JULIE: Yes.

ANGELS: So your job is clear to you and you are doing a wonderful job. The other thing that will be essential is, as you begin to develop your land and work, absolutely essential—they're actually getting a little serious here. It's a change. But they're saying, "You have a kind heart," yes?

JULIE: Yes.

ANGELS: "And you don't like to say no," yes?

JULIE: Yes.

ANGELS: What they're saying is that this is very serious—is that you're not to invite anyone into your community, as you are working this community, if you have any feeling or any doubt of their purity, is the word they're using, or intention. It is essential, particularly in the early stages, that the frequencies remain as pure as possible and that you do not allow those who are carrying darkness to subterfuge you—or lead you off track. You will develop a relationship with Samuel, who is your guide, and only when you feel his approval will you say yes to those who want to join you. Do you understand?

JULIE: Yes.

ANGELS: So it's essential that you actually remain in control. You must be the leader. That is important. Do you understand?

JULIE: Yes.

ANGELS: That's not easy but you understand why there would need to be a leader. Learn to trust your instincts, your guides and your own feelings. If something doesn't feel right to you, it's okay to say no.

JULIE: Yes.

ANGELS: Don't worry that you're being bad or blocking energy. If it doesn't feel right, listen to it and sit with it for a while and allow yourself to say no if necessary. That's the issue. You are going to meet, they're saying, many people who have many different visions or agendas. Do you understand?

JULIE: Absolutely.

ANGELS: This is your vision and your agenda, and you are to keep it pure. So that is going to be important, that you don't allow others to take over the helm from the captain.

JULIE: You know, I wonder how that's going to sit with my partner that I'm looking for the land with. Not that anything is written in stone here because it isn't.

ANGELS: No. Well, we're not saying that you can't have a partner. That is okay. What we're saying is that there is a call going out energetically, both of you, and all of the Wee People, as we said—the signals are being sent out and many are receiving it throughout the world. They're going to be drawn to you and to this area. What we're saying is that as your community forms and as this vision unfolds, it is going to be essential that you bring people you feel comfortable with, that are sharing a similar vision, and that do not have their own egos first but have the collective vision as their consciousness. Do you see?

JULIE: Absolutely, yes.

ANGELS: That is what they're trying to say to you. So if you feel that someone is coming but their ego is going to get in the way, then don't allow that.

JULIE: Absolutely.

ANGELS: The call is going out and it's being heard, and you're going to get more and more energies and people who are going to be attracted to you and coming to you to create this vision. So someone has to stand for the vision, you know?

JULIE: Yes.

ANGELS: And say no to the egos, and that will be you.

JULIE: Okay.

ANGELS: That is what they are trying to say.

JULIE: Okay.

ANGELS: That makes sense, yes?

JULIE: Totally.

ANGELS: Okay.

JULIE: Do you have anything to say about this person that I'm looking with?

ANGELS: Please give us the full name.

JULIE: His name is ______________. He is a friend. We're not involved romantically at this time and we haven't been.

ANGELS: He is not the Wee People. He does love the land. He has more human story than you do. Do you understand what we're saying by that?

JULIE: Yes, absolutely.

ANGELS: His motivation is more like a human motivation to take the land back. In other words, he feels deep inside that the land was taken from him. Do you understand that feeling? And it is time for him to reclaim what he feels is his, the land. In other words, that's more of a human. Do you understand that?

JULIE: Yeah.

ANGELS: His karmic consciousness is: "The land has been taken from my people." You see that idea?

JULIE: Yes.

ANGELS: And it is time for it to be claimed by those who care for it and love it. His motivation is one of wanting to get the land back and care for it and love it, so that part is good and it is a human motivation. But he is not a Wee Person as you are, you know?

JULIE: Absolutely.

ANGELS: So he is more serious.

JULIE: Yes.

ANGELS: He doesn't have the light heart that you do in that way. He's not closed to the idea of Wee People but it's not his reason for joining forces with you. He would not say, "Oh, my job is to make a home for fifth dimensional beings, once the Ascension is made, you see?"

JULIE: Correct.

ANGELS: He would say, "My job is to bring back sacred earth." So, it is a different motivation. The only trouble you might have is if he cannot understand and respect your vision. You respect and understand his because you understand that it is time to claim the sacred earth, yes. But he needs to understand that you will be working with the Wee People and fairy realm. And if he cannot take it seriously, then he might not be the right person.

JULIE: Yes.

ANGELS: Because you are not going to want to be hiding these people, your people from him any more than he should have to hide his guides and people and his spiritual guides and his Native American guides and so forth from you.

The time is to bring all of those energies harmoniously on to the land. But he carries a human karmic story, even carrying energy from the time of Atlantis and the destruction of Atlantis in his consciousness, so he carries much more of the human conflict, you see, than you do.

JULIE: Yes.

ANGELS: But that's okay as long as there's mutual respect for your different frequencies. If they both can find a place together, then it can work. But it's important that it's made very clear why you are both setting up this land and what you expect from it and how you're going to call and work on it and who you want there with you, before you get into anything.

JULIE: Yes.

ANGELS: We suggest that you make sure you take much time to clarify motivation and so forth.

JULIE: Yes. I've been feeling that that was almost our next step is to have that.

ANGELS: By the way, we sense that he is assuming that you are like he is.

JULIE: Okay.

ANGELS: Do you understand what we mean by that?

JULIE: Yes. And I wondered that, too, because if his consciousness doesn't go to these other places—it's not familiar territory to him, so he wouldn't—to

ANGELS: It is not familiar to him.

JULIE: Yeah, so he can't go where his consciousness hasn't gone yet.

ANGELS: He would be more likely, in blessing land, for example, to call upon the Native American energies or different earth energies and those kinds of things. That would be more comfortable to him than to say, "We're going to get the Fairy Folk and the Wee People here and we're going to be dancing with them and they need a village here." But if he's willing to understand that it's time to allow them to have their villages on earth and that your job is to create a village so that when the transition happens, POP, it's there, if that is okay with him, then it can be a beneficial thing as long as mutual respect is afforded.

JULIE: Right, because there's nothing about the Native American way that I don't honor and respect. I feel that I could honor and respect what he would bring to it.

ANGELS: Yes. You were a squaw in the Native American life, so you know that and so it's familiar to you and you're comfortable with it. So you know how to do the rituals and call to Father Sky and to the ancestors.

JULIE: But it isn't what holds magic for me.

ANGELS: No, it is not, but you understand it.

JULIE: Yes.

ANGELS: So it's just a matter of, can you bring those worlds together; that's all.

JULIE: And is it best for the situation?

ANGELS: And because you're going to be calling a lot of fairies to you: Is he comfortable with fairies? That is something he needs to answer. Fairies are pretty spacey and they're pretty gentle and they have trouble with harsh human reality. Fairies can be annoying sometimes to serious human folk.

JULIE: Yeah, although he does get light-hearted, especially around me, you know?

ANGELS: Yes, and that is good. As long as there is mutual respect and understanding and no veiling of who you really are, it should be fine. As long as he loves you truly for who you are, it can be a good blending. We don't sense that you wouldn't ever respect him for who he is. It would be more of an issue that he would have trouble understanding you and thinking it's a little flaky, so it's time for him to take off the flaky glasses.

JULIE: And get down to business.

ANGELS: And get down to business with the Wee Folk and the Fairies. They're laughing. They're just showing us a funny image and they're being very mischievous. They're saying they can come around and one—they're going to be kicking him on the shins and the other one is going to be biting him and holding on (laughing). They say, they will win in the end, so he'd better be giving in. We find that humorous as well. In the end, they're going to win anyway because they can do that.

JULIE: They can also just charm him into their world, you know?

ANGELS: Well, they say, but don't forget, they can also do those things, Ha, Ha, Ha! They have a mischievous side—they say, that's why the Leprechauns get their reputation.

JULIE: Since I have my Irish background—to

ANGELS: You know them well.

JULIE: Oh, yeah!

ANGELS: They like to play tricks. They're saying that one of the favorites for the Leprechaun is to make a drunken Irishman think he is seeing things. (Laughter). He thinks it's the alcohol but it's really them. And they move things, too. They like to move objects on a drunken Irishman. They say, "Where did I put my glasses?"

JULIE: Uh-oh, I'm drunk again.

ANGELS: Yeah! They're very humorous that way. So they feel superior to men because they can do that.

JULIE: And also because maybe there are fewer men who would be open to them, as far as our world, but maybe that's not true.

ANGELS: They know that they have some power over the human race in certain ways, in that way. It lets them feel better because some of them feel there's a division there and it's a way of them getting back at the humans and playing with them.

JULIE: Messing with their heads.

ANGELS: Messing with them a little, yes.

CHAPTER ELEVEN

THE PLEIADIAN KARMA

CLAUDIA M.

ANGELS: We are delighted to have this opportunity to be in your presence and to speak with you today. This is the Archangel Ariel who is speaking with you. But as you are well aware, any and all angels are also available to you at any time.

We wish to begin today by speaking about the fragmentation of your soul—the fragmentation of your Self; and the idea that you have split yourself into many pieces. What we see as healing yourself at this time is finding those pieces and those fragments and reunifying them. Of course, each human being would say, "Well, my job, if I'm to be healed, is to be whole." Very often, they do not even know what they're saying. They don't understand what that means. They think perhaps what that means is that they have to forgive this individual or they have to find places and ways to heal certain parts of their pain.

But what we're talking about is actually finding and relocating pieces of yourself that you have left behind in various places or various lives. In order for you to know yourself better and in order for you to get your power back and to feel comfortable with the idea of being in a state of empowerment, you need to know a lot more about who you are, about where you've left some of the pieces of yourself, so that you can integrate them comfortably and feel yourself to be complete.

We're going to address today the first issue of many, which is the idea of trying to help you to feel complete, to feel whole, to begin the journey for you of reattaching, reunifying the pieces and the parts of yourself that have been scattered throughout time. We're going to pause and ask you if you understand what that means.

CLAUDIA: I think so, yes.

ANGELS: As you can imagine, you are not what we would call a youthful soul. In other words, there's wisdom, there's experience behind you. You know much, but you've also chosen to forget much. This forgetting has left you divided; it has left you feeling not whole. The forgetting has allowed you to enter into agreements that are not of your best interest, that are not serving the higher version of you, but instead they serve what you might call a lower version or a lower vision—perhaps we're happier with that word—a lower vision. It's not really a lower version, it's just a vision that you have of who you think you are that is not the highest vision that we wish to see you embody.

What happens to individuals over many lives and many traumatic events, if you will, is they fragment and they don't want to remember or know or feel parts of themselves, so they leave them behind. What happens then is that there are a lot of holes in the auric field as a result of those pieces having been removed and those holes leave you feeling vulnerable and disempowered. What we believe is that collecting the pieces of yourself and reunifying them—finding yourself integrated—makes you feel more empowered. That is why we have mentioned that; it is not to drag you through the mud again, but to help you to not be afraid of where you've been and who you are and what you've seen, so that you can carry it with you without fear.

We're going to pause for a moment and ask for your comment, if you understand what we're talking about.

CLAUDIA: Yes, and I very much desire to feel again my own empowerment.

ANGELS: So, you can resonate with this idea of leaving pieces of yourself behind?

CLAUDIA: Yes.

ANGELS: Part of the problem is because you have been traumatized in very profound ways, although it is not in this life that we're talking about. We're talking about in previous lives or previous places and existences; those places where the ground beneath you was, how we should put this, so shattered, you don't even know where you belong or where to place your feet. It's as if you forgot over time even how to find safety or what safety means. So, the trauma of your soul, to try to explain it simply, has been that you have forgotten how to access a safe place, a safe haven, and how to integrate yourself and find a way to feel safe. Do you understand what we're saying?

CLAUDIA: Yes.

ANGELS: Part of that problem is because in the many battles that you have suffered, what happens very often when you die in any particular life is that the consciousness that is being manifested at the time of your death is with you profoundly and it can cause a difficult passage from being incarnate to being disincarnate. It can cause a soul to leave pieces and parts of itself "behind" and feel quite lost—feel like it's wandering.

Many times, those energies are called ghost energies. Those fragmented pieces of the self or the soul are left behind and are like ghosted parts of the self that are just wandering, without knowing how to find home. This happens often during particularly traumatic deaths and at war time, which is why often, if you visit a battlefield, there are many ghost sightings, because so many of those fragmented pieces are still wandering and lost and not unified with the soul.

What we want to make you aware of—so that you understand why at times you feel so empty and lost—we're going to ask if you agree that there is an emptiness and a feeling of "lostness" quite often inside of you?

CLAUDIA: Absolutely.

ANGELS: Okay. So what we're trying to help you understand is not to feel bad or ashamed about that, but to understand it's because there's a lot of fragmentation. You also have had, in your female lifetimes, a great deal of victimization. Your human female tends to carry a lot of victim energy. It is particularly difficult for you to get a sense of empowerment while in a physical human body that is female.

One of the things that we wish you to do is to work with the idea of feeling very proud of having a female body and being in the female form and having female emotions and consciousness—that you remember what you knew long ago, which was the power of the Divine Feminine. You do hold deep within you a profound resonance to the Goddess cult or the Divine Feminine or the power of that energy; the female, feminine, divine energy. In many ways it is your strength: if it can be released, remembered and re-empowered. Then it is your strength.

But through many of your lifetimes, you have suffered wounding and you have suffered from the belief system that being a powerful woman is going to lead you into pain, to struggle and to trouble. So when you find yourself trying to re-empower yourself in your female form, often you come up against what appear to be blocks. It's like you get so far and then you get afraid or you just stop and you have trouble getting further. Do you understand what we're saying?

CLAUDIA: Yes.

ANGELS: And the reason is because when you have attempted to be powerful as a female you've often been punished for it. Back in ancient times, what you would think of as the Biblical, Hebrew times—

CLAUDIA: Yes.

ANGELS: Women were stoned to death and this happened to you. The reason that it happened to you was that you stood up for a young girl, a younger woman, and it was actually your daughter. This woman was to be killed due to having had sexual intercourse inappropriately for the times, and they felt that she was to be punished for her transgression. You tried to stand up and to defend because you felt that this daughter of yours was the victim and not to be punished. But unfortunately, what happened was that you were stoned to death for the defense.

Your anger and your rage are deeply buried in you in that experience, and it frightens you sometimes. You know that anger, yes?

CLAUDIA: Oh, yes.

ANGELS: Well, that is not the first time as a female that you were hurt and punished for speaking up. You were punished in the Inquisition times, and it was a very dastardly torture. In that life, your tongue was literally cut out, pulled out, cut out, and you were slowly killed. So for our purposes, what we feel is that it is a lot about your regaining your voice, okay?

CLAUDIA: Yes.

ANGELS: Now, the problem is of course that it's not been safe for you to speak up or regain your voice. Also, whether you are completely aware of it or not, you still harbor a great deal of anger at men for what they've done to you and also for those who are in power.

CLAUDIA: Yes.

ANGELS: It's important for you to begin to look at both sides, so that you can tame some of those feelings, because you've spent so much time as a victim and you've spent so much time being pulled under and pulled down. One of the things that you have in your auric field as an energy imprint is the image of a woman who is being dragged down into hell by her feet. It's the idea that there is some horrible thing down there that has reached up and grabbed your ankles and is pulling you as you claw against the sides to resist, down into someplace of darkness. That is your greatest energetic fear, the idea that something is going to get a hold of you and has the power to throw you into a deeply dark place, where you're afraid you won't get out of. Do you understand what we're saying?

CLAUDIA: Yes.

ANGELS: The first thing we need to get you to feel and to understand is that that dark place, which although very real to the human mind and the human existence, is still a part of the human creation. So to free yourself, realize that no matter where you get dragged to you can always get out of. Although it can feel, certainly with the power and the profound nature of mental illness, depression, darkness, rageful thoughts or suicide thoughts or angry thoughts, or all the other ways that these claws can drag you into a dark place, all of those places that they can drag you to are only manifested in human astral, lower astral plane.

In order to free yourself you must know and understand that these places are completely within your control to exhume yourself from. Nobody and nothing can take you anywhere that you yourself can't get yourself out of, okay? Not really. The illusion may be of helplessness, but from our perspective it is an illusion.

CLAUDIA: Okay.

ANGELS: The first thing to getting out of the feeling of helplessness or hopelessness is to reframe what's in your energy field. From lifetimes of being told about hell and feeling the darkness that can envelop your consciousness, there's such a fear that I might disappear into something I can't get myself out of, that great fear of being overwhelmed by that sheer misery of the dark places.

We want to remind you that you are always able and capable of exhuming yourself from this darkness. It is a human creation and it can be destroyed. So, anytime that you start to feel that your anger or your rage or your depression or your hopelessness is acting like a force to drag you down, remember to get rid of the fear that it's going to drag you someplace that you won't be able to escape. There is always a way to escape the darkness, okay?

CLAUDIA: Okay.

ANGELS: Does that help you a little?

CLAUDIA: Yes.

ANGELS: Okay. When you're feeling the most helpless, remember that it's still a part of the human creational realm. There's nothing in the darkness that is part of this realm. Because of that, you can escape it. If you can recognize it as the human fear realm, then you can recognize that you are capable of drawing yourself from that place to something else.

Now, these lives that we talk about have been also filled with other experiences where you have witnessed those who have been in power deeply abusing the power. You have witnessed, quite honestly, some very, very dark places. This is nothing you don't already know somewhere inside of yourself, yes?

CLAUDIA: Yes.

ANGELS: You have taken yourself to some of the darkest places that have been manifested on the earth. As a result of that, although you do fear the darkness, you're also aware of it and not naïve to it. Unfortunately, when it frightens you, one of your defenses has been to try to become more what we're going to call like a "normal" human and pretend you don't know what you know. Do you see what we're saying?

CLAUDIA: Yes.

ANGELS: It's like, "If I can try to be like the average Joe, maybe I can forget everything I know and I can just slide through this life easy." Do you see what we're saying?

CLAUDIA: Yes. (Laughing)

ANGELS: Unfortunately, what happens is you don't fit into that world very well. Do you know what we're saying?

CLAUDIA: No, I sure don't.

ANGELS: It's kind of a false community for you.

CLAUDIA: Right.

ANGELS: The problem with being in a false community is it's not satisfying the depths of your soul and your heart, and they can't really help you with the issues you're struggling with because they don't understand or know about them.

CLAUDIA: Yes.

ANGELS: So, your approach to life—suppressing all these feelings inside you isn't working because it's making you feel alienated on top of feeling the heaviness, you see?

CLAUDIA: Yes.

ANGELS: Then there are both feelings to deal with. We want you to be proud of what you know and to begin to speak it without fear. Begin to associate yourself with those who are as wise as you are, who have as much knowledge and wisdom and understanding as you do, so that you can speak freely of some of the things that you sense or that you know and you can find deeper souls to communicate with.

You're also finding at times a little bit of discomfort with those who you feel only want to look at Light. Do you understand what we're saying? You're feeling that if you dump some of this dark knowledge on them, they might not like you.

CLAUDIA: Right.

ANGELS: Okay? You understand?

CLAUDIA: Yes.

ANGELS: We're getting at—you're hiding this but you know this is true, too.

CLAUDIA: Yes.

ANGELS: The problem is: you're trying to find people who understand the Light and the dark, so you can speak about some of these fears and some of this knowledge you've gained in some troublesome places, without "freaking people out. "

CLAUDIA: Right.

ANGELS: Now, there are people who understand both sides, who don't get afraid to speak about both sides, who don't feel that it's something that has to be hidden, because you give power to the dark when you believe in its power and when you try to hide from it and you run from it.

CLAUDIA: Right.

ANGELS: But your experiences through many lifetimes have contained so much wisdom that the "dark" has given you that if you deny it, then you feel empty again. So we're here today to free you up a little bit, to go ahead and feel free to talk about some of the fears and some of the darkness; it won't upset us, you won't shock us, it will give you a place to vent those thoughts and feelings in safety. Okay?

CLAUDIA: Okay.

ANGELS: Now, the wisdom of the dark experiences you've had, like we talked about, where you were tortured and your tongue was ripped out and you were stoned to death, if you can look at it and try to find out how it strengthened you, you won't be quite as angry at it. We're going to take you back to that life where you were stoned to death, okay?

CLAUDIA: Okay.

ANGELS: If you close your eyes, you'll be able to see it pretty easily. You can see that you're standing there and you're a strong woman. You really have a strength about you. A younger woman stands next to you. The two of you are singled out and you can see that there are people who are standing in front of you and they're angry. They're yelling at you and they want to hurt you. Do you have that image in your mind? Can you find that one?

CLAUDIA: Yes.

ANGELS: What's in your chest at that moment as you stand there?

CLAUDIA: It feels very cold and hard.

ANGELS: That's the anger.

CLAUDIA: Yes.

ANGELS: When you look at those people, what do you feel about them? What are you thinking about them?

CLAUDIA: I feel rage that they won't open themselves up to truth.

ANGELS: That they're so ignorant?

CLAUDIA: Yes.

ANGELS: Yeah, okay. That's a common theme for you. You know that theme, right?

CLAUDIA: Yeah, it sure is.

ANGELS: You carried that through many lifetimes. It's very frustrating to be among people like that. Let's just take you through the experience of your death in that lifetime. If you wish to re-experience it, you can. It was important for you to hold the hand of that daughter while you died. You wanted to give her your strength. She was not anywhere near as strong as you. You can feel that, right?

CLAUDIA: Yes.

ANGELS: She was frightened. She also died with the feeling she had done something wrong and that was deeply upsetting to you as well because she blamed herself, you see? Can you see what she carried with her?

CLAUDIA: Yes (crying).

ANGELS: Yes, okay. It's okay, you can cry. You need to regain these parts of yourself.

CLAUDIA: (Crying).

ANGELS: Do you see how you've blamed yourself?

CLAUDIA: Yes.

ANGELS: You've held that in.

CLAUDIA: She was so afraid and I couldn't help her.

ANGELS: But she does not blame you. She does not blame you, does she?

CLAUDIA: No.

ANGELS: You've been your worst enemy. You blame yourself. Can you feel that your angels do not blame you?

CLAUDIA: Yes.

ANGELS: You need to invite that piece of yourself back into yourself. That's a part of yourself that you have kept apart because you have felt so guilty and bad and angry from that lifetime; you need to reunite that. You are forgiven. Forgive yourself, she forgives you—and forgive them. We do this to heal you because these lives are really in need of healing for you to move forward.

CLAUDIA: Yes.

ANGELS: Already it feels a little lighter, doesn't it?

CLAUDIA: Yes.

ANGELS: Invite that person that you were and invite that daughter to join with you so that you can feel she's forgiven you. She never blamed you. You can look back at them and realize that all those people were just reacting out of their own fear, because they had been told by others that they had to protect themselves from you. Do you see?

CLAUDIA: Yes.

ANGELS: It was their own fear of you that caused them to destroy you. It was fear run rampant on everyone's part, and nobody was really evil. There was just a lot of fear, wasn't there?

CLAUDIA: So much.

ANGELS: We're going to just help you feel that, so you can forgive that life a little bit and feel lighter. That's one of the fragments we were talking about that really needed to come home. We want you to recognize, too, that there are times when your heart can get that hard when you're angry. You know that feeling as well.

CLAUDIA: Do I ever! It's horrible. It's a horrible place to be.

ANGELS: And the next one—and we're sorry to have to move you so quickly. But we're helping you to get through these quickly, so you don't have to sit there.

CLAUDIA: Okay.

ANGELS: The next one is the story we talked about, which is even more painful. We're sorry to have to take you there but you need to heal this.

CLAUDIA: It's okay.

ANGELS: The problem with that life was when they tied you down with your wrists they cut out your tongue. They did that so that you couldn't speak and you gagged on your own blood, swallowing it. It was horrifying and we are sorry. We are not crying but this conduit feels the pain and that is why she has tears. But the rage was so powerful that it almost exploded your head; if you understand what we mean.

CLAUDIA: Yes. (Crying).

ANGELS: And again, you felt: Why are you doing this to me? How can you be so evil?

CLAUDIA: (Crying).

ANGELS: They were lost in their darkness and their fear so badly that they were living in hell. And they dragged you, you see, into their hell.

CLAUDIA: Yes.

ANGELS: Just like you feel those arms carrying you down into hell. They dragged you into their hell. But we want to remind you that it's man-made, and you know that. So in your mind, in order to be "whole" yourself we want you to see that body, which suffered so much, being made "whole." Okay? It's important. See that body; how it was restrained. We want you to loosen the bonds on your wrists, okay? Just go ahead and loosen them. Empower yourself by re-growing that tongue; it never had to be cut. We want you to just feel all the mutilations disappear. Stand up out of that position. Stand up and be whole.

Look upon your abusers and realize that they were living in hell and they dragged you to their hell, but you can leave it at any time because it's not your home. It's not your real home. They tried to convince you that that was your home but it was an illusion and it isn't your home. Tell them that now; with your tongue intact. You tell them, you're trying to take me to your hell but you can't succeed because I always know where to find heaven. I always know what the truth is. You face the Light and you walk away from them. Imagine that as you died in that life, you died whole, you died proudly and you walked as a fully intact woman up to the Light, okay? They did not drag you into hell but you walked fully intact. Change the story into the Light. Get your power back. You can leave them behind in hell. It's the hell of their own making but you can leave now. It's good to be done with those stories, isn't it?

CLAUDIA: Yes.

ANGELS: They taught you. They taught you. And now you understand things that you wouldn't have known. Ultimately, because you understand the hell they live in, when it's time for them to return to the Light, you'll be able to help them, you see?

CLAUDIA: Yes.

ANGELS: When they're ready. We do not deny your pain and your darkness but we try to help you move through it, okay?

CLAUDIA: Yes.

ANGELS: They liked to call you a witch quite often.

CLAUDIA: (Laughing). But I'm a good witch.

ANGELS: They did not know that (laughing).

CLAUDIA: So much blackness. It's so good to let it go.

ANGELS: There is an angel that is associated with forgiveness. Her name is Stamera. She's often used to bring in the energy of forgiveness, if you would like to invite her into your life to help you clear some stories. She will be a companion as long as you need her.

CLAUDIA: Yes, I would like that.

ANGELS: We ask you to be proud of what you know about the darkness and not pretend that it doesn't exist, but also to help teach others how to understand that although it feels very real, that it is still part of the human realm and can be escaped, okay?

CLAUDIA: Yes.

ANGELS: We're going to let you just breathe for a moment, breathing in the White Light, breathe in your oxygen and be glad to be in human body. Feel glad that you are here, having this opportunity to heal old wounds. Let's talk about now how to be an empowered woman on this earth, okay?

CLAUDIA: Yes, please! Okay, let's talk empowerment.

ANGELS: How does one get empowered? Well, one understands, first of all, the illusion of the darkness. The darkness wants to make you believe that it's something it's not. The only way it gains power is by trying to trick you into believing that it has more strength than it actually does. It can't work without trickery because it's basically an illusion. It's an illusion to trick you into believing that whatever methods or ways that you have of discovering Light, are not enough or are not successful. It did its job well because over a number of lives it made you very afraid of bringing your Light into the world.

CLAUDIA: Yes.

ANGELS: Because you're afraid if you shine too brightly, you're going to be attacked by the darkness.

CLAUDIA: Absolutely.

ANGELS: So, it did its job well. We'll give it points for that. Now, the question is of course: Why is it that you kept that happening to you? In some ways, it only needs to succeed one time in one life to get you to do its work for it. In other words, once it's convinced you in one life, in one episode, that it's dangerous for you to let your Light shine, you'll keep recreating that for yourself over and over. Your consciousness will continue to create your own hell for you.

What happens is you become so wedded to the idea of victim and the fear-based thoughts that they often have power enough to create that reality over and over. In order to free yourself, you have to realize that you're not creating out of nowhere. You're creating for a very good reason. You've suffered much and who wouldn't create darkness out of that suffering? Of course, anyone would.

Now that you're a more wise soul you're further along in enlightenment, you can realize that all they've ever had is smoke and mirrors. That's all they've ever had is smoke and mirrors. We're not saying they can't play a really good game of smoke and mirrors with you but we're telling you that's all they've ever had. The Light of God is very, very bright. But when you're in human form, you're so far from it in terms of your vibrational state that sometimes it's very, very easy for you to forget the truth of that Light.

Begin to realize that it's all been smoke and mirrors. They've counted on that; the darkness has. The fear has counted on you believing in it, in order to keep creating it. So, now you're going to realize that, okay, fear exists if I'm in third dimensional mind. It exists if I'm in fourth dimensional mind; which is the lower astral realms. But all I need to do now is get closer to God vibrationally and it will start to dissipate because I will have stepped out of the lower astral, the third and fourth dimension, and I'll come into a place of non-duality, a higher vibrational. I'll be able to "look down" from that higher place on the earth.

Then you'll start doing what people are telling you, which is you become a Master, you become a co-creator. But you cannot create or co-create from the place of the third or fourth dimensional mind, or you will be creating and co-creating fear and darkness. You have to get yourself out of that, understand that that's just another one of many levels of consciousness that you're capable of manifesting. Manifest the Higher, look down and say, "Okay, I don't want to create from that place anymore. I'm not denying it; I'm not saying it doesn't exist. It certainly does and I'm not being so arrogant as to say I'm not capable of going there again, should I choose to, but I'm not going to choose to be there now. I'm going to choose to be up above it, look down at it, as though I was above the world and the earth, looking at that lower consciousness, and I'm going to start to say, I'm not going to create from there."

The way that you do that is that every time you feel a lower thought, a lower, fear-based thought or a thought that is restricting your capabilities, you immediately understand: Oh, that's my lower self, my lower astral self. I'm not going to reinforce it. I'm going to find a mantra, if you will, to override it. When I find myself saying, "You can't do that or that's not safe," I'm going to say, "That is just part of my lower mind but I no longer live there." My Higher Mind can create anything it wants, and I create empowerment and I create safety and I create beauty and I create ease and I create love. I do so not from having to deny the darkness, not from pushing it away out of fear, but from choosing to step out of it and vibrate someplace else. Do you see the difference?

CLAUDIA: Yes.

ANGELS: That's where you gain empowerment. But it's a long process sometimes because the fear on this planet is so thick that there are plenty of places to step back into it. You know that.

CLAUDIA: Yes.

ANGELS: If you step back into the fear with the awareness that it's just another illusion and that you don't want to be in it anymore, then choose a higher illusion to work with, you're going to find that you attract energy that will support that higher vision and you're going to be releasing energy that supports that lower vision. You have been wedded, as we said, through many lifetimes to that lower vision and it's very happy to spring back into place at a moment's notice, as you know.

If you can get the point of view that you're looking down at it from above, almost as if it's below your feet now and you're above it, then you can say, I can see that old mucky muck but I'm not going to play into it anymore. I'm going to know and create something higher and attract something higher. You'll feel much better but you won't be feeling that you have to just deny its existence, which also doesn't sit well with you. You see what we're saying?

CLAUDIA: Yes.

ANGELS: Because then you're denying a part of who you are. You're denying how you've learned, how you've experienced. You've done much of your learning in the darkness and learning through the darkness, so why would you want to cast that out if it's taught you? Otherwise, it would have been a completely useless thing and there would be nothing more horrifying than experiencing some of the sufferings you have and get nothing out of it. You see what we're saying?

CLAUDIA: Yes.

ANGELS: That would be a horrifying thing. We don't want you to just say, "I never experienced those things." We want you to say, "I experienced them, I don't have to re-experience them. They were my teachers but now I've learned in that way for so long, perhaps I'm going to try to learn from the Light for a while." With that belief system, we think you'll start re-hooking the pieces of your soul back to you and not feel so fragmented, as if there's such a war inside you between the dark and the light parts of the self. Do you see?

CLAUDIA: Yes.

ANGELS: We're going to just pause here and ask for any comments or questions. It's a lot we've thrown at you but we're good at that. We want to get to the heart of the matter in the small time we have.

CLAUDIA: It's such a relief to be able to claim those parts and not keep running back and forth between the two.

ANGELS: And feeling completely at war inside yourself in a way or not even having a home, or having to be at home here with the dark and here with the light, but how do I find somebody who understands all of me?

CLAUDIA: Yes.

ANGELS: That's what you're looking for, and that's a good thing to look for. Eventually, it's not that you will want to dwell with somebody in the darkness but you will find somebody who is of light but understands that the darkness can be a teacher and is not afraid of it.

CLAUDIA: Yes.

ANGELS: That is what you're looking for. Would you have any other questions at this time?

CLAUDIA: I have this gift of singing and the fear has kept me from truly using my voice in the world the way that I want to. I feel deeply called to it and so I very much want to find a way to express myself and really shine that light into the world.

ANGELS: Well, part of the problem of course is having one's tongue ripped out is not going to help you speak, of course. We can laugh about it now to some extent because it helps to lighten the issue. And you can say, "Well, I can see why I'd be afraid to speak up and sing and make noise because I've been so punished for it and told that women should never do this." But you also have ability and it might be important to start in a way that feels safe to you.

One of the places that you feel particularly safe and that doesn't frighten you at all is with the fairy realm. In other words, you feel safe with the idea of walking into someplace beautiful by the ocean or in the woods with the fairy realms and the mermaids or merpeople; those who are fairies of the sea. It would be the idea that you could sing to them and begin to listen to how they sing back to you. This will sharpen and re-awaken your ability to sing to nature, sing to crystals, sing to trees, and sing to the fairies. You'll begin to sharpen and remember how they sing back to you and how you receive back the vibrations.

You'll begin to feel a way of opening that feels safe to you because part of the problem is that there was a time when those who had the ability to use sound and energy to transmit ideas and thought were harvested and utilized as slaves by Darker Beings. What happened was, you were also involved with being drugged in another life, in being drugged and kept enslaved through drugs, your mind being clouded, enslaved and so forth, with the hope that they could control you. But unfortunately, what happened, they found, is that when they drugged you, you lost a lot of your abilities. You became lost in the drug state and you lost a lot of your abilities. So it didn't work so much. That was not useful to them. But you've been utilized for some of these abilities in some very strange ways.

It scares you. It's okay again to utilize it in an "average Joe way," and that's the only way you feel safe. You understand what we're saying.

CLAUDIA: Yes.

ANGELS: In certain realms of musical expression that feel to be "mainstream" you feel safe.

CLAUDIA: Yes.

ANGELS: But what scares you is the idea of opening up in a more what we're going to call New Age kind of way or the way of just using pure sound for toning or frequency or healing, to impact others or to impact the world, because you understand the power of it and you understand that the dark forces also understand the power of it.

CLAUDIA: Yes.

ANGELS: They're brilliant at that and there are ways they have utilized these frequencies and so forth to actually control other humans. They know and understand—and we're talking about through hundreds of thousands of years of manipulations; many galaxies, not merely on the Earth. Pure toning, pure frequency experiments have been done to make people go mad by inserting certain frequencies. That terrifies you. You understand that deeply.

CLAUDIA: Yes.

ANGELS: The idea of making—controlling people's minds with certain frequencies so they have to behave in a certain way. In other words, if you insert a different vibration or a certain frequency into someone, you can almost enslave them that way. There's been much terrible use of frequencies by the dark forces.

Those who are here to liberate mankind can also use these sounds and these frequencies and these tones to liberate mankind. But often they are also afraid that if they start they're going to be imprisoned or enslaved by dark forces; and it's not even conscious. They don't even know why they are afraid because they're remembering soul history from so long ago. And the other thing is that they're afraid that they might harm someone and that stops them as well. It is a very difficult gift and those who have the ability to work with pure tone and sound and frequency must free themselves up to do it.

One of the things that's going to help you is to remind yourself of very light, lovely energies, like the fairy realm. In other words, begin by just walking through the woods and just making a sound or a tone and using the tone to say, with just tone, "Are you there, fairies? Are you there? I've come to awaken you and to speak with your realm and to understand and to know the sparkle of light and the love that you feel for Mother Earth." You just begin simply that way.

If you feel a fear rise up as you do it, stop and you don't make any more sound. Just walk. Use your heart to feel love. You use your heart to feel the love of Mother Earth. When you've regained the love in your heart again, you start to listen and you start to hear the light sounds and tinkles and voices of that realm, the energy that the trees are emitting, the energy the flowers are emitting, and you begin to sense and feel those energies and vibrations and frequencies. In the beginning, that's enough. That's all you have to do is just enjoy and feel and re-establish. Slowly, you'll get to the point, when you do it over time, that you won't feel fear rise up when you say, "Are you there, fairies? Are you there, Mother Earth? I wish to hear you and send you love. "You'll just feel the love and you'll know you're beginning to be liberated because as you do that, the first thing that will come up in your heart is a feeling of love and not the feeling of fear. Once you do that and you feel love and no fear, you can know you can progress along your path. Do you see what we're saying?

CLAUDIA: Yes.

ANGELS: But anytime you begin to do work with vocal toning or vibration and communicating on that level and you have a feeling of fear, we suggest you immediately stop, sit, go into your heart, try to feel love in your heart and when that fear has been transformed to love, you can begin again. Don't go on and try to push your way through the fear because it will only bring up more fear for you.

CLAUDIA: Okay.

ANGELS: By the way, the love is the higher vibration, so if you're going to be doing the work in fear, you're going to be attracting the lower vibrations that you fear. But if you're doing the work in love, with higher vibration, they aren't going to be there. They're not going to be vibrating at that level. So you are protected from the lower vibration and you'll be working higher. Do you see?

CLAUDIA: Yes.

ANGELS: That's what we would suggest there. Eventually, you can get to the point where you could just use your lovely voice to start things vibrating and awakening love in the hearts of others. But first, you have to push through this fear in your own heart so that you can awaken love in your heart before you start to sing.

CLAUDIA: Yes.

ANGELS: That's what we see as your calling or path. But tiptoe and be aware of your body; it's sending you signals. How you feel will let you know how to proceed. Does that assist you?

CLAUDIA: Yes.

ANGELS: We would welcome another question.

CLAUDIA: As I continue to follow this path of singing recognized forms of music, as I go along, will I then be able to—I guess it's the same concept, that even though I'm not just making tone and I'm singing in a way that people recognize, will I be able to get across the spiritual element as well?

ANGELS: Yes. Once you have learned how to be a vehicle for love as a frequency, then you will be a vehicle for love as a frequency, and anything you do will have that frequency of love attached to it, and you'll be sending out love. And that's what you're really trying to do is become an open conduit for Love and Light, which is synonymous in our realm, with the idea of God or the

Source in its purest, loving form. You send it through there and it just comes out and everyone feels good because they've been touched by love. That's really what it is to be a true vocalist.

CLAUDIA: Okay.

ANGELS: You move people to tears because they feel the love and they feel how much they are loved by God. That would make you feel good, if you could help others to remember that, and yourself to remember it as well.

CLAUDIA: Yes, it would. I've been experiencing certain physical symptoms that I'm wondering if there's something I should know about them. One of them is very powerfully, this feeling of too much heat in my digestive system, which I imagine is connected with the anger and rage.

ANGELS: That is blocked energy.

CLAUDIA: Yes.

ANGELS: Yes. And the lower chakras have been very closed up in you. You know that.

CLAUDIA: Yes.

ANGELS: There's a need to move the energy through and to feel it's okay or safe to be on the earth plane because you certainly don't really feel that. As you begin to clear and connect some of these old fragmented pieces, you will begin to feel more and more that it has no power over you, so the fear can dissipate. You'll feel that you've moved energy from your lower body more and more. That's what we sense, too. Yes, it's a blockage. It looks to us to be red hot, like a fire.

CLAUDIA: Yes.

ANGELS: That's what it looks like; it is the rage. We feel that if you just pour water on it with your mental images, it's not going to do much good. In other words, your best bet is to do what you did with the past life images. Go ahead, put your hands on there and let the feeling or emotions come up; go ahead and just express them by crying or weeping. Move it in an emotional way. Don't just try to—"Oh, it's hot, I should throw water on it. It's more like I need to get this out of here!"

CLAUDIA: Yes.

ANGELS: It needs to know that you're listening. Otherwise, it will feel you're just trying to—it's like putting a gag on someone who is trying to tell a painful story. They need to speak. So, these stories that are in there, as you know, the idea of rape and torture and other things have deeply wounded those lower chakras.

CLAUDIA: I've been lately reading some channeling books of the Pleiadians and I feel a real connection there and I'm wondering if there is some deep connection.

ANGELS: Yes, you are Pleiadian. Your soul matrix, if you will, is a Pleiadian form. You have a strong resonance with and you understand that culture. Many of the Pleiadians have very similar paths on this earth and many of them have been here in many ways; in many guises. Some of them have been responsible for the damage on the earth and some of them have been responsible for the victimization on the earth, and some of them have come back at this time to liberate the earth, to assist the earth to liberate.

The Pleiadians are one of the groups that realize that if in fact some change is not made on the earth at this time, some profound change in liberating the earth from fear and moving into higher consciousness, then the ramifications for not only the earth but what would spread out into galaxies ahead in time, in linear time, ahead in the future would be profoundly vicious and difficult.

The Pleiadian agenda is to reinsert itself into human consciousness through Pleiadian humans and to help human beings lift their vibration from one of fear to love. They are doing this so that the human race will not be so dense and caught in its fear—killing one another and destroying one another and being enslaved by fear.

So, what you are here to do at this time is to liberate your human self from fear, and in doing that, to teach other humans how to liberate themselves from fear. By using your vocal cords to channel pure love and the vibration of love, you can tone love into people. Others have been toning fear into them; but you can shift the vibration from one of fear to one of love. Do you see what we're saying?

CLAUDIA: Yes.

ANGELS: But you have to do that for yourself first.

CLAUDIA: Yes.

ANGELS: Not by denying, but by liberating those dark places and reconnecting those fragments of yourself. The Pleiadians have been involved in the earth's history in many ways; both in the future time and in the past time, and are linked deeply to the human experience. They are responsible in many ways for some of the karma upon this earth, and it is their duty to help liberate the earth from some of the karma. But they are peaceful, loving beings and they are very evolved and understanding; albeit they are an emotional species. The Arcturians are less emotional but the Pleiadians are highly and deeply emotional. They study and are masters of the arts, of music, of dance and understand creative expression, and have embraced the energies of the Divine Feminine and have understood the power of the feminine self. They are wedded to those belief systems.

CLAUDIA: I had an experience last week where I have begun to work with the image of the Merkaba; which feels like an image that's very powerful for me. Last week, I received a necklace that is the image of the Merkaba, and that evening, I had an ecstatic experience of orgasm over and over and over again, and I was wondering what that might have been about.

ANGELS: Well, that's another thing that the Pleiadians understand and that they are Masters at. The Pleiadians understand that the human experience of orgasm is extremely powerful and creates portals, and it can create a portal for divine ecstasy—but it can also create a portal for darkness to enter. One of the things that the Pleiadians became Masters at is the idea of using the human sexual experience to connect to the divine frequencies of love and Higher Self. They can actually utilize that to travel. It is a Pleiadian gift and it's one of the reasons that the human beings have been enlightened into the idea of what's called Tantric sex, which is using sexuality as a sacred and divine act rather than as an act of humiliation or degradation, as has been utilized on the earth. You are just awakening to what you have known as a Pleiadian and experienced; the idea of using that energy which is released during orgasm for a divine expression.

Now, when doing your Merkaba exercises, we want to make sure that all who do Merkaba do the Merkaba as self-directed. In other words do not allow others to tell you how to create your Merkaba. It should be a creation that comes through you from a divine source at the proper time, when your body is ready to receive and hold it. Do not allow others to tell you how to create a Merkaba because it needs to be something which is organically built between you and your divinity.

The Merkaba is something which must not be abused or misused, and it must be divinely inspired to be created. If you feel the love and the ecstasy and the freedom associated with it, you know you're on the right track. Again, your heart will know the truth, so allow it to be a natural creation for you, but don't let anyone else tell you what you should do to create it. Do you understand what we say?

CLAUDIA: Yes. Does that mean that the image of the Merkaba itself would come from within me?

ANGELS: Yes, it will come to you and through you from your own divine guidance.

CLAUDIA: So it might not look like what others have said it looks like, basically.

ANGELS: Well, it looks like this holographic interweaving of the triangles. It will have that, but your divine, sacred geometry needs to be fashioned by you. Unfortunately, there can be a misuse, if others are trying to utilize—just like they can utilize sound; saying they're making you feel good but you don't. You know what we're saying?

CLAUDIA: Yes.

ANGELS: They can utilize sacred geometry to say, "Oh, we're making you feel good," but you don't. If you always work from within, with your own divine guides and feeling what feels good to you, you'll know you're on the right track. Then nobody can enslave you with their thoughts. Do you know what we're saying?

CLAUDIA: Yes.

ANGELS: Allow it to be your organic experience. It will come to you when you're ready, it will come to you how you're ready, and it should feel ecstatic to you. If it does, you're on the right track. If you're feeling any fear or darkness, you know you need again to stop and pause until you can clear your field and once again feel light and love before proceeding.

CLAUDIA: I have had some past relationships that have been very difficult, you know, intimate with men. Obviously, it makes sense now, given what you've explained to me about past lives and anger and darkness. I have been getting used to being on my own for a while and not looking outside of myself to get—that it was so important for me to feel love from men and not to feel love for my own self. Yet at the same time, I do very much want to have a deep, intimate connection with another human being, and I'm just wondering if that is something that you see happening for me.

ANGELS: The problem is that when you are needy, you send a signal. When you're needy, you send a signal to all the dark ones that there's a good, needy soul here that can be manipulated. Do you know what we're saying?

CLAUDIA: Yes.

ANGELS: It sends a signal that there's a "ripe one here for the picking." Unfortunately, because sex is such a powerful energetic sharing when you are having sexual intercourse with one whose sole purpose is to manipulate or overpower or demean or make you feel bad, the energy cords that are established are very powerful and can be utilized to almost enslave another and make them feel powerless. It's particularly important when you're working to come into Light that you make sure that your sexual partner is of a similar vibration and not allow your neediness to be the motivating factor in relationship because it attracts the dark forces, not the light forces. There's never been a human in the Light who wanted to have a needy person clinging to them. You know that.

CLAUDIA: Yes.

ANGELS: So, the ones who are attracted to that, they think: Oh, it's someone weak I can manipulate. You need to strengthen yourself, find your own sense of love, and release the need. Eventually, when you're in your own power, you're going to be with another empowered human, and it will be a good relationship at last. That's why it is needed for you, and you can't do your work to heal others if you are being sucked dry. Do you understand what we're saying?

CLAUDIA: Yes, absolutely.

ANGELS: In a negative relationship you're only involved, in an almost self-centered way, on your own problems. You are focusing on your own out-of-balance relationship; and it's a good way to keep you from doing the growth you need to do. If someone can keep you focused on your own pain and unhappiness in relationship, it's a great way to keep you from bringing Light to the world. Could you see that?

CLAUDIA: Yes, absolutely.

ANGELS: So, it's better to be alone and be a Lightbearer. Do not accept anything other than a relationship that will give you pure and total freedom to be a Lightbearer; that supports you and uplifts you and gives you energy to do your Lightwork and does not drain you.

CLAUDIA: I've been hearing much and reading much about this time on the planet and what's happening: The Ascension. I do have certain fears that come up because I feel that I've been held back by my fear and am now just starting to become aware of my multi-dimensional self, I do have fears come up that I'm somehow going to be left behind or that I'm somehow out of synch with what's happening everywhere else.

ANGELS: Well, if you are in fear then the dark forces are doing their job well. They're brilliant and never underestimate the dark forces. They are far more brilliant at manipulation and cunning and trickery than you can possibly imagine. Everything always has been and always will be decided vibrationally. It is no different than when you die. When you die, your vibration decides where you go, and you go where you're comfortable. You don't go anywhere you're not comfortable because your own vibration is creating your reality. It's no one else—nothing else.

The first thing we need everyone to understand is that it is all about self-empowerment. Your vibration is always taking you where it is that you are. Whether it is on the earth plane, in a body, or whether it is in a transitional state, between life and death, whether it is in a disincarnate state—it's all about your vibration. The reason to release the fear is because it lightens you up. It makes you feel less heavy and you find yourself easily vibrating places that feel good. So, you're on the right track.

But it's not about your being left behind or not being good enough or not being empowered or not having any control over your destiny. The idea is that as you progress, as you have always progressed and as everything has always progressed, your vibration determines where you are because dimensional consciousness *is* consciousness. If you are sitting in this room with an angel, the angel and you are together but perhaps you don't see the angel. The angel is vibrating at a different frequency than you are and is holding more love and more Light than you are, but it does not mean that you are not taking up the same space.

So, you are on the right path. Everything that you do to make yourself hold more love is a benefit to you, so that you will always, no matter where you go, no matter what time, no matter where you are in the earth's history or your own soul's history, you will feel more love and more light and better. Understand that it's always been true that parts of you exist simultaneously everywhere. For example, those ghosts we talked about. There are parts and pieces of you everywhere—even in the angelic realm. Those parts and pieces of you are where your consciousness is. As you begin to integrate those parts of yourself, those parallel selves, and you can hold all those parts in Higher Light, you become a Living Master.

It's true, you can be alive and in a physical body and hold more light and more love and feel like a Living Master, freed from fear. You should never be afraid that you are being rejected or judged or cast out. The only question that is ever asked of a soul is how much love do you hold? That is why love is the only thing that really matters.

Now, we're not trying to be someone who says, "Oh, there's no darkness, there's only love." To you, in this realm, for this consciousness and where you are, there's plenty of darkness. We're not denying that and we're not denying its gifts and its teachings. But we are saying that it feels better to be in more of a state of love and harmony. It feels better to give up the victim in you. It feels better to give up the judge in you. It feels better to be in a state of self-Mastery.

As you choose to integrate more pieces of yourself and bring those pieces into your Higher Self, those pieces begin to vibrate at a Higher Light, those parallel selves become unified, and you find yourself really feeling better. That is really what this is about. This is really about stepping from the illusion of the fear into the reality of love and Light, so you can all treat each other better and stop being so mean. You've done plenty of that.

We were asked a very wise question once and that was, "Well, but doesn't earth depend on the dark and the light and the duality? Doesn't the light depend on the dark to know itself and doesn't the dark depend on the light to know itself? How does light know who it is if it does not have dark to compare itself to? So, if you're eradicating all the darkness, then isn't it true that the light doesn't know who it is?"

We're not telling you that we're eradicating the darkness. We do not do war against anything. But those of you who have lived plenty of lives, as you know, in the darkness, you know the darkness. You don't need to be there anymore. You see what we're saying?

CLAUDIA: Yes.

ANGELS: You know it. It's ***not*** that you're eradicating it and becoming so forgetful that—and by the way, that was one of the problems with the Pleiadians. They cast the darkness away from them and they were afraid of it, so it became a fear that could be manipulated. That's another story. But your job now is to have learned from the darkness and yet not want to live there anymore. Why would you want to repeat that, you see? It's not that you deny its existence but you step from it into the Light, and that's what you're trying to do. Do you see the difference?

CLAUDIA: Yes.

ANGELS: And that's what freedom is for you and that's what freedom will be to all of those who want to choose to free themselves. Does that assist you?

CLAUDIA: Absolutely.

ANGELS: You're not going to be left behind anywhere. You're going to go to the perfect vibrational place for you, as all always do. No different. Each of you on this earth is simultaneously creating. Some are living in true hell, some are living in heaven. Those who have perfected love on this plane exist and feel themselves to be in heaven, and then there are many in-between those levels. So, it's not different. Each person is vibrating and creating and causing other vibrational similarities to be attracted to them, and that's all. It doesn't change. You're just choosing to step into a higher vibration, so that the hell realm is no longer where you live. That's all.

CLAUDIA: Okay.

ANGELS: And hell realm can be on earth and it can be of your own making, as you know.

CLAUDIA: Oh, yes. I know that place very well.

ANGELS: So we would welcome a last question. She's growing a little tired at this time but if you have another question?

CLAUDIA: I'm about to embark on a trip to Italy to sing. This is a big step for me. I've never done something this—I've been too afraid before to do anything like this. Do you have any advice for me in terms of—?

ANGELS: Well, you're going to a karmic place to free yourself. Do you understand that? You're going to one of these old stories.

CLAUDIA: Okay.

ANGELS: Okay?

CLAUDIA: Is that what this is about?

ANGELS: Yes. So you're going to a place where before, you were shut down, to come and be opened up, to heal that old wound.

CLAUDIA: Okay.

ANGELS: Your job is going to be to sing like a bird, free, in the place where before, you were encaged or enslaved or hurt, okay? And then you'll feel yourself finally healing some of that old wounding. That's what it's about.

CLAUDIA: Wonderful. Thank you.

ANGELS: If fear comes up for you, realize the gift. Oh, good, you're coming up as old stories so I can transmute you to freedom and love. Don't believe in the fear of it, but realize it's going to be like a homeopathic gift. Okay, the old disease is coming up. Now I can lift it to heaven with my beautiful song. And it will no more be a vibration on this earth of darkness but now you can say, "Where I left a vibration of darkness, I'll be leaving a vibration of Light." Do you see?

CLAUDIA: Yes.

ANGELS: That's the idea.

CLAUDIA: That's beautiful. Thank you.

ANGELS: It's about your healing, but you're doing a very good job and we hope that you are feeling more integrated and more peaceful.

CLAUDIA: Yes.

ANGELS: And understanding a bit more of yourself. We are going to be enjoying working with you off and on throughout your journey. Remember that your journey is to transmute all these places of your darkness to Light. Because in doing that, you help the world move to Light, okay?

CLAUDIA: Yes.

ANGELS: It's not that you deny them; it's just that you heal them.

CLAUDIA: Thank you so much.

ANGELS: So if you are alright with that, we would release her now, unless you have one quick comment.

CLAUDIA: I just want to say I feel so safe here and so much love; and it is such a gift to feel that. Thank you.

ANGELS: You are loved and remember that you were never abandoned, you were never dragged down. It was just an illusion that you chose to embrace for a while, but this should feel a happy time because now you're realizing, I don't need to be there anymore. I learned a lot but it's time to move on. That way, you empower yourself from old habits and patterns of belief and habits of behaving. And we see glorious things ahead of you, so feel excited for your own empowerment.

CLAUDIA: Thank you.

(After Note: When she came back from Italy she told me that the opera coach and director/guide of the trip said, "We are going to visit a house of the Inquisition where they tortured witches. Her fear immediately was stimulated but she remembered what the angels told her—that she was there to heal the wounds of the past. When she stepped into the same place she had been tortured hundreds of years ago she knew it was the story where her tongue had been cut out. The actual chair they had tied her to was in the middle of the room. She worked through her fear with forgiveness and when it came time to sing she sang a song of freedom.)

CHAPTER TWELVE

SPIRITUAL TRIAGE

RHONDA R.

ANGELS: We are most delighted to have this opportunity to speak with you today. And as always, this is Ariel who is speaking, and Michael and Gabriel are also with this conduit and delighted to be in attendance.

We thank you so much for the work you are doing upon the Earth and, also, the work that you are doing on the other side of the curtain or in the other dimensions. We want to remind you that you are loved and you are needed and that at times you forget your own importance. You forget that what you do matters and that you have a role to play that is of great importance. From our perspective, sometimes we would say you negate your contributions a bit and you humble yourself and you try to stay small or quiet or in humble service. But, we want you to remember that what you do is important, so that you understand and do feel the pride in your accomplishments and you feel the pride in the gifts that you have to give, because that feeling and that sense of pride is not arrogance; it is a sense of feeling your own self-worth—feeling essentially what it is you are and what it is you have to give. That is not arrogant; that is an essential component of being able to function well on the Earth.

We want to remind you of how important you are and remind you that some of the gifts that you have hidden or even squelched are important to the Earth. You have tremendous, astute powers of observation and understanding, and we want you to know that you use those in the task which we call triage. When on the other side of the curtain, or in your spiritual body, you can understand and access wisdom so that you can see and fully understand where the soul should go after passing. This is spiritual triage.

One of the reasons that you are here on the Earth now is to broaden your knowledge, so that you can do your job even better—your job of what we would call triage for incoming souls. The knowledge and wisdom that you are gaining on the Earth at this time and removing your blinders to see more clearly is obviously going to help you a great deal with the passage and understanding more clearly what each soul has endured and where their hearts lie, and where they need to go to best suit them for their continued growth. So, each and every thing you do, every task you are given, is giving you the wisdom and the knowledge that you need to do your job better also in the spiritual realm.

You do have a nursing function. But we're going to put it this way: you're growing out of your nursemaid function and wishing to take on and studying and learning the triage function. And it's requiring you to be more astute in wisdom and knowledge and to understand the nature of the dark and light and so forth. That's not so necessary in the nursery, the nursery of the souls, but it is essential in the triage units. So, to use human terminology, it's the best way we can describe it.

We're going to pause now and thank you, welcome you, and invite your questions and your comments at this time.

RHONDA: I've been thinking a lot about this present life that I've been in, and I feel like I've been derailed repeatedly. I'm wondering if the people that have seemed—when I look back on it—that they've been on a mission to derail me. I'm wondering if they have followed me in other lives and if, when they do that, if that is true, then I'm wondering are they here purposely trying to sidetrack me or destroy me? Are they just innocent in that or are they intentionally—are they innocent and just misguided and they don't understand the impact they have on other people or have they purposely derailed me?

ANGELS: Well, both are true. Both are true. There is a Family of Dark and they are in opposition to your family, which is the Family of Light. There is an oppositional, conscious family called the Family of Dark who work to stop the Family of Light from succeeding. There is a battle and that's true. Simultaneously, there are many, many people, as you are well aware, who are wounded and innocents, who are themselves in a sense victims of the darkness in which they find themselves on this Earth, and they lash out from fear.

Now, those who are lashing out from fear, from old karma, who are unconscious of it, have a motivation very different from those who are wide awake and consciously working to stop the Lightworkers or the Family of Light from doing its job, and you have encountered both. This takes us to our opening message: you are trying to answer that question to better understand what to do in the triage unit.

Do you understand what we mean by that? When an incoming soul dies and they're wounded, and they're dying because of innocent wounding, well, you would put them into a different place for healing. If a being comes in who is Family of Dark, it's a totally different situation. You're seeing and learning and discerning on what you call your human side of the curtain, the physical plane, what it means to be Family of Dark, what it means to be a wounded human, what it means to be a wounded Starseed. You're learning and understanding all the different categories. And as you understand and get clear in your own wounding, you are better equipped to do your new job on the other side, which is the idea of triage. Do you understand? Does it make sense?

RHONDA: It does make sense.

ANGELS: You started or you spent much time on the other side of the curtain in the nurseries, in the comforting zones, which allowed you to remain pure and merely work from that level of innocence. But in order to grow up yourself or to increase your wisdom, you've made an agreement to step outside of your comfort zone and begin to look at and participate in the battles of duality.

And what you are experiencing are direct examples or hits from the battle of duality. And you understand that humans become wounded and, as you say, strike. You are also beginning to understand that there seems to be an intelligence behind some of these strikes, that it's almost as if they were operating wide awake versus sound asleep. You're beginning to understand what it feels like when someone hits you sound asleep and when someone hits you wide awake. You understand what we mean by sound asleep and wide awake?

RHONDA: I believe so. Sound asleep means they're not aware of what they're actually doing, they're just reacting.

ANGELS: Or being manipulated.

RHONDA: Or being manipulated.

ANGELS: Yeah.

RHONDA: And wide awake, they full-blown know what they're doing and are really participants in it.

ANGELS: And they have teamed up in a consciousness with dark forces, to derail any and every being that is trying to carry light or bring light to the Earth. And those hits feel different, and you're beginning to understand, as you begin to understand humankind at a deeper level and analyze it at a deeper level, rather than your previous desire which often was just to escape it into the nursery. Previously you would say, "I'm going to escape this and go into a place of healing and light and peace and calmness, what we call the nursery, the transitions, the places where they're coddled, where souls are coddled." You say, "Oh, I'm ready to step out of that place and move ahead in my work and my studies. I want to be awake and strong and I think I can handle it." And at times, you feel you want to run back to the nursery, but at the same time, you've come too far now to ever be in that innocence again. Do you understand?

RHONDA: Yes.

ANGELS: And you're in a little uncomfortable place because you're in the transition place, if you understand that meaning. The transition place means that you haven't fully gotten into your full power or strength or "awakeness," but you're not asleep and you're moving there.

So please, if you would like to give us an example of someone that you believe was a conscious attack and someone that you believe was derailing you unconsciously, we will help you to analyze, to increase your studies and knowledge in this area.

RHONDA: There was a particular time period in my life where it seems like everybody turned on me, one after another. I go back and forth about the motive of my mother, because my mother was an alcoholic, so it's hard to figure her motives out because she could have really been an innocent, just a misguided innocent person who just caused me a lot of difficulties in my life. And of course, her impact on me would be more than somebody else's because she was my mother. So, I really don't know about her but I feel like a lot of it started with her.

Both my daughters turned on me. I think they were innocent. I think they were manipulated. I think they just were in a period in their life where they—it's normal, I guess, to be against your mother, but they were swept up into this thing that I feel like still has affected their lives not for the good, you know, that taught them wrong lessons rather than good lessons.

But there were a couple of people around the same time that were—one of them was named Blanche and she was a self-proclaimed prophetess in a—well, she wasn't really in a church. She was in her own ministry and she went from church to church but then she ended up doing her own ministry. I was drawn to it because I was taking care of IV drug abusers; I was taking care of AIDS patients down in South Carolina. And we had this connection about wanting to help the destitute and the down and out, but she totally abused me spiritually.

ANGELS: She casts a web like a spider. Her trick is to cast a web, draw the prey close and then entangle it just like a spider. That is truly what she does. One of the reasons that we feel she's attracted to certain types is because it's easy to get them into her web. Now, do you understand? Do you see the image? Is that clear for you?

RHONDA: Absolutely.

ANGELS: Now, why does a spider. What does a spider do to the victims in its web?

RHONDA: It eats them.

ANGELS: Well, what does it really do first? Take it step by step.

RHONDA: It entangles them.

ANGELS: Cocoons them, yeah. And then what does it do?

RHONDA: It devours them. It lets them starve to death?

ANGELS: It sucks the blood and fluids.

RHONDA: Oh, it does? I didn't know that.

ANGELS: Yes, and then drains them of their fluid. And then, yes, it can eat them, but it isn't a quick death. It slowly cocoons, it poisons and it paralyzes, so the prey becomes paralyzed. And then it is able to slowly draw the nourishment. So it isn't a quick strike, correct, like your friend? It wasn't a quick strike, correct?

RHONDA: Correct.

ANGELS: It is a means or a method for energetically feeding off of other people. It is a way, when someone does not know how to get nourishment from God, to nourish themselves, to create a web, to draw the prey and it becomes very good, that spider soul, at figuring out what is good prey, what is easy prey; and you were easy prey. It then cocoons it, which at first might even feel loving but soon becomes smothering.

RHONDA: Yes.

ANGELS: And then once you are fully unable to move, it will try and paralyze you, so you can't escape and draw and kill slowly. And unless you are very strong as a human, it can be very hard to get away. So it is a type of vampritic action.

RHONDA: That's actually—I've actually even thought of a psychic vampire. After I got away, sometimes that's exactly what would come to mind, like a psychic vampire.

ANGELS: The Family of Dark are vampires. They are the vampires. They are led by the Lord of the Family of Dark, who is the greatest vampire of all time—Vlad Dracula. He is the devil.

RHONDA: When I did leave, I actually really suffered when I left because I really did feel like I loved her. The last time I met with you, you reminded me that I was connected to Mary Magdalene when she walked the Earth with Jesus, and I've wondered since then if my attraction to a woman who I thought might be a strong spiritual woman and me being a supportive role to her and a friend was maybe me wanting to relive that life I had with Mary Magdalene, except that Mary Magdalene was legitimate. Is there a possibility that that's what I was doing?

ANGELS: Well, yes, but it's teaching you that you need to be your own strong woman, that you need to be the head of your own church, that there are no more disciples, no more beings to worship, no more ladder of who's better than whom. It's time for you to be the head of your own church, and that taught you that. So, as always, when looked at the right way, the Family of Dark gives great gifts, because they strengthen you. If you survive, you will never, ever be that weak and gullible again, and you learn very important lessons through the Family of Dark. So, the Family of Dark is allowed to operate in a sense because of the lessons they give. If you can be taught by them and learn from them, you can progress.

RHONDA: There was a pastor who was also a friend of hers, and he and his wife and I and some other people had kind of that bond, where we had been through that cult really that she had, that web or whatever.

ANGELS: The spider web, yeah.

RHONDA: But then they ended up turning on me, too. But I don't feel that was the same .

ANGELS: No, it is not the same. They are weak souls and it is different. They are very weak souls, who are guided tremendously by fear. They have a great deal of fear of God. They fear God, so they make comments or statements that they believe will keep them from being cast into hell. They push people away or do things from their weakness, but it is not the same energy at all.

RHONDA: After I left Blanche, she absolutely tried to destroy my reputation with everyone. She said awful things about me.

ANGELS: Well, the fly got out of the web, which angers the spider. Do you understand?

RHONDA: Yeah.

ANGELS: Terribly. These Draculas, these vampires, are very, very powerful, on their terms, on their level, and not to be taken lightly.

RHONDA: You've said I've learned very important lessons and I believe that I have, but I also feel like I have scars from it that I'm having a hard time healing from. I feel like I have a hard time trusting people. Is that just because I'm still in that transition and I need to hone my discernment, so that I know who I can trust before I can allow my heart to trust people again?

ANGELS: Yes.

RHONDA: It feels very isolated and lonely.

ANGELS: Yes, because the problem is that you don't trust yourself yet. It's not about trusting other people; it's about learning to trust you. And one of the things that all the Lightworkers go through is an experience similar to yours, where someone who pretends to be working in the same path or being in the light, who is really a Family of Dark member—the Family of Dark always cloak, because if they came in and declared themselves to a Family of

Light member as a Family of Dark member, obviously, it would be easy, right? They wouldn't be able to get in and weaken all of you.

So, what they do is they're very wise. They have a great deal of information and access to a great deal of information, and they come in disguised and they attempt their work under the guise of being of Family of Light. So the innocent Lightworkers who are all open-hearted and in love welcome them, thinking of course, if someone speaks the speak, they must be of the Light. They learn the hard way that not everyone who claims to be of the Light, when the chips are down, is of the Light. They often have just been masquerading themselves or masking themselves but they are really of the Dark. That is not just your lesson. Every single Lightworker learns that lesson, okay?

RHONDA: Okay.

ANGELS: And will learn it and has learned it. It's absolutely essential to understand and learn discernment. You are teaching yourself that and learning to trust yourself. As you can see, it's going to help you a great deal in your triage work. As you begin to understand the levels that people work from and why they do what they do, you begin to understand where it is they need to go to heal, and you begin to understand those who don't want your services, who just—we'll put it this way, just refuse, on the other side of the curtain, your services, to keep it simple. You can see that you don't coax them, you just leave them alone.

Others who are asking for assistance or help truly from the Light, those are the ones that you embrace and help. But you have to learn and really understand the difference. That's what all these experiences are teaching you, not to—as we said, as you step out of the nursery and you get your wisdom wings, not to just trust anyone. That happens by learning the skills so that you trust yourself to immediately be able to pick out who is intentionally harming you and who isn't.

RHONDA: Is there anybody in my life right now that's intentionally awake, doing this?

ANGELS: Well, we sense that there's a woman that you work with, not that she is intentionally doing this but—

RHONDA: But she's doing it.

ANGELS: She's doing this. What we sense from this woman is that she is very jealous and very angry, and has been very jealous and angry with you for many lifetimes, and that is her motivation. Do you know of whom we speak?

RHONDA: I know exactly of whom you speak.

ANGELS: Okay. Besides her, it feels right now, at this moment, like it's relatively calm. But you need to get your power back with this woman.

RHONDA: Okay.

ANGELS: She's a more hateful heart. She doesn't love herself, so she projects outward from that lack of self-love.

RHONDA: She's very two-faced so I find it very difficult to be—she's not in my face confronting me. It's not adversarial like that. She gets moody sometimes but she's very back stabbing.

ANGELS: If you can realize that it's all coming from her own self-loathing, that it's not anything else, then you can forgive her more easily. It's really about how she hates herself, not about how she hates you. She hates you because she hates herself. So when she hates you, she actually hates herself, from our perspective. Realize that when you feel her hating you, just say, "Wow, she hates herself that much." Then send her love, and that should help a little bit. Someone like that needs a lot of love.

Let's just imagine—we're going to play a game with you. You're on the "other side of the curtain," and you're doing your triage, and the two souls are incoming. One is the woman we just spoke of, who hates herself and the other is your spider friend, and they're coming into you, in soul form. Now, what do you see? What would you do with the first one we're going to address: the one who hates herself? How would you triage her?

RHONDA: I don't really know. I'm not really familiar with what happens in-between lives. You mentioned that there's a nursery where people are coddled and stuff, so I would think she would probably need a lot of love, so she would probably need time to heal from some of the wounds from her lives that she's had.

ANGELS: Right.

RHONDA: And learn to appreciate herself and love herself so that she can love others.

ANGELS: Good. So you would send her to that unit, yeah?

RHONDA: Yes.

ANGELS: Okay. Now the spider woman comes in. What does she look like when she comes in?

RHONDA: Mean.

ANGELS: Black, right?

RHONDA: Yeah, dark.

ANGELS: Black energy. You don't want to put her in the nursery, do you?

RHONDA: No.

ANGELS: Where do you want to put her?

RHONDA: I'm not sure.

ANGELS: Think about it. She wants to go to her own family, doesn't she?

RHONDA: She wants to go to the Family of Dark.

ANGELS: Can you feel that?

RHONDA: So would you send her there?

ANGELS: Yes.

RHONDA: Oh, you would.

ANGELS: Yeah, because that's her home. That's where she's comfortable. She has said to you, "Send me to my home, I want to go where I'm comfortable." And you agree because you do not override her free will, correct?

RHONDA: Okay. So she goes to the Family of Dark. So that's hell?

ANGELS: No, that's only hell to *you.*

RHONDA: It's not hell to her.

ANGELS: It's hell to *you.*

RHONDA: I just wondered if that's maybe what Jesus meant when he spoke of hell.

ANGELS: It's what you think of as hell. It is hell to anyone who knows the Light.

RHONDA: That's what I meant. I didn't mean like eternal damnation. I meant that interpretation of—

ANGELS: But to someone who considers that their home, they're comfortable in the dark. If the two souls come to you, as they will, when they come to you, you feel their energies. You feel and you sense and you know, that one goes here and that one goes here. This can assist you in your human life. Imagine this game: the soul is coming to me in triage, and then begin to imagine—play that game. Where would I send them? It will teach you a lot about their wounding, who they really are and their motivation, which was your first question, right?

RHONDA: Yes.

ANGELS: If you can triage them, it will help you to know what it is they really need. They can be working for the Family of Dark but if they are working against their will, even then, you're going to have a sense that you'll want to heal them somewhere. But if they're working in will alignment with the Family of Dark, you'll say, that's their will, that's where they want to go. Some are manipulated and you'll feel differently. It will help you to decipher the motivation of the incoming while you're on the Earth. Interesting way to think of it, yeah?

RHONDA: Yes.

ANGELS: Different for you. But it's what you're training to do, so it will be helpful.

RHONDA: Okay. Now, as far as the scars that I feel, I don't need—I just need to give myself time or is there something I can do?

ANGELS: You need to give yourself time and you need to realize that as you start to really trust yourself, so you don't think you're going to be fooled again, you'll be able to open your heart without fear. It's the idea that if you peak out of the shutters with fear, you're going to keep everything a little closed up. But once you feel very sure of yourself and know that you can take care of yourself and be the "head of your own church" and no one will fool you, there's no reason not to have the shutters wide opened. It's quite a job, though, because the Family of Dark is good at masking.

RHONDA: And, apparently, good at manipulating, too, because I feel that all of the people who were close to me are the people who were manipulated against me.

ANGELS: Some by their own volition, as we said: the "spider woman" is in willing work and others are being manipulated energetically to do the bidding. Because they cannot hold a high enough frequency of love, they are easy prey for the Family of Dark to vampire off of and use them.

RHONDA: Is that my mother?

ANGELS: Well, we're going to help you triage her, okay? Let's triage her. So imagine now you're in your angel self, your Higher Self. You're welcoming her in. There's a little resistance there, isn't there, immediately?

RHONDA: On my part?

ANGELS: Not your part. Feel her. She comes in and what does she do? What does her energy, pure energy do?

RHONDA: I don't know.

ANGELS: Feel the resistance. There's a resistance.

RHONDA: A resistance to me?

ANGELS: Yeah. Feel that? What is she saying to you? "I won't let you do anything. I don't want you." Do you feel that?

RHONDA: No.

ANGELS: You need to go into your angel body more.

RHONDA: Okay.

ANGELS: You're doing it from your human. You're too attached to her as your mother. She's not your mother. She's just a soul. She's incoming.

RHONDA: Okay.

ANGELS: She's incoming, she's standing before you. What do you feel?

RHONDA: She's pulling away.

ANGELS: Resistance, right. Now, pretend you're triaging her. What does she do when you start to reach out?

RHONDA: She pulls away.

ANGELS: She runs, doesn't she? Now, where is she going? Watch her as a soul, soul to soul, no attachment. What is she afraid of? Why is she running away from you? What is she afraid of?

RHONDA: I don't know.

ANGELS: Life review. She's afraid of live review.

RHONDA: She doesn't want to look at her life. She's afraid of the truth.

ANGELS: The life review, do you see?

RHONDA: Okay.

ANGELS: Now, you're triaging. You've got an incoming soul. This is an important lesson for you.

RHONDA: She doesn't want to look at her life.

ANGELS: They will run, right. Now, where do they go when they run? You're triaging them. Where do they go? They're not ready for life review. Where do they? They go to ghost realm, right? She's just going to float. She's not making a commitment yet.

RHONDA: Right.

ANGELS: Now, what do you do when she sees you? She feels that you force her into life review. So when you are with her on the Earth, she runs. She hates you. What does she do? She resents you. She resents you there because in her mind, she feels that you are pushing her. You see? Do you understand?

RHONDA: Okay.

ANGELS: She fights back at you or she runs away, but she is never comfortable in your presence. Do not see her as a mother. See her as a soul in trauma—in turmoil.

RHONDA: And she's just going to do it until she's ready?

ANGELS: Ready to do her work, her life review. At some point, she will have to come up and face you at the triage unit, and you'll have to take her hand and say, "It's time for your life review, you can't run away anymore." She has to be ready. By life review, we mean many lives, a review of who she is. What she hates about herself is her weakness. She hates her weakness. Do you understand that?

RHONDA: Yes.

ANGELS: Okay. She hates her weakness. She hates the fact that she's so weak that she has to run from the life review. She hates the fact that she's so weak that you have power over her, even though you do not mean to. That is how she perceives it, you see. She can't get away from you, so she has to beat you down or beat you back as a result. But in truth the thing she hates is her dark core—her shadow. As a result of that, she's easily manipulated as well, because anything that makes her feel better about herself or tricks her into thinking that she will be more empowered by working with the dark, she will grab on to, because it's an easy way for her to feel empowered.

But the trouble with the dark side is that what it does is that it may temporarily empower you but, ultimately, because they are all vampires, it destroys you. Do you understand? Eventually, she is going to have to step it up and look in the mirror and do her own life reviews. But that is what she is most afraid of. Do you understand?

RHONDA: Yes.

ANGELS: She's a manipulated figure, due to her own weakness and fear, but she would not be someone who would be incoming and you would say, Family of Dark member over here. She would be somebody who would be there and you would have to let her go, until others can convince her and work with her to come and begin to heal. She's not ready to heal with the Light yet. She still believes a little bit in the power of darkness, is how we would put it.

RHONDA: Other than my own learning and my own growth, do I have a purpose for this life as far as healing or helping others? I mean, I know everybody does, all Lightworkers do, but is there something I should be working towards?

ANGELS: Well, first and foremost is that you are always attempting to do your own soul work, and we have pointed that out to you today, right?

RHONDA: Right.

ANGELS: What you are learning, so that you can begin to do better work in the triage unit, if you will. You needed to understand both sides. And that is, first and foremost, your work upon this planet. And as you begin to understand and get discernment, what you had called discernment for other souls, you will also begin to be able to help them more, because you'll really understand who they are more. Rather than having to either paint a picture of them as being something they're not or believing that the same thing will work for all beings, which you might have done before. You might have thought, for example, the same reaction on your part would be appropriate to all beings. So when spider woman met you, your reaction was, "Oh, well, act this way because that's the loving way—I would put everyone in the nursery."

RHONDA: Right.

ANGELS: Now, what you're realizing is you can help others because the discernment is allowing you to choose the path of assistance, so that you don't just put everyone in the nursery on the Earth, either. You're learning how to help people better by that discernment: what does this person need, what does that person need, what does that other person need? And if I help this person, will it harm me? How do I help them, how do I keep them at bay? Is this someone that just wants to work with the Family of Dark so that I don't bother with them, just like when you triage them, you don't bother with them. Let them go where they need or want to go. Or is it somebody, as we said, like your mother, who needs another kind of work?

So your discernment can help others more then, because you aren't just shutting yourself down. How can you help, as you say, when the shutters are closed? Your job first is to strengthen that discernment, that core, and be the "head of your own church," so your shutters will open wide. Then you will truly be able to help each person exactly as they need to be helped, without it harming you. Does that help you?

RHONDA: Yes.

ANGELS: At this time, you are doing the perfect work for your own soul's growth, so that you can do even better work in the days to come. Would you have another question for us?

RHONDA: About my job. I go through spells of feeling like I just need to learn what I need to learn from being there, and then I go through spells of feeling like it's really a negative place and it's not doing me any good. I was just on vacation last week and I felt really good. Even the energy in my house was beautiful and the energy that I was carrying with me was beautiful. I went back to work on Monday and by the time I came home from work on Tuesday, I just felt like I was surrounded with all this negativity, and it takes me all this work to get rid of it. And I'm wondering, am I learning through that or is that bad for my progress, because it doesn't feel like it's good for my progress. It feels like it hinders me.

ANGELS: What you just spoke of was in a sense a type of learning. What you're realizing is that the work that you're doing is the third dimensional, old matrix work, yeah?

RHONDA: Yes.

ANGELS: We're going to ask you to make the connection in your brain. When we say it's the old, third dimensional matrix work, what do you hear? What does that mean to you?

RHONDA: It means that it's limited to this time and space, and that it's maybe—

ANGELS: What is the thought that goes along with what you do? What is the thought that you are surrounded by? What are the thought patterns that people around you are holding? What consciousness?

RHONDA: That's not what you're looking for.

ANGELS: No.

RHONDA: Okay.

ANGELS: Victim.

RHONDA: Victim. Everybody is a victim?

ANGELS: What does that mean? They're not self-empowered, correct?

RHONDA: Right.

ANGELS: And they have to go where to be empowered?

RHONDA: To me?

ANGELS: Or to others.

RHONDA: Or to others.

ANGELS: Yeah.

RHONDA: To others, okay, in one way or another; so it's just draining.

ANGELS: Right. They don't understand self-empowerment, correct? They don't understand self-feeding, self-healing, self-loving. So, what do they do? We talked about the one woman. What does she do?

RHONDA: She sucks it from everybody else.

ANGELS: Vampires, yes. So, what you're feeling is what? What is it you are feeling?

RHONDA: Drained. I feel drained.

ANGELS: And that is because why?

RHONDA: Because I'm allowing them to drain me?

ANGELS: Well, in part, but what are you surrounded by? What are those people thinking? Again, discernment. We're trying to help you really go deeply into your understanding and your wisdom. When you look at people, you'll understand who they are much deeper now. Look at these people, understand them. What do they think? What is their process?

RHONDA: See, I think they're all different.

ANGELS: Pick one.

RHONDA: I think my boss uses everything to make herself look better or feel better about herself.

ANGELS: Which is fear, of course, always from fear, always from insecurity.

RHONDA: They're all in fear.

ANGELS: Right. And what are they afraid of?

RHONDA: They're afraid of exposure?

ANGELS: They're afraid that everything outside of them can destroy them. They're victims. They have no "self-power." So you felt, as you say, empowered, yes, in your vacation? You felt what? I am receiving energy directly, I feel good. And when you go back into a place where the consciousness which is held is about always something bad is going to happen because everyone feels like a victim constantly, not even just here and there temporarily but operating from the idea of being a victim of circumstances all the time and having to manipulate your environment to make the circumstances suit you. Do you see the difference? It's not how masters operate.

Well, of course the third dimensional, victim consciousness is very alive right now. You are in transition. You are in the overlap right now between the old and the new world. You are in the overlap between your new and your old self, you see? You're in the overlap time, where you are outgrowing where you used to be, but you have not yet firmly established what suits you at a higher level. And the world itself is overlapping right now; so the old is destroying but the new has not been established yet. That's the same thing in your life. You are, "Oh, I feel good, I feel my fifth dimensional, empowered self," and then you go into the old world, where it is still manipulation, me against them. I'm a victim, I have to protect myself, you see? And you start to feel the pull of that again, and then you are in discomfort because the new you and the old you are at war. But you understand that if you were to take your new you on a job search, you'd say, "Where can I go?" Because the institutions haven't shifted yet. Do you understand?

RHONDA: Right.

ANGELS: The institutions are still hooked into a lot—there are institutions which are pushing and trying to establish themselves in a higher consciousness but as you can see, it's a transition. So there's a deep sense of discomfort, not only for you but many Lightworkers who have lifted themselves up but there's no place for them to go. The old world is still too much with you, you see. But, as you say, you can learn there, because what you can learn is: "Can I maintain my Light and my fifth dimensional self in a lower density environment?" If I can, I can trust myself to hold it no matter what's thrown at me. Then I am a Master because a Master doesn't need everything around them to be perfect to hold their mastery. A Master can hold the mastery when things around them aren't perfect. That's the test and that's what you are all undergoing is that initiation. Things around you will become imperfect and if they throw you right off, you've still got more work to do. All Lightworkers are encountering that right now.

RHONDA: Okay, good. I just wanted to make sure it isn't a bad place for me to be. I thought maybe—you know sometimes when something is dark, you should stay away from it, or no, maybe that's not even true.

ANGELS: Well, you should not allow it to drain you. If you cannot be there without dying inside, you are correct, you must leave. But if you can learn to be there and just use it as a temporary test of your own mastery, then you can use it for the time being, until the next thing presents, and then step into the next thing, knowing that you're not running away but you were empowered and now choosing from an empowered place, not from a place of a victim: "Oh, I'm a victim, I need to get away," because then the next thing will come and victimize you and you'll have to get away from that, you see.

RHONDA: That's my pattern, I run and hide.

ANGELS: So, it's about establishing your strength and your mastery until the next thing comes along that's truly the fifth dimensional world that you can step into because you vibrate but not because you're escaping. Do you understand?

RHONDA: I do.

ANGELS: But you are capable of doing much more discernment work than you do, and it will give you a much, much stronger feeling of trust rather than run and hide. You do this when the dark person comes or the negative. Do this. Go directly into it. Look into it. Go into the heart of it. Understand it. Imagine, "Oh, my goodness, this is coming to me. Dark energies are going to come to me. I have to triage them, so I must know them, understand them. What are their motivations?" And then you won't be afraid. You won't have to do that. You'll go in and that will empower you.

That's what we're trying to really impress upon you in the session today more than anything is that new way of bringing the energies to you. We used the idea of triage and we think it's something you can relate to, so you don't run from the emergency room, like so many do. What is that wound? What can I do? How can I help it? Each one comes in, they are different. Then you'll feel empowered and you'll trust yourself, and you will be able to hold your

Light because you will have such great powers of discernment, you will be in your mastery, you see.

That's what we feel is our most important message. We want you to leave today behaving differently from this point forward. This will be so empowering for you. So that's going to be very helpful to you.

RHONDA: Okay.

ANGELS: We're going to just pause and ask you to close your eyes. Before we end today, we want you to imagine yourself on the other side; in your spiritual body. You are one of the greeters in the triage unit. Feel and see yourself in your highest spiritual self. Now feel how strong you feel, empowered. Can you feel that? Can you allow yourself to be that empowered? Good. Now feel how wise you are. Feel how clear you are. Feel how there's nothing that frightens you, right? Good. Hold that in your body.

Now imagine that someone you know from work is coming to you. They've died. Someone from work is coming to you. Just let them come to you. Look into their soul. Feel and sense. What do they need? Send them to the correct place or the correct person, the next place to go.

RHONDA: They're going to the nursery.

ANGELS: Okay, so send them to a nursemaid. Now, do you feel differently about that person?

RHONDA: Yes.

ANGELS: And will you relate to them differently now at work?

RHONDA: Yes.

ANGELS: Do you feel that you can be with them without a closed heart?

RHONDA: Yes.

ANGELS: Okay. So it doesn't mean you have to let them in to destroy you, but you can feel and see and understand, "Ah, wounding. I know what I need to do. I can be powerful, I can have my heart open, not weak. It doesn't mean to be weak to have my heart open. It means to be discerning, it means to be in my strength, it means to be my greeter in the triage unit and to really use all that wisdom and strength so that I can see these souls as they come to me and know what they need, clearly." Then you're going to have an open heart, okay? That's your task, okay? It will shift you.

RHONDA: Going back to the Spider Woman, if somebody like that comes to me on the other side, I would let them go to the Family of Dark, but what do I do with somebody like that in this life?

ANGELS: You do the same. You understand that they have no other intention but to destroy you. So as a result of that, you don't have to hate them. You bless them and you send them away.

RHONDA: Okay.

ANGELS: That is not an unloving act, you see? It's a loving act to send them someplace else. You love yourself. You love yourself by sending them someplace else.

So, we thank you. We hope that you will be helped from this day forward to be able to be open, clear in your vision, your wisdom, your ears, your eyes, your senses, your higher senses wide open. And as people come to you, you can feel and trust and have the tools so that you can discern, understand and be comfortable in the world, without having to be alone or shutter yourself, all right?

RHONDA: Okay.

ANGELS: That was our great intention for today. We love you and will release her now.

CHAPTER THIRTEEN

PLEIADIAN PERSPECTIVES AND THE HOLOGRAPHIC GOD SELF

NATALIE J.

ANGELS: It is with great delight that we speak with you today, and we understand that you have had much on your mind, and that you have been going through a great and difficult period of time, and that your soul is purging, as that is how we look at it. We see it that you are purging, and you understand well that you have been given this opportunity at this time in history, if you will put it that way, to purge much of what has weighed you down and kept you from your own personal integration and ascension.

We wish to remind you that as you work through your karma and your issues, you affect every part of yourself, as it is everywhere throughout time and space. That is why you have chosen to be here at this time; because you saw that there was no better or more perfect time for your soul to do what you felt was the karmic cleansing, clearing, and healing. Integrating is one of the words we particularly like for what you are doing, integrating yourself. You chose to come here to do that integration work.

You do know that it is impacting all of your selves, as they have been scattered throughout time and space. As they heal, they do integrate; they come back into oneness. The shattering of the soul, the shattering of the self is being healed. As you bring your many pieces back into wholeness, it reintegrates and gifts you with many abilities which are thought of as being beyond human range or human capability. Where you falter is in your discomfort with carrying some of those abilities and trusting yourself to carry them, but you are pushing onward, moving forward and healing nonetheless, despite your fears and despite your blocks.

As you do this healing, what you begin to understand is that the wisdom you have also carried through many lifetimes throughout time and space is also being integrated. So, unlike previous lives, where the experiences, the knowledge, the wisdom in terms of metaphysical abilities to manipulate space and time were quite alive and utilized by you, what you had not integrated fully in those other lives was the wisdom of your heart. This is the opportunity for you to integrate now the wisdom of your heart and the wisdom of your skill set, if you will.

What you are stopping yourself from doing, what you are overcoming is perhaps the better way to put it, is the tendency and the desire to escape or to run away. As difficult as your work is to do this integration, you realize that there is not going to be a better place or time for you to do it. So you stay around and you stick to it, knowing that the ultimate reward for sticking and staying will far surpass any temporary relief you would experience by utilizing an escape route.

So, we want to begin today to encourage you and applaud you for sticking around and staying to do this integration work, even though it's difficult at times. We understand what it is you are up against, even more than either you or your friends do. But you are aware, as we said; there is no better place or time for you to do what you need to do. You have, in fact, accomplished much.

We thank you for what you are doing and for being with us to speak, and we would enjoy hearing any comment on our opening message, as we begin our discussion today.

NATALIE: Can you elaborate on the abilities that are beyond comprehension for humans, because I'm not actually sure what they are. I mean, I know the singing is one of them and the ability to feel literally the vibrations around me as they come, but I'm not sure I understand how everything comes together.

ANGELS: Well, you are not ready yet to fully awaken all those abilities, so you must not push because you will not gain anything by pushing. You have noticed that the other abilities that you have so far acquired have come on their own, when they are ready, and so too will your further abilities.

We want you to understand that what you and other Starseeds who are ascending are working toward is literally being able to manipulate matter, and to manipulate matter in ways that, prior to this time, for quite a long time in human history, has been thought of as evil or witchcraft and so forth—but you are beginning to realize that it is the right of every Ascended Master to channel through them the ability to manipulate matter.

What is actually done when this is accomplished is an interesting integration of the Self, the human self, into what you like to think of as sacred geometry. In other words, if you think about the way that the molecules and atoms and so forth are rearranged in one item, one object, and you insert your hands within that reality and you literally manipulate it in a way, you can shift, as Jesus did, the water to wine. You enter the sacred geometry with the God-Self and you shift the object, the matter, to a different state.

Ultimately, that is what the human race, in its ascended form, is working toward. When that is happening, when that is able to happen, it can only happen through a purified vessel, a purified human. All doubts and fears must be erased. All tendencies towards ego expressions such as arrogance or self-doubt must be erased, and the human is in a state of unity with their God-self. The integration of all the pieces of yourself brings you ultimately, as it is bringing others as well, to a place where things such as teleportation, materialization and restructuring matter, which was thought of as impossible, begins to be more possible. So that is what we are speaking of in terms of skill sets. Do you understand?

NATALIE: Yes.

ANGELS: But you know that that will not happen until the full integration, and the full integration is what you are trying to prepare yourself for. And from your Higher Self, you don't care where in the time/space continuum it occurs. You don't care if it's in this particular body or in any other body that you've ever had, or where it is that you integrate your God-self to your human self. It doesn't matter, from the perspective of your Higher Self. From the perspective of your Higher Self, all the pieces of you which are scattered throughout space and time come together and create a new time, a new place, a new space, in which to integrate and "relock" and "rehook." Once that happens, the miracles that, for example, Christ and other avatars have performed begin to be possible.

But you are already beginning to see changes in your abilities. Things which had been impossible for you, such as seeing and hearing energy or guides, colors and things like this are now possible, so you realize that the skill set is growing as you do your work.

NATALIE: Yes. Can you elaborate on what is still blocking those abilities because I -- I mean, I realize the karmic history is what carries the light and the shadow. And from what little I know, I have spent a lot of time doing good, doing bad, doing good, doing bad, having this yo-yo, some of them going back all the way to the Orion/Reptilian/Pleiadian wars. I mean, even if they're still happening as we speak, it's still—it's like now, I want to go ahead and just not burn the steps. I know it's not good to do that. You can only walk one step at a time; leaping is no good, and you won't leap for very long anyway. But what is it—what are the major blocks that I'm still banging my head against that either I don't want to see or I just don't know what they are, so I wouldn't see them?

ANGELS: Well, the first thing that we would say to you is that rather than thinking about this as a movement ahead or behind, we would ask you to change the picture. The picture is you, as you envision you, and you're in the center or the hub of a wheel. And around you in time and space, scattered around you, are all these pieces of you. So you're not leaping anywhere, okay? You're staying where you are and you are calling to you all these pieces of you, okay? It's not that you need to move anywhere or leap forward but that is why we call it integration.

The question is then—it's never been whether you are willing to move forward. In our paradigm, in our template or picture, you can see that it's whether you've been willing to integrate or call to you bits and pieces of yourself, okay? Now, what if the things that are the most frightening and scary to you are not actually outside of you, what if they are pieces of yourself, you see? So what if instead of these pieces that have been coming to you of different—you call your little Asian Buddhist monk your guide but what if it is you? Do you see what we're saying?

NATALIE: Yes.

ANGELS: What if these are just pieces, if you use our template—and it's okay, you don't have to, but it's just another way for you to understand that as you already are open in your frequency and ready to call them forth and heal them and love them and integrate them, they begin to pop up around you. They begin to present—they begin to act as guides. They begin to act as ways to push you, open you is perhaps a better word, and integrate.

From our perspective, it's more you in the hub of the wheel calling out to different pieces of you, and they respond when the frequency or the landing pad that you create for them is right. They bring with them many different issues, wisdoms, skill sets. When they're ready to be integrated, instead of feeling that they are outside of you and a guide—some people feel, oh, that guide disappeared. Maybe the guide disappeared inside of you and so is now integrated and become a part of you, and you now carry the gifts and the wisdom, so you don't need it outside of you.

So it's a little bit different. It's not that we feel that you are moving forward or you're afraid to see things, it's that your Higher Self, which is at the hub, knows exactly what pieces of you need to be called to you in order to maximize this time for you to heal without overloading you and without being too stagnant. It's like you're the puzzle being put back together as you call pieces of yourself to you. Do you understand the different image?

NATALIE: Yes.

ANGELS: So you don't need to worry too much about going out there and slaying a dragon here or a dragon there. It is more that you feel yourself at the hub and you are calling to you, as you do naturally, the stories and the images and the beings and the feelings that you know need to now come home and be integrated.

NATALIE: Well, I always thought my spirit guide, Little Monk, was the joyful part of me that's—I do understand what you're saying because I feel it is part of me. I haven't looked at the other guides quite that way but from your perspective, it is quite magnificent to think of it this way.

ANGELS: And you are a microcosm of what God is doing, and that is because everything is holographic to everything else. As you call pieces of yourself together to become the one God, God calls pieces of His/Herself together to become the One. Do you understand?

NATALIE: Yes.

ANGELS: You are a microcosm of the hub and are creating and integrating on your cellular level, if you want to think of yourself as one cell in the body of God, as God at the larger level is integrating all cells of His/Herself. Do you see? Do you understand?

NATALIE: Yes, I understand because it reminds me of the analogy I had about the snow the other day, which is what you're saying.

ANGELS: Yes, God is like the Central Sun. All the creations of God are now being called back to God; as you are calling all creations you have made. So that is how we envision it and you are ready as well to envision it. When you change that template, then you begin to see that you are not moving anywhere but you are calling to you. When you begin to understand the great farcical illusion of the idea that you have had that you could run away or escape—in our paradigm, our template of you in the center of the hub, where would you be running away?

NATALIE: Right. Well, very much like the hamster in its wheel, going around, trying to either lose weight or write poetry, to just find its way out. But, yes, it makes perfect sense. And, yes, those feelings of wanting to occasionally bail out and be done with it can be very strong. That's the way I feel about the last few weeks, where I really felt weighed down.

That dream I had the other night of being dead, which was kind of nice—I'm not sure that's what it was but it felt like it. Wanting to integrate and understanding that everything was mutual. There is no feeling, no emotion, and no conflict. It seemed that no conflict is the greatest part of that dream. There were no conflicts.

ANGELS: Because you were in your God-self at the hub of the wheel. And from there, all these pieces of you are just equal. You love them all as God loves all the pieces of Him/Herself equally. Do you understand?

NATALIE: Yes.

ANGELS: So, you are in your God consciousness, without judgment, and that is why it felt free.

NATALIE: But what if some of the parts of the wheel are in the shadow?

ANGELS: Well, from God's perspective, with you in the center, none of them are in the shadow. From Natalie's perspective, there are obviously shadows. But from your Higher Self perspective, which we call the hub of the wheel, everything is perfectly illuminated and no --

NATALIE: But what about from Natalie's perspective; what about all the fears that I still carry?

ANGELS: Well, Natalie is asking herself to be the conscious integrator and step into this wheel hub. In other words, Natalie is the place, the being, the expression that is asking itself to do the work. In other words, the best description we can give you—perhaps we'll come up with a better one in a moment. But think about Christ. If you think that Christ was one of the offshoots of God, as many think, right, the Son of God, just as you are the son or daughter of your Higher Self, correct—your God-self?

NATALIE: Yes.

ANGELS: And in that life, Christ was wrestling with human fears and used that body called Jesus to draw to him all pieces and things and to integrate and become the God-Self through that piece of the human self. The idea or the ideal is that as one works towards enlightenment, one is utilizing one expression of one's God-Self, just as Jesus was to God, to be the vehicle through which the God-Self is realized and all parts are reintegrated. Do you understand?

NATALIE: Yes.

ANGELS: It's a little complex.

NATALIE: It is complex.

ANGELS: But we think you do understand.

NATALIE: I do understand.

ANGELS: One piece has to take responsibility for integration, and that is where the idea that through Christ, all are saved—because Christ was the piece in that perspective that allowed others who wished to use him as a passageway to integration. It's complex, we understand.

NATALIE: Yeah, I understand. Well, speaking of Christ, can you tell me more about the life I had during that time because I have obviously not wanted to look at it because I only acknowledged it very recently. Why was I so angry at him? Why was I so rabidly angry at him?

ANGELS: Because you have a life with this individual–Jesus—in another place and time. And in that life, he was your teacher. We're going to talk about it in another place and time because it's not a human, third dimensional life, okay? This life we are speaking of takes place in another dimension.

NATALIE: Okay.

ANGELS: But it did exist. And in that, you were an apprentice is perhaps the best word, and he–let's look at this way. If you were a student and he was the teacher, you challenged him and he did not pass you. He did not pass you up to the "next grade" and you were angry at yourself but you used your emotion of self-hatred and anger to be arrogant instead and to lash out. So in failing your studies, you blamed him and did not want to look at your own issues. In that life you wanted to rush ahead, to do more, to prove that you could do better, even challenging him and so forth. Do you understand?

NATALIE: Yes, I do.

ANGELS: What happened was when he came to earth and he was being given that task and role to be a mirror for humanity and that is, in many ways, what his task was, what he agreed to do, which was to provide—a mirror is a good word or just an icon almost—he became an image through which others could fathom parts of themselves by looking at him.

When you looked at him, you were extremely distraught because you saw your own failings and once again created the same exact dynamic in the life when he was Jesus Christ that you had had as the student/teacher life. Do you understand?

NATALIE: Yes.

ANGELS: It is hard for you to look at because you have to look at a part of yourself that makes you upset. Do you understand?

NATALIE: Yes, but arrogance is something I struggle with, something that I don't even see sometimes, until something or someone points it out.

ANGELS: You do this, though, when you feel the most vulnerable. Yes? Do you understand? It would be like a young child who acted out or did incorrectly, trying to bolster and so forth, and who was then admonished in front of the class by the teacher. Instead of being able to take the correction, the student is so upset and heartbroken they act out and they start saying, "Well, the teacher is just stupid." You see? That response.

NATALIE: Blame the teacher.

ANGELS: Yes, because it's hard to be humiliated, which is what you felt, in front of others, and you fear humiliation a great deal.

NATALIE: Well, yes, I do fear humiliation. Can you tell me about—I have little flashes of past lives, and this was one that I will go and look further into. But the other one that has been intriguing me for quite a long time, and I actually don't know if I was that person or not, is Little Wolf. I know I lived in the Dakotas—what is known on this planet as the Dakotas. The phrase that came with that life is: "I am condemned to live alone forever." Looking at the pattern in this life, I start to be able to integrate how it has been for quite a few lifetimes for me—obviously I carry a lot of baggage there. But who is this --

ANGELS: Where was the pride in that life, what you call Little Wolf? Where was your pride? Where was it carried in you?

NATALIE: My pride was in being able to "assist the tribe" in escaping the white world and going back to their land. I think that's where his pride was.

ANGELS: And where was your humiliation?

NATALIE: When we went back but we were still—it was never the same and I wasn't able to bring back the old days. I mean, the white world had taken over and we were still treated like cattle, and it was very hard to accept.

ANGELS: Could you see the humiliation of the idea of being not good enough again? Do you understand what we mean by that?

NATALIE: Yes.

ANGELS: When you wanted Christ to suffer, you wanted him not to be good enough. Do you see?

NATALIE: Yes.

ANGELS: To save his people, just as you were not good enough to save yours. Do you understand?

NATALIE: Yes.

ANGELS: It's that kind of pattern that does keep you locked up a little bit and that you're trying to break inside of you. When you stop blaming yourself and forgive yourself for your being kicked out of the classroom, and you start realizing that you are being given the opportunity at this time, as you integrate again that piece of yourself, to whole yourself, and you will become or you can, you have the potential to become the idea of your living, ascended or Christed self. It needs to be healed, this part of you, so that you will accept yourself being whole, shining and being accepted into the classroom.

NATALIE: Is this why I'm so reluctant to teach, because I don't want to find myself in—I don't want to be in the paradox of being the student and the teacher?

ANGELS: Well, it is true, but you also don't like to be a student. It's not just a teacher role. You don't trust yourself as teacher. But you also resist—every time you are a student, you fall back into your old pattern of the Christed schoolroom; learning with the Ascended Masters in their schoolroom—Christ's classroom. You're healing that piece. You had asked us, what was the piece you needed to look at, and this is it.

NATALIE: Okay. I will look at it. So the next piece is: How do I go about not falling back into the old patterns—not backsliding? Because I see it in this life. The tendency is to move two steps forward and then backslide.

ANGELS: Well, from our perspective, it's more—we're going to go into our paradigm, our template, so that you don't get too linear. From our perspective, it's that you pull a piece to you, you integrate a piece, and then it gets whole, you feel good, and then you call the next piece to you, which shakes you up again. But it's never a backsliding because you've integrated –it's not that the puzzle was messed up on the table. A new piece of yourself comes in and shifts the energy, and then you go searching for the next piece. And as you search for it and it comes, you become aware of where you still have a missing piece.

During the process of looking for that piece, realizing where you're empty and eventually sticking the piece in the correct place is what you think of as two steps back, but it is not. It is just another piece falling into place that makes you feel that way, because you suddenly realize, oh, I thought the puzzle was put together and you realize it isn't. Do you understand?

NATALIE: Yes.

ANGELS: So, it makes you feel "un-whole," but it's just an illusion. The puzzle hasn't changed, just your perspective on it.

NATALIE: Can you tell me more? Someone mentioned once when we were doing sound healing for the earth that I was releasing energy that I had programmed into crystals in the past. Of course, if we step out of linear time, it makes perfect sense to me.

ANGELS: That is what it is. It releases frequencies that are similar to energies throughout time and space that you have programmed or created and it explodes them, draws them to you; however you wish to see it. Suddenly, you see them, you feel them. They are part of you, as they were before. That is what is really happening with you.

NATALIE: Can you tell me more about what is going on when we actually do energy resonance with that part of the earth? If we send high frequencies into the earth then what about the Reptilian world underground? It obviously opens a Pandora's Box.

ANGELS: Well, you're opening portals and the portals are allowing higher frequency vibrational energy to insert itself into pockets of dense, low vibrational energies. What happens is that when the portals are open and the frequencies are sent in there, the dense energy gets extremely stirred. It begins to awaken, it begins to vibrate, and the energy, the consciousness that is connected to those dense energies comes alive, becomes awakened in a fourth dimensional realm, if you wish to put it that way, and then it can be vacuumed up, cleaned up. It's hard to find the right word. It's not really what happens but it's the idea that it dissipates. That is the word we feel better about.

If you think about it as being an ice block and the energy that you send to it shifts it to liquid and then it heats it even more, until it starts to boil, and then it turns to steam, and then eventually, it dissipates. The blocked energy is literally shifting its form, going from a denser state to a higher frequency, which is allowing the incoming vibrations, which are being sent directly from the galactic center, to be received more completely by the earth herself.

NATALIE: Is it dangerous for us to do this, considering that we are dislodging dense energy?

ANGELS: It is not dangerous unless you believe it is.

NATALIE: Okay.

ANGELS: And if you believe that it is and your fears feel that it is, then you are correct not to do it. But it is only stirring up the density in you and that's all. So once it is healed, you won't be so afraid.

NATALIE: One of our concerns is, is it creating karma with the other side; with the Reptilian world?

ANGELS: With the Reptilians?

NATALIE: Yes.

ANGELS: The intention, which is to move dense energy and to wed it with energy from the galactic core, is not a karma producing state. It is just assisting the earth herself and the human race, if you will, to hold higher frequencies. However, those who do not wish to do so, to hold higher frequencies, are being impacted negatively, and that is where you get the question of karma. But your intention is not to harm anyone or anything, and that is an important fact. It is not a small thing. Intention is important. Those beings who are in the—you're calling underground caves, perhaps is a good word.

NATALIE: Yes.

ANGELS: —are being bombarded one way or the other. One of the things you might find interesting is that an earthquake or crack in the earth would energetically facilitate the frequencies from the galactic core reaching the center of Mother Earth or into regions. So an earthquake would be one way to allow these frequencies, these higher frequencies access to the underground world and the core of Mother Earth.

What you are doing is finding a less violent way for these frequencies to make their way into these denser places and integrate, without, hopefully, the need of such earthquakes of such magnitude that the earth is split because the earth is in conflict between the dense and the Light energies coming in. Do you understand?

NATALIE: Yes.

ANGELS: Your intention is to try and stabilize her so that such grand seizures would not be necessary, and a grand seizure would be caused if the density is not moved at all and suddenly, the energy from the galactic core is so powerful and profound that it causes a ripping or seizure. Do you understand?

NATALIE: Okay. This brings me to the next piece, which is a bit of an open wound right now. Taking into consideration everything you say before, I understand. But why the loneliness? It has been something the last few weeks that has deeply affected me, and I would like to understand which part of the puzzle am I not getting to fit in correctly?

ANGELS: Well, perhaps it's just being aware, as you wake up, of all those empty pieces that have not been put in place yet. Suddenly, you look down at yourself and you can see the holes in your integration process, and you long for union and integration. But you are not going to allow yourself to have a relationship with another until you fill in your own holes. Do you understand?

NATALIE: Well, it's the paradox. I see so many people around me who are mirrors to each other for healing and—well, I don't think I know how to play that game. I do see the holes in my own but I just don't know how to appeal to anyone who would help me look into this. My illusion is to think that there is somebody out there who has that ability but there's a part of me that says, think again.

ANGELS: Natalie, would you allow anyone else to put a single piece of your puzzle in place? No. There is not an ounce of you that would allow someone to put this piece here or that piece there—you would balk at that.

NATALIE: Yeah, but how do I change this?

ANGELS: You do not need to change this. This is you and this is good. But you need to get all of those pieces in place yourself, so that you feel integrated, so that the person who is with you stands next to you and you don't need them to put a piece in place because, simultaneously, you are saying you want someone to come and help fill you up, to make you whole. But at the same time, you do not want this at all. You resist it.

NATALIE: I know it doesn't work that way. I've tried that and I know it doesn't work.

ANGELS: You are waiting until you feel whole to attract a mate. That is what we see. Do you understand?

NATALIE: Well, that could take a while.

ANGELS: Well, that is what your Higher Self wants is your own wholeness—to be secure and solid and well-integrated. There is nothing you will do to stop that task at this time because it is the most important thing to your Higher Self, to your soul. Your soul does not want anything other than to be whole and it's all that matters to you, in truth. If something else did matter to you more, it would be the thing consuming you, but it has not been the thing that's consuming you. Getting yourself healed has been your consuming issue, yes?

NATALIE: It has been.

ANGELS: So, why would you doubt that that is anything but first and foremost on your menu of items or things to do? And that is what you will continue doing. Once that is fulfilled, then you will begin item number two on the menu.

NATALIE: Alright. It's just that I get so overwhelmed with sadness about it and I frankly don't know what to do about it.

ANGELS: From your Higher Self perspective, the sadness is coming from the holes in you, not from someone outside of you (that you do not even know) being with you. It is you looking at the holes in you that causes your sadness. Your Higher Self knows that what you must do is keep putting these pieces together until you are solid and whole and do not feel the sorrow. At that point, you will trust yourself and be healed enough that you will invite another into your life. From your Higher Self, it is not sadness for a lack of a companion; it's sadness because of your own lack of integration. You have come so far that you're almost there. Don't give up now.

NATALIE: I don't want to give up.

ANGELS: You are not far from completion at this time.

NATALIE: That's one thing I can say about myself: tenacious is fully part of my vocabulary.

ANGELS: It is both your strength and your weakness, as you know.

NATALIE: Yes, it's my worst quality and my best fault.

ANGELS: It's your best quality as well.

NATALIE: It is.

ANGELS: And it serves you well when it serves you.

NATALIE: I'm not about to let it go now. I do feel I have come too far in the last couple of years to give it up now; nor do I want to. But there are those moments that feel incredibly empty and lonely and not very comfortable to be Natalie. I understand that I'm doing what I can with the help of everything else around, bringing myself to completion.

ANGELS: Then you will feel that it is done. You can strike that off your list. You are whole, you are complete, and then you will stop needing. The minute you stop needing your number two item—a life companion—you will attract one. But you cannot jump forward as you call it. You need to be where you are now and that is what your soul desires, this healing and completion. It will take what it takes, and you know this. So do not feel sad. Feel joyful that you are doing a profound amount of work that is bringing you to a place that you know you need to be at this time.

NATALIE: It feels like as you said earlier when we started, which was time to fix up and put together and clear up the housing. This is exactly how I feel, whether it's at the Natalie level or the cellular level or Higher Self level. I feel that it has been such a long time coming and that this life is the opportunity and it's a fabulous opportunity to just finally get it together. But those places I feel so vulnerable—it's so hard for me to be that vulnerable. It is such an uncomfortable place to be, I'm sure for many reasons that I cannot fathom, but that's what it is.

ANGELS: But in that discomfort, it creates movement, and in your movement to eliminate the discomfort, you integrate more of yourself. Do you understand?

NATALIE: Yes, because it's dealing with the will.

ANGELS: Exactly, so it's serving you in your work.

NATALIE: It is.

ANGELS: If you were satisfied and as they say, everything was comfortable, well, not much gets done then. Humans often work better from a place of off balance and discomfort, as they try to heal that, yes?

NATALIE: Yes. Well, I can only speak for myself. Yes.

ANGELS: It can be a way of trying to urge you on to fix that which is broken.

NATALIE: Yeah. If you have a burr in your shoe, chances are you want to take it off.

ANGELS: Yes, exactly.

NATALIE: Because it becomes uncomfortable. Is there anything else about the Reptilian/Pleiadian story that you wish to share with me at this time? Anything else that would just help bring more understanding to this?

ANGELS: Well, it's interesting because the Reptilian/ Pleiadian hatred and integration is often one of love/hate for many. The Reptilians envied the Pleiadians very much, although they would never admit it, due to their arrogance. They wanted the gifts that the Pleiadians had. They wanted to own them, to enslave them and to create their own species, but they never quite understood that—they have never been able to let go of their arrogance enough to fully understand how to acquire these gifts in a way that they want.

What they do, in using frequency control, and in using some of these abilities metaphysically is that many of them are falling prey, if you will, to their own creations. They are creating realities that they think are going to only harm their enemy, when they are finding that they, too, are falling prey, as we said. And they are not escaping their own evil creations.

It's the idea that you can have a war and in the war, only the opponent gets harmed. Well, where has there been a war where only the opponent has been harmed? In war, one harms one's self as one harms one's opponent. So what they are beginning to understand is that their desire to harm others in a warring attitude has also harmed them.

In other words, what we are trying to tell you is not to worry so much, that karma, in its infinite wisdom, the energy of sow and reap, works on all sentient beings, all energies, all beings who are third and fourth dimensional. So don't worry, you don't have to do much. All you have to do is worry about integrating yourself, so that you can become the Miracle Master yourself.

NATALIE: Okay, Miracle Master, that's cute.

ANGELS: Merlin likes that, so he added that.

NATALIE: Does Merlin have anything to say or add to—?

ANGELS: We will allow Merlin to speak. She is growing tired but we'll let him have the final word.

MERLIN: Do not mistake human creation for Divine Creation, for human creation will always fall short of Divine Creation, when it is done in a consciousness of separation. It is always essential that to make and create miracles one must step into the Higher Being, the Higher Self. It is only when one is one's God-Self that these miracles can be created without harm. When one is outside of one's integrated God-Self and fooling around, it is then that harm is created, as you saw in Atlantis and what is called the rips in the space/time continuum seen on earth, as in your Bermuda Triangle. There is harm.

Do not mistake these earthly "playings" for the Divine Being Creator. It will serve you well to worry only about, as the angels have told you, self-integration. From that place, you will feel secure, you will feel healed and whole or, as the angels call it, like your "Christed-Self," and you will not worry about all the things that are troubling you now. They will dissipate. So, your task is integration. All other things will take care of themselves.

ANGELS: So, we will release her now and we thank you so much for the opportunity to speak with you, and we have given you, we hope, a new perspective. Always hold the idea of yourself in the center or the hub of this wheel. And as you integrate, look down upon yourself, look at yourself; however you wish to do it. Stand outside and look and say, "Where is there still a piece missing? Where is there still a place?" Ask that place, "Okay, are you ready for your piece to come home?" And it will come in and integrate.

You will get used to the fact that it's a little rocky journey sometimes, sometimes during the integration, but it will smooth out, as you are now more aware of what's happening, and you can just say, "Oh, come home, its okay." If you have a few little thoughts or feelings of that new part of you that comes home, you look at them, you heal them and you move on. Do you understand?

NATALIE: Yes.

ANGELS: That is the template we think will serve you best at this time.

NATALIE: Thank you very much.

CHAPTER FOURTEEN

THE GALACTIC WARS: KARMA WITH THE REPTILIANS

VICTORIA B.

ANGELS: We wish to begin with this important information: From our perspective the movement to claim yourself, to claim who it is you truly are and to unify yourself, is one of coming out of hiding; knowing ,feeling , believing and sensing that it is safe to do so. This belief is deep-seated and has gone back much further in time karmically than you are consciously aware of.

You have been destroyed for a long, long time. To be able to come out of hiding for you, to trust yourself to come out of hiding, it has been a requirement for you to know without a doubt that you can stabilize your energy and your frequency at a dimensional level, at a place high enough that those who would do you harm in the past cannot find you, cannot reach you. Until you trusted yourself to be in a place of—we're going to call it dimensional freedom—until you trusted yourself to hold frequency at a high enough level, you would not allow yourself to fully come out of hiding. Your fear is that if they see you fully empowered, they will once again enslave you, capture you and harm you. That is where you operate from, that deep fear.

It is a testament to your progress that you are beginning to be willing to come out of hiding. It is an indication to yourself that you are beginning to lift and stabilize your frequencies high enough that you feel that you are no longer afraid. We want to begin today by speaking about what we believe is going to be the theme: re-empowering yourself, stabilizing yourself, transforming yourself, and being aware of what it takes for you to hold the frequency that allows you to feel safe, to feel that you can no longer be harmed.

We welcome this evolution so that you can step from your protective, artificial shell, which has been dimming your light and allow it once again to shine and to feel yourself ready to be fully who you are and not be afraid of that. We welcome you and enjoy seeing you this way.

We also ask you for your feeling about what we've said. How do you feel both about coming out of hiding and stabilizing your frequency and your field so that you can trust yourself to vibrate high enough, as well as the idea that by doing this the lower or denser energies can't "find" you? Does that resonate for you?

VICTORIA: It does, and I guess I feel so comfortable in my shoes now and I feel that no one can harm me at this point. A lot of my insecurities are diminishing, and I really feel like I am coming into my own and feeling a lot more confident and loving myself more than I ever have.

ANGELS: We are going to jump right in. Is that okay?

VICTORIA: Yes.

ANGELS: We're going to hit you with something that might be difficult for you to understand, but we're going to start there and ask you to comment, okay?

VICTORIA: Okay.

ANGELS: Now, what we want you to understand is that there was a time when—you are aware of what happened in the experience humans call The Orion Wars, yes? The idea of the Reptilians, the Pleiadians and others; the battles that have happened between good and evil, yes?

VICTORIA: I've just started hearing about them.

ANGELS: Okay. One of the things that happened to you was that you were originally what would be thought of, for lack of a better word, you were royalty. You were highly placed. We don't know how else to say it but you were royalty on your planet. Let's put it that way.

VICTORIA: On planet earth?

ANGELS: No, we are speaking about being extraterrestrial. Pleiadian.

VICTORIA: Oh, okay.

ANGELS: Off the earth, in, as they like to say: "a galaxy far, far away," a place far, far away. You are aware that you are not human, yes? You are aware that you carry energies, as you say, from other systems, yes?

VICTORIA: Doesn't everybody carry energies from other star systems?

ANGELS: No, not necessarily in the same way that you do. In other words, although the human race has become genetically intermixed and is a "mish-mosh" of various types, there are those who are a direct link having done incarnations upon other planets or star systems. Not every soul chooses to incarnate in other places or in the same places. Every soul has their own choices that they make. Some do not even incarnate at all. So, what we are speaking about is your incarnations which were done off-planet.

We're going to speak for a moment about your incarnation that was done on the Pleiades, okay?

VICTORIA: Okay.

ANGELS: You were royalty. We speak about it this way, but when you think of royalty as an earthling it's quite different than what we mean. We don't mean it the way you think of it as an earthling. It was very different in the Pleiades. How could we best express it? There were beings on the Pleiades, in the apex of their existence, who were in complete and total harmony and in a state of grace, to the extent that they understood how to work with what humans think of as subtle energies. They understood how to communicate with the world around them, the life forms around them, telepathic communication, teleportation, oneness and being in harmony with nature and beauty and All That Is. They understood the oneness and lived in an extremely pleasant, if you would, and exalted environment.

In that place and that time, what your role was: You were one of the beings whose job it was to hold and stabilize the frequency and light so that others could partake of it. As a member of this "royalty" it was your job to hold and stabilize the high frequencies of the planet.

VICTORIA: Kind of like what I might be doing now?

ANGELS: Well, it was different. Currently there is no human equivalent. How can we look at this? Imagine if you think of a hive of bees and imagine that there are beings in that hive, bees in that hive whose job it is, through the frequencies they emanate, to stabilize the hive. It's a very strange concept. Do you understand, though?

VICTORIA: I do.

ANGELS: So, those beings, those bees who hold and stabilize the frequency for the hive are considered to some extent to be royalty. You could see that, yes?

VICTORIA: I get that, yes, definitely.

ANGELS: That is why we would use that term. It is not governing like a king or queen on the earth but a different type of governing that was needed in that day, in that place. So, you were the frequency governor, one of those who held the frequencies at that level.

Now, what happened to the Pleiadians was that when the frequency started to dip and started to plunge past its apex—we're going to put it that way—the vibration began to get interference. This lowering of the frequency brought the vibrational dimension of the planet down to a lower level; suddenly it was "on the radar." That is what allowed the Reptilians to locate and find the Pleiadians. When the Reptilians came and overpowered and enslaved the planet that they took over, they did it with frequency modulation. They jammed the frequencies and lowered the frequencies so that the abilities that the Pleiadians had prior to the frequency jamming could no longer work. You understand what we're saying?

VICTORIA: I do.

ANGELS: What happened is they captured you as one of the royalty. You were the prime and supreme—among a few others, not just you but among others. Those of you who could do this, well, wouldn't it be that you would be enslaved and kept as a specimen? Do you understand what we're saying?

VICTORIA: Yes.

ANGELS: Now, what happened was, in those periods of time, as you can imagine—we won't go into detail at this time unless you ask us for specifics—but you can see that you were harmed and enslaved and so forth. What happened with you particularly was the desire or the attempt to reproduce with you. The idea of working on reproduction and making a mutated species was one of the things they were interested in. There was much DNA work being done and mutation being done.

One of the things, too, was to steal your abilities, because the Reptilians understood frequency control and they felt that the Pleiadians could give them even more of an understanding and empower them even further. You being a master of that lead them to say: "what a catch."

One of the things that started you going very deeply into hiding and being afraid of using your gifts was that they were used against you, and you were actually desired for your supreme gifts. Do you understand?

VICTORIA: I do.

ANGELS: So, this is something that has dogged you, if you will, for many thousands of years. That is one of the major reasons that you have been in hiding and your karmic issue is to come out of hiding and to use your gifts. The gifts of what you call the medium are to some extent child's play for your soul. It's child's play for your soul. Do you understand that?

VICTORIA: I do.

ANGELS: It's a great gift and it's a great service but it's still a fourth dimensional service. So you're working fourth dimensionally when you do that work, and the frequency is still much lower than what you're capable of moving through you. But it is the beginning to your work of coming out of hiding. Do you understand?

VICTORIA: So is this part of my path? Could this be part of my path, my desire, my want, my passion for being—?

ANGELS: Of service again?

VICTORIA: A psychic, intuitive, medium, whatever. Is that okay to do?

ANGELS: Absolutely, because you need to begin to get comfortable and feel safe again, working with frequency and what we said, "coming out of hiding," so that's easy for you. Ultimately, as a frequency modulator or generator, you would actually get to a point where, if you were to repeat your Pleiadian abilities, you could see that you would be working even much higher than that. Do you understand?

VICTORIA: Yeah, but what do you mean by much higher?

ANGELS: Well, do you understand that when you work with dead humans, it is a lower frequency than when you work as a direct conduit for Languages of Light, or as a frequency modulator, for example? Dead humans are going to be working with you in a fourth dimensional realm. Frequency—Language of Light is sixth dimensional. Do you understand?

VICTORIA: I do.

ANGELS: What you're doing is working now in fourth and occasionally fifth dimensional work, which is what you need to be doing now. Yes, it is absolutely what you need to be doing because you can't get to the sixth until you go through the fourth and fifth.

VICTORIA: Okay.

ANGELS: But what we're saying is eventually your work is going to move past that. Do you see?

VICTORIA: I do.

ANGELS: But, you need to be there at this time.

VICTORIA: I could feel it. I could feel that it's time.

ANGELS: What happens for you with the Reiki is that it brings you back into, to some extent, what you were capable of in the Pleiades, but it's so muted compared to what you were once capable of transmuting. Do you see what we're saying?

VICTORIA: I do.

ANGELS: That it just frustrates you because you know what you're capable of. But you can't achieve it yet. Begin to work towards where it is you ultimately want to go.

VICTORIA: Yes, that's exactly what I'm thinking and feeling. And then later, I can go back to what I did.

ANGELS: Except that it will be something different. You won't be going directly back to that. You will be going to a new form of being a frequency modulator.

VICTORIA: Can I just ask a kind of maybe off the track question? When I was a child living in Long Island, I felt very alien, and my mother had this obsession with UFO's. Was I a Starseed then or was I a direct product of my mother and father, or was there some intervention with the Pleiades at that point?

ANGELS: Well, your mother has ties to Reptilians. Do you understand what we mean by that, way back in the karma? Do you understand that there's a link in terms of your karma with this soul? Can you understand that karma is brought on to the earth from other places?

VICTORIA: Oh, I see.

ANGELS: You see? It didn't begin on the earth.

VICTORIA: Okay.

ANGELS: So, we're going to just help you work through this so that you can understand it. What happened to you in the Pleiades? What happened? Begin to feel that in your body. What do you feel happened to you? Feel your body. Begin to go into your body. Where are you afraid? What starts to happen in your heart chakra?

VICTORIA: My heart chakra?

ANGELS: Yes. They literally began with shocking the heart. That's how they began their frequency control. Close your eyes for a moment and imagine that you're wide open. Then imagine that these beings come and they begin to mess with your vibrational field. What do they do to you?

VICTORIA: Torment.

ANGELS: That's good. Keep going. What does your body feel? What does your body start to feel?

VICTORIA: That they're just taking everything out of order.

ANGELS: Okay, keep going. That's good.

VICTORIA: Disassembling me.

ANGELS: Good. Confusing you.

VICTORIA: Yeah.

ANGELS: Disturbing your field so much that you've become confused.

VICTORIA: Chaotic.

ANGELS: Chaotic, very good. They're considered masters of chaos. They understand chaos as well as the Pleiadians understood order and harmony. So, when those two meet, what happens? It's quite the opposites, yes?

VICTORIA: Yes, definitely.

ANGELS: Good. What happened was these bringers of chaos came into a completely harmonious world and they stirred it up and created chaos in intensely fear-based ways, okay? Feel what they did to your system, as if it was shocked. Do you understand that feeling?

VICTORIA: Yes.

ANGELS: Good. Now as you close your eyes and you go within, what did they do to your being? What happened? Begin to feel and follow where your body went.

VICTORIA: With my physical body?

ANGELS: Yes. What happened to it, suddenly, in that chaos? What did it do? It froze.

VICTORIA: It froze. Yes, that's the word I see in my head, froze.

ANGELS: Yes, it froze. Good, go there, go to that freezing.

VICTORIA: I hate being cold. I hate it, even today.

ANGELS: Yes. It froze, good.

VICTORIA: They froze me.

ANGELS: Good. So the chaos—it was as if suddenly, all the vibrations went chaotic and then you froze—you couldn't handle it anymore. Do you understand going into freezing?

VICTORIA: Yes.

ANGELS: You just shut down is a good way to put it. You froze. Exactly, you froze, went into freezing. And once they had you there, what happened? You couldn't send any signals, could you?

VICTORIA: No.

ANGELS: Good, you didn't. You slowed your vibration.

VICTORIA: Yes.

ANGELS: Good, okay. Then you realize that fear, which had been foreign to you prior, suddenly became a quick reality, didn't it?

VICTORIA: Yes.

ANGELS: What did you also think? We're going to just help you with that. In your head, you thought two things that have karmically been with you. One is, "Oh, my God, my people! What's happening to my people?" You see? Fear for what was happening to your people. The other was, "Oh, my God, I let them down!" You blamed yourself for lowering the frequencies and letting this come in.

VICTORIA: That's my big issue.

ANGELS: I let them down. You felt a deep and powerful responsibility because of who you were. You were one of the royalty, the bees who held the frequency for the hive, to keep it elevated and safe. If this is happening, whose fault is it, you see?

VICTORIA: Exactly.

ANGELS: That's a big karma, isn't it?

VICTORIA: Yeah.

ANGELS: That's a big karma, so you have a lot of self-blame and you felt you deserved to be punished after a while because you had let everyone down. And it goes all the way back to all those many, many thousands of years ago on the Pleiades, okay?

VICTORIA: Okay.

ANGELS: So, we want you to understand that.

VICTORIA: Was my mom one of the Reptilians at that point, during that?

ANGELS: Let's help you to find that. How did you feel when you were around her sometimes?

VICTORIA: Never close to my mother. When I was a little girl, I used to think that she and my father would turn into monsters; but maybe they were the Reptilians.

ANGELS: They were Reptilian shapeshifters.

VICTORIA: I never felt comfortable in my own home.

ANGELS: Do you understand that human Reptilians are shapeshifters? They can move into what you might call monsters. They can do that.

VICTORIA: And I used to feel that as a child.

ANGELS: And you used to see it as well, but it was so frightening that you blocked it.

VICTORIA: When I was a child in this life?

ANGELS: Yes. If you can imagine a time when you saw them actually change, it came from somewhere. For a brief second, they would shift when they got angry or upset.

VICTORIA: Yes.

ANGELS: That was the Reptilian. Do you see?

VICTORIA: Yes. So, my father was Reptilian as well.

ANGELS: One moment, please. Your mother is clearly Reptilian and your father—this is an interesting karma. Your father was the byproduct, originally—we're going back now to your Pleiadian life. When they used you for reproduction and they combined the Reptilian and Pleiadian DNA, your father was your byproduct; he was your child and a mixture. So your father holds both of the DNA's. Do you understand?

VICTORIA: I do, because there is a closeness with my father that I don't have with my mother.

ANGELS: Your father was your child. Your mother was the Reptilian that impregnated you and your father was the byproduct of that genetic pairing in the Pleiades. Is that helpful? The karma goes all the way back to there.

VICTORIA: Yes.

ANGELS: So he is both.

VICTORIA: So, is this why my mother has this fear of me being who I am? When I talk about being an angel or being a medium or anything intuitive, she's a little excited but there's this—it goes against her grain.

ANGELS: If you become fully empowered, she is terrified that you will harm her as she harmed you. If you get your power back fully, you are so much more powerful than she is that she fears you will turn on her and destroy her because of the karma, which as you know, was carried on to the earth as well in other ways.

VICTORIA: Right.

ANGELS: So it is in her interest to keep you asleep and disempowered, so that you will never understand. She knows, if anyone does, because she saw you in the Pleiades. She knows your full ability to be a frequency holder, modulator for a species, for people. If you wake up fully, what will you do? You'll do it for the human race. You'll hold frequency to awaken the human race. And if that happens, the Reptiles cannot be in hiding anymore. Do you understand?

VICTORIA: Yes.

ANGELS: We want to make sure you truly understand.

VICTORIA: Yes.

ANGELS: This is complex information.

VICTORIA: Yes, I'm getting it. I'm definitely getting it. It's making a lot of sense.

ANGELS: That's why we decided just today to cut to the chase and get you all the way back to the beginnings here. You can begin to understand things more clearly once you understand what we've told you. Now a lot more makes sense for you.

VICTORIA: Yes.

ANGELS: When you are with her, it is in her best interests to keep you enslaved, you see?

VICTORIA: This might not make any sense but she's been an alcoholic for thirty years, in recovery. She's tried to get me to go to AA meetings with her.

I'm not going to go to A.A. meetings for the rest of my life. She's always tried to control me.

ANGELS: Well, you can see, she was your enslaver. If she can control you, she keeps you powerless. And if she keeps you powerless, then she believes that she is the one in power. She sees it as either she is up and you are down or you are up and she is down. Do you understand at a deeper level why? The Reptilians could only be powerful if they had enslaved the Pleiadians and gained their gifts. If the Pleiadians regain their abilities with frequency, sound and modulation and tone and awakening the human race with this, then the Reptiles see themselves as being the powerless ones, you see?

VICTORIA: Let me ask you, in this life with her, how I safeguard—because I'm going to be who I'm going to be, regardless of her fear. And I saw her fear tonight, just talking about having a conversation with you. I made a joke saying—

ANGELS: Because she knows that you will be told.

VICTORIA: I see so much fear in her. I said to her, "I'm going to speak to God myself because I know God is all of us."

ANGELS: Yes.

VICTORIA: I said, "I'm going to speak to Him myself." She just laughed, like how absurd, but I meant it. But there's this fear.

ANGELS: Yes, because she's afraid that if you get fully empowered, it means the end of her. She does not understand love and equality, she sees in duality and polarity. If you are up, she must be down. If she is up, then you must be down. She does not understand the idea that you could both be up. Do you understand?

VICTORIA: Yes. So, as her life today, as who she is today, she still works in that way.

ANGELS: Essentially. You would agree, yes?

VICTORIA: Yes.

ANGELS: Essentially, yes. She has not overcome her fear. Her fear is what keeps her captive. Her fear is so enormous.

VICTORIA: Her fear is enormous.

ANGELS: It is enormous, and she will not look at the truth of herself. Her own shadow is her own undoing. If she would be truly at peace with who she is, it would not matter that she is Reptilian in her origins. There is not a denial by God for the Reptilians to join the human ascension. But we want to explain something else to you.

Many of the Reptilians have rejected the human soul progression. They have hosted in a human body rather than fully accept the human karmic cycle. They have believed that they are above that. They have believed that they can control the human experience. Do you understand what we're saying?

VICTORIA: I do.

ANGELS: They have to surrender and humble themselves completely and reunify with their God-Self in a human body, but they believe that human beings are very inferior. And in order to accept being fully human, they must accept the human piece of themselves which they reject because they feel that they are above that. In rejecting it, they weaken and sicken themselves and do not become as empowered as they could be if they would truly join the human race and become one with the Divine template that has been given to the human soul journey. Do you understand what we're saying?

VICTORIA: I do.

ANGELS: It's their arrogance that keeps them separate. So, their shapeshifting abilities come from their hosting in the body rather than fully accepting their bodies.

VICTORIA: I see. So, in this lifetime, did I come from her? How did I get here? How was I brought on to the earth in this incarnation?

ANGELS: This is how we see it. You were born to her but not fully awakened until later. In other words, you agreed to do the work on this karma. You knew that you had to heal this karma, this deep rift and this Pleiadian/ Reptilian rift, but you understood that you would not be capable of healing it and regaining your power until later. So, it was not until later that you integrated what we're calling this part of yourself into your human body, in order to begin the karmic progression.

In other words, the karma was there from the beginning. It was in there but it was not activated. You were not ready to do this work. You were not fully willing to accept being human. You were ready to bail out. You weren't sure if you wanted—you were afraid. You see what we're saying? You kept part of you outside until you were fully sure that you were willing to take on this difficult task. It was almost as if you were not fully integrated. You gave yourself an easy way out or an exit point early on as a weak life force. You were a weak life force. Finally, you said, okay, I'm willing, I'll come fully into my body, and I'll do this. I can do it. You integrated more of yourself and decided not to take the exit but to actually come in and do the work you've come to do.

VICTORIA: At what age was that?

ANGELS: We're seeing it around the age of three, somewhere in there.

VICTORIA: Okay.

ANGELS: Three or four, somewhere in that age. You started early with a lot of exit points. Do you understand what that means? Death points. You could have chosen to leave very early. Your life force was much weaker. Do you understand that?

VICTORIA: Yes.

ANGELS: Then it was that you made a choice in early childhood. You said, "Okay, I'm ready to do this, I think I'm going to hold on and I'm going to be fully here and I'm going to take this ride." But in the beginning, it was too frightening, so you made—you kept a part of yourself out of your body, a great part of yourself out of your body early on. That's truly—it's almost as if, from our perspective, you were split. You put enough life force into your early infancy to stay alive—and that's why it's like a walk-in. Because the life force was very weak and you always were outside of yourself for a lot of your earliest years, and you were looking at the life from the outside. Finally, you said, "Okay, I'm willing to jump in and do this." So it is like a walk-in in many ways, because if you had not done that, chances are you would have died. You would not have survived. You would not have had enough energy and life force to keep sustaining that body, that initial, original body, is the best way we can put it.

VICTORIA: I see.

ANGELS: It's a different way of looking at it but it is like a walk-in. So your early years, your earliest years were much less vivid or intense in terms of your life force. Does that resonate?

VICTORIA: It does.

ANGELS: So that's how we feel about it. Then once you began to be willing to integrate, you started stepping in slowly, testing the waters. You actually would pop in and out a lot in childhood, yes?

VICTORIA: Yeah.

ANGELS: You popped in and out a lot. You didn't fully solidify or integrate until much later. You kept your options open but you were a much stronger life force, we feel, from about the age of three or four onward. You began to solidify.

VICTORIA: I see.

ANGELS: You said, "Yes, I think I can do this," and you began to bring more and more of yourself and your gifts alive and tested the waters, but it was brutal for you. It was brutal. So you kept an opening. You kept ways of getting out. You knew how to get out. You knew how to escape.

Oh, this is interesting. What your guides are saying to us is that—what we're hearing is that it was actually the safest way. It was safer for you to be weak earlier. It was actually safer to keep most of your—okay, this is it. Because they were after your gifts, you believed in keeping most of yourself out of your body until you were fully integrated and ready because what they had always enslaved you for is your gifts. So you kept the gifted, higher part of yourself able to slip in and out of the body, eluding your captors, and kept a weaker life force always available to draw back in.

VICTORIA: I see.

ANGELS: It's an interesting scenario.

VICTORIA: I kind of do that even today. I want to be hidden so much that I—I don't want to say it in the wrong way but I like to hang out with the very ordinary people, maybe to hide myself.

ANGELS: Yes, it is camouflage.

VICTORIA: There's something about me where people just have an instant reaction but yet I still like to hide myself.

ANGELS: Well, you can see where it got you in your Pleiadian life to be royalty or a queen bee, or to be able to do these gifts that got you a horrible karma for many, many hundreds and thousands of years. One of the typical Pleiadian scenarios was that once so much trauma had been done to your soul, you didn't know how to regain it. You had been messed with—fragmented. They literally tore your energy apart. You know that. You see that. Your heart and your soul. You went into what is called the fairy realm—this is a very common Pleiadian story—to heal. That is why you carry what is called fairy energy. The only way you could be on the earth safely was to be in the fairy realm because it was the closest to your Pleiadian. To be fully embodied in a human body was dangerous—you could be found. But as a fairy—

VICTORIA: Have I had a lot of human lifetimes?

ANGELS: You've had a number. You did few but it was so terrifying to your soul. The frequencies for you have been so dense that you often hide in-between for long periods of time. You also have some shadow work. In other words, what you did out of terror was you went berserk. You have those stories as well, going crazy, yes?

VICTORIA: Yeah.

ANGELS: Going crazy and going berserk. There was a story where—you just go nuts sometimes on the earth in other lives. That's why you would gain the most peace by being in the fairy realm. But in one life, what we are seeing right now, was that you went crazy and you grabbed a knife and you just went slicing and hacking at whoever was around you.

VICTORIA: I can see that.

ANGELS: Insane madness, absolute madness. Then you turned it on yourself. Then when you died, it was so painful for you; you would go and hide again in the fairy realm. That is a common Pleiadian story. There are others who share a similar one because where else can you feel the same frequencies? So many of the fairy energies on the planet today—those who resonate with fairies have a very similar story, having come from such overpowering enslavement karmas and such torture and horror and being messed with that they had to heal. One of the best ways for them to heal was to find "soothingness" in the fairy realm. So they feel an affinity and a love for nature because of that.

VICTORIA: Wow, this is so much.

ANGELS: That is where all these pieces of your soul are beginning to fit together now. Do you see?

VICTORIA: Yeah.

ANGELS: Making sense more. So we're going to ask you, what is it that you fear the most?

VICTORIA: Not being able to deliver information.

ANGELS: And being—

VICTORIA: At this point, I can't get hurt. I'm feeling more and more confident and I love my work, and I'm willing to come out. But I want to do it correctly. I want to—meditating and upping my frequency, so that I can help people, if that's what I'm meant to do.

ANGELS: Exactly, and it is a wonderful thing. One of the things happening on the earth as the frequency is rising is that it is giving the Starseeds who came from other planets, who have these gifts but have suffered for them, it is giving them the strength that they need. The frequencies help them and support them, and it is a beautiful thing to watch the unfolding of the humans who are waking up, the Starseed humans who are waking up and helping other humans to do the same. Those who are feeling the increased vibrations and frequencies—sometimes the denser humans are fighting the frequencies and they don't know how to integrate them and they are afraid of them.

VICTORIA: Everyone is feeling ringing in their ear but I don't feel that anymore. Do you know why that is?

ANGELS: Yes, that is a stage that is often gone through and begins to dissipate because the receiving of information begins to come in other ways. Occasionally, you still might feel it off and on but it will shift into other things now. You don't need that. Do you know what we're saying?

VICTORIA: Yeah. That's what I kind of felt, that I was beyond that, the ringing.

ANGELS: Yes.

VICTORIA: I want to know about a friend of mine. Am I supposed to help him "wake up?"

ANGELS: You knew him when he was an elf.

VICTORIA: I so get that.

ANGELS: Truly. You knew him when he was an elf. You met him in one of your fairy journeys.

VICTORIA: He's cute and boyish.

ANGELS: Yes, he is an elf and you met him there. We're going to tell you about that because it's quite beautiful, if you would like to hear it.

VICTORIA: I would love to hear it.

ANGELS: When you came and you were deeply traumatized and you went to the fairies, to the fairy realm, you asked them to heal, protect, and to hide you. Perhaps a metaphor for that if you will, a way for us to help you visualize it would be the idea that you came in and they hid you under the beautiful overhanging flower petals, you see?

VICTORIA: It's beautiful. It's so beautiful.

ANGELS: One day, when you had healed and your soul was feeling stronger, you ventured out. And when you ventured out, you came upon this soul that was what we're calling an elf in that realm. He saw you and he saw the delicacy of you. He saw how wounded and hurt you had been, and he took pity on you. He felt deep love for you and he fell in love with you instantly at that moment. You were afraid of him in a way because you trusted him but you were a little what humans call gun shy. You were a little shy. So he slowly wooed you. He helped you slowly to heal. He helped you to trust again. He helped you to feel that it was safe to even exist. You were hoping that you could eradicate your very existence.

He said to you, "There are things that we cannot understand and there are things that we cannot know yet, but I believe that if you hold my hand, I believe that if you walk with me and stay with me, then one day, together, it will all make sense and we will truly know and understand why it is that you had the journey that you had. But in the meantime," he said, "I love you and I want you to be happy here and happy with me, so I ask you to stay with me for a while, as long as it makes you happy. And when it no longer makes you happy, I free you to go on your journey and on your way."

You were the thing that coaxed him out of hiding or agreeing to take on the human soul progression. He actually came in search of you and began to incarnate as a human because of you.

VICTORIA: So our love is that strong.

ANGELS: From our perspective, it is. It has always been his belief that love must be free and that love is not to be owned.

VICTORIA: That's how we feel in our current relationship.

ANGELS: That is the essence of how you've been, always. It is true. Even though it sounds to most humans that it is a fairy tale, this is a true story.

VICTORIA: That's the most beautiful story I've ever heard in my entire life. That's so dear to me. Were we Indians in a life together, like Native Americans?

ANGELS: He was younger. He was a boy and you were a woman. He was younger, we sense like a son or a brother. One moment. No, a brother. You cared for him. You were paying back the karma that he gave you in the elf life. You took care of him. That is the energy.

VICTORIA: That is so sweet.

ANGELS: You watched after and cared. The connection is very strong.

VICTORIA: When I meditate what should I do and who do I pray to? You know how they say, please God, help me, but God doesn't work for me and Jesus doesn't work for me. I'm a little confused about the whole meditation or what I should do to begin.

ANGELS: None of these are—one moment. Just let us stabilize within her body for a moment as she's growing tired. Because your connection to the human race is not solid, as we said, you do not have the same deities. You do not have the same beings to worship that work for you in the same way as others. That is why it is difficult for you. When you were in the Pleiades and you were a frequency generator, you did not have to call it by a name. You knew it in your knowingness and channeled and held it through your body. In that, you were experiencing God rather than knowing or understanding with your mind, as a mental exercise.

VICTORIA: That makes sense.

ANGELS: So, for you, it doesn't resonate to study God. For you, it resonates to feel or experience God, and you don't understand how to translate your understanding of God to the human understanding of God. That is where you get into trouble, if you want to put it that way, where you feel a little troubled. It is okay. You're going to have to carve out or fashion your own individual expression of your God consciousness. Don't try to make it a human one, allow it to be arising from within you naturally. Once you do that, you'll feel that you can communicate directly with your God consciousness, your Higher Self.

The idea that the humans have that God is outside of the self, that these deities are outside of the self is foreign to your Pleiadian soul. Do you understand?

VICTORIA: Yes.

ANGELS: It makes you feel separate. It's absolutely the opposite from what you naturally feel. Certainly in your fairy realm experience, you just were an expression of the God energy. Fairies don't have to worship anything, fairies are that thing. Do you see?

VICTORIA: I see.

ANGELS: And that's more comfortable for you. Do you understand?

VICTORIA: Yes. Do you recommend me meditating or—

ANGELS: We recommend you closing your eyes and lifting your heart center, this area directly to the sun, to the Central Sun that is the Light that feeds you, and to communicate directly with that and allow it to feed you and fill you and know that, I am God. Know that, I am one with that. Once you are there, then it moves through you in whatever expression that it does. That is what, for you, keeps your frequency high.

VICTORIA: Okay.

ANGELS: Because as we said, you were a frequency modulator, if you will. If anyone could do it, you can.

VICTORIA: Just one more question because I know she's tired. Is Eagle Feather still with me? If he's not, what guides do I have? I kind of feel just kind of alone because I don't know who I have for guides.

ANGELS: Well, you can call your fairy realm to you at any time and they tend to be circling around your feet, from your knees down. They're there to support you and love you. It would be very wise for you to always thank them and look down and say," Hi guys, I love you, I call you to me," because they comfort you in a way that you need sometimes, okay?

VICTORIA: Okay.

ANGELS: So, that's important as well. And certainly, your Native American energies are sacred to you and help to give you that love of the earth and sky and a grounding that is particularly useful to you. But we do sense that feeling of emptiness, which is strange because there was a time you didn't need to call in a thing. You just felt that energy that animates all. Now that it needs to be *called something*, it's confusing for you.

Perhaps we're sensing you might be best to do direct, what you think of as God- link or God communication, because that is where you're going to get the energy from the Central Sun of God. Try that and speak directly to God and see if you can't hook into your Higher Self that way.

VICTORIA: Okay. So Eagle Feather is no longer with me?

ANGELS: Always. Certainly, you can call upon that energy or any other energy. It's very happy to help you and assist you, any energy. But do not worry that you will get too arrogant. That's a bit of a worry for you as well.

VICTORIA: Yeah, I don't like that.

ANGELS: Allow it to humble you but not denigrate you, when you work with that higher frequency, when you work with the Central Sun of God. Allow it to fill you and humble you. It will never denigrate you. Because what we feel is when you do that, you will begin to step into your old role.

VICTORIA: Okay, and just do it in the morning?

ANGELS: Yes, put your hands out and feel it come in. Then sit quietly and say, "God-Self, do you have a message for me today?" Let it speak to you.

VICTORIA: Great.

ANGLS: So, we are going to release her now. It was a lot of information.

VICTORIA: Thank you.

ANGELS: A lot of, information, ideas and feelings, and sensations, for you to now translate into whole. As you begin to feel and understand a little bit more, you'll hold these in your body. When we speak to you again, you'll be ready for the next piece of the puzzle, okay?

VICTORIA: Thank you so much.

ANGELS: We welcome the work you do on the earth. We welcome the work you do in this realm, with all realms, and we thank you for being who you are today and always.

VICTORIA: Thank you.

CHAPTER FIFTEEN

THE SEEKER

JOHN R.

The first time John ever came in I did my "prep" work and went into the Akashic Records and could find no "human story." When he walked in I felt it was best to tell him right up front that he was not going to get a "normal" reading about human karma but that I had seen him in all sorts of different galactic incarnations. It seemed clear to me that they wanted to talk to him about his "other" incarnations. Although he appeared "conservative" in his suit carrying a briefcase he said, "That seems about right."

We are delighted to have this opportunity to work with you, and we look forward to enlightening you, a little bit. It is, from our perspective, time for you to wake up; it is time for you to step into a greater understanding or knowledge of who you are. It has been appropriate for our purposes, to keep you "under wraps" for awhile, because the time has not been right for you to awaken. It would not have been advantageous for you to have awoken sooner than this, for up to this point, it was not necessary for you to understand more fully, who it is you are, and why you are on this earth.

The Earth is not your natural home and it is a place that is extremely foreign to you, and this conduit is correct in her understanding if you will, or correct in hearing us, prior to your arrival, that you are in fact, not of this planet.

What you are known for, or are, perhaps we would use the human term, your task, or your true identity, or how you are most comfortable expressing yourself, is as a go-between, we are going to call it a go-between; you are what might be called on earth—a diplomat. You are a being who understands or has studied, in your case, and experienced in your case, an extreme number of extraterrestrial experiences or lives; has studied the civilizations of many other planetary systems and has attempted to forge bonds or gateways, if you will, of communications and even at times what humans might even call, the idea of exchange or trade between various beings or species.

You are utilized often by others—it is hard to speak of in human language for there are not always very good words to describe this method of existence off the planet, so we are going to try to keep it somewhat simple for you today without overwhelming you.

But, the idea is that you have learned how to shape shift, how to change your form into various different forms at will, when necessary. In human terms, the closest would be, what humans have seen or experienced with a Shaman, one who understands how to shape shift or change. You have done enough experiences in other realms or forms that you are comfortable, and do not over identify with one particular extraterrestrial or galactic civilization. There are things that you like about particular ones more than others, but as a whole you have found or you feel that the problems that exist not only on this planet itself, but also in what you have seen, in what has been dubbed the Orion Wars, or intergalactic wars between species, have come from a place of deep divide—a sense that there is a forgetting of the unity. It is not just on this planet that this separation has happened, but on other planets or with other species there has also been this forgetfulness of love or togetherness.

What is particularly fascinating to you about the earth plane is that the humans are able to experience a wide variety of unity and separation consciousness. What is interesting to you is the idea that if you can figure out how a human can go from deep separation to deep unity you are hoping to be able to pass it on to other species, off-planet, and help them with their evolutionary lift. You feel that if humans are doing it, it must be possible for others to do it. In other words: if humans can do it it's got to be possible to take other species in deep separation consciousness to help them find their unity consciousness. So, your mission is: you are learning the human ways in order to broaden, or bring them to other experiences off-planet. So, we are going to stop now and ask if you are with us so far.

JOHN: I understand what you are saying. I can't say that I had a consciousness of this before I came here. You know, I don't really know what my origins are, though I had suspicions they are not human.

ANGELS: Well, you have to be given a human body and a human template in which to operate. If a human, or any being comes into human existence, when they take on human form in order to what you might say "fit in" it as best as possible, it's necessary to give them enough of the human consciousness so that they can operate. But unlike other humans who have more of a sense of history, what has been almost lacking in your soul is that feeling of human history. Would you agree? Do you understand what we are saying?

JOHN: I do agree with that. I don't seem to have a great deal of attachment to the Earth.

ANGELS: To being human.

JOHN: To being human.

ANGELS: And that is correct because you are not human. You are primarily here on a study mission. You are here to gather information; and now let us explain to you that you have seen in other civilizations different ways of living. We will explain to you how the Arcturians have managed their unity consciousness. There is a part of you that already knows this but we are waking it up in you. The Arcturians have achieved their unity consciousness for they have created a civilization over time that contains very little separation by outward appearances or so forth. In other words they have managed to find great peace with great uniformity.

But what you strive for is how to find great peace without resorting to everything being alike or everyone looking alike. Because in your heart what you believe is that that is almost a false unity. In other words it is easy when everyone looks the same, but what about when everybody looks different? The thing that you find interesting about the Earth, and by the way, the reason you chose to take on a human form that stood out, and is so different, is because it wouldn't have fit your research if you fit in easily. Do you understand?

JOHN: Do you think this is a form that stands out?

ANGELS: Because you are so tall.

JOHN: Oh.

ANGELS: You see? You can't hide; you are not in the crowd. You stand out from the crowd; you don't fit in. This is a reflection of how you feel. But the real reason is you need to understand and experience the human experience in a form that doesn't allow you to go unnoticed or just fit in because you are trying to research how to be a little different and at the same time find peace and unity. As we said you are trying to study how human beings can find peace so that you can bring it to other extraterrestrials that greatly lack peace.

We are going to ask you then for example, what is it that you do to find peace, as a human?

JOHN: I generally seek solitude and silence. It seems to me, where I feel most peaceful is essentially, by myself.

ANGELS: What you are trying to do, from our perspective, is learn how to find peace by going within. That is what you believe you can teach. Peace is not found externally, correct?

JOHN: That's my experience.

ANGELS: Yes, so can you see that if you can master that here—there is a part of you that is also working to take the knowledge you are gaining here and bring it to other places and try to teach them how to find inner peace. Now you have experienced a number of different places because you are on a quest. And your quest is to discover ways to help your own people and other planets—to help them stop warring.

JOHN: I would say that I carry anger inside of me. I don't know if war is unfamiliar to me.

ANGELS: Of course it is not. Because look where you come from. Do you know where you come from? If you close your eyes and do not look at your human and you imagine yourself as not human, how do you imagine yourself? Anything is fine. Can you get a picture of yourself, perhaps on another planet, or as a non-human?

JOHN: I don't have an image of myself—I have an image of a uniform, like a, it's almost like a Samurai's uniform.

ANGELS: But it is not on a human body. Can you see that?

JOHN: Well.

ANGELS: Try to feel or imagine another type of body. What we sense you are picking up is a Reptilian life. You have done many types of species like we said, almost like you are capable of shape-shifting, having done many different species.

But you know discord, you know war, as you said, and you are trying to bring knowledge of how to find this peace back to those planets where there is so little peace. You are an intergalactic searcher, but also wishing to be like a diplomat to help others to find peace within them; that is why you are searching, trying to find peace while human.

We don't need to go into your other lives. Let's just stay with your human one at this time. Let's talk about finding peace as a human because this is what is going to be what helps you. When you can analyze and figure out the human progression from discord to peace you are going to be able to help many others to do the same. It doesn't matter whether it is on Earth or off Earth. It just matters that you learn that lesson. Do you understand?

JOHN: Yes.

ANGELS: And you can see that this has been a lesson that you have been trying to teach yourself, yes—to be peaceful?

JOHN: Yes, absolutely.

ANGELS: Yes, you can see we are telling you that your mission is ultimately grander than just you. You are on a large mission. You don't know that yet but it is going to start opening up for you from this point on. You had to figure it out for yourself, otherwise how would you pass it on? How would you help on a larger mission if you weren't able to help yourself? Do you see what we are saying?

What is particularly important is what you learned about being a human being—answering the question, "Where is peace found in the human soul when there is so much to be angry about?" Correct?

JOHN: Or, seemingly so.

ANGELS: Yes, how does one find peace as a human?

JOHN: When I discuss this—it is not as if I have mastered this—but it's coming to a state of acceptance of the events and the things that revolve around us. It's trying to understand first what seems to be reality but then what is most likely the reality behind the scenes. In some ways it is like a theatrical play but really, there is a real reality behind the visible.

ANGELS: And what do you think is the real reality behind the visible?

JOHN: There are a lot of motivations—what would be considered negative motivations that would be considered fear.

ANGELS: Correct. It is the idea that when one is working from one's fear place—or the idea that you have to fight or struggle—that all these issues become troublesome. People fight, or war or struggle to survive because they do not know or trust in a Higher Power; they are incapable of taking a larger view. Do you understand what we are saying?

JOHN: I do.

ANGELS: It is because they are in their small mind. What we are going to share with you, as Margaret would share with you, is how she came to an experience today that would be most appropriate for your channeling, at this moment. She was witnessing some fish who were attempting to swim upstream in rocks and they had been, in a sense, pushed out of a larger lake and there was a rocky stream, and below the bridge below the stream there was a deep pool and if the fish had just let go and gone with the flow of the water, and let go they would have been brought to safety, down in this deep pool. They were struggling and fighting and struggling and fighting to try to get back to someplace they thought was safe, which of course, was the least safe thing they could have done. And she looked at them and she thought they were like the human race. If they would just allow and trust that this water, this flow is taking them someplace safe and let go, they will be much happier and less exhausted, and they won't be their own worst enemy, you know?

And so she said as she looked down at the fish: "I'm kind of in the perspective of an Angel or Higher Self. I can see where they've come from and I can see what's waiting for them is good, but they can't see so they fight and fight, because they don't trust. If they would just trust, they would be helped."

Well, she tried to help them by lifting them with her hands but they were in such fear that they could not trust her and they would fight and swim out of her hands instead of allowing her to help them to a safer place. And that is, in many ways, how an Angel feels when an Angel tries to help a human you see? Saying: "Well, just trust, have faith, and know that it is a benevolent universe that will help you if you can just allow it to; know that there is a higher perspective even if you can't see it."

Letting go, as humans call it, and letting God—or letting the flow. So, peace is found in surrender. What it is that you are trying to teach both yourself and ultimately to those who war anywhere whether on Earth, or off-Earth, is the concept that peace and happiness is found not in fighting but in surrender.

Now there are species, particularly ones that you are familiar with, who are unfamiliar with this concept, that don't want peace and don't know how to surrender—they always want to be the victor and to feed off their enemies. They need to conquer constantly, to be fed.

What is unusual or interesting about the human species, is that the human species can do both. The human species can understand deep surrender, tranquility and peace and find complete and total union with the God consciousness as your Enlightened Masters have shown you. Or, they can work as some of the lesser beings, and fight, and feed off their enemies—creating disharmony.

Earth is a place where all levels of consciousness are allowed simultaneously which is why it makes a perfect training ground for the soul, as well as for you, as a field scientist. It is a perfect place to study all the different ways of being, without becoming too attached to any one way. It's the idea that you can look and see and understand, and bring back to others the information, but what you are trying to do is master it for yourself here, so that you can help others master it.

Ultimately, you could even help other human beings by teaching them more peaceful ways—ways of not getting caught in their own drama, or controlling dramas and feeding off one another. You've witnessed this. Yes?

JOHN: Yes.

ANGELS: It's interesting because it's been a study ground for you. You can see how the Enlightened Ones on this planet are teaching others to let go of their control dramas. You are trying to teach yourself so that you can teach others. You have the potential to be a great teacher if you desire.

JOHN: So those are the issues that I have to really develop—that sense of connection with God, so that there is ...

ANGELS: Well, for you, it is going to require—because of what you are trying to teach yourself—you are going to require yourself in this lifetime, to get to a place of surrender. That's difficult for you in many ways. Yes?

JOHN: Yes.

ANGELS: Because it is foreign to you. But, it is what we said, why you are here, you are here to study that. Now, on all the other planets it's so interesting because either it's already been mastered and gone to uniformity as in Arcturus; or they are all in their different stages. But here, as we said, you have this wide range in one location—Earth. The idea is that you have to find your God Consciousness. That consciousness is a Higher Consciousness—it is above the consciousness of all the different species from all the different planets that you have studied. In other words, you have been looking for the answers by studying many different galactic species. But, now you are beginning to realize that the answer to unity is not going to lie in incarnate beings, but is going to lie in something that does not have a body, in Pure Spirit. That's the piece that has been missing for you. Do you understand what we are saying?

JOHN: I do.

ANGELS: Let's give a human equivalent: like a human who is really interested in studying anthropology and archeology. A human would go to different sites and try to understand the meaning of life by studying this tribe, and their bones, and their way of life. Then they would go to another site and they would see another particular experience. They would go to Egypt and Stonehenge and perhaps to South America, and Africa and Australia and they would learn a great deal, you see, about being on the Earth and how different beings or species did it. They would study how they worshiped, or what they worshiped and how they connected and what they connected to. But the anthropologist or archeologist is still looking to understand the Nature of All through incarnate or physical objects. But suddenly, one day, this archeologist suddenly begins to realize that maybe he/she is looking in the wrong place, he/she is looking through bones and creation when he/she needs to look past that, and that's where you're at—do you understand what we are saying?

JOHN: Yes.

ANGELS: You've been looking in a wider field. Instead of going to places on the Earth, you've gone to planets where beings look like insects. Then you've gone where they look like lizards and then you've gone to the Pleiadian home and experienced being Pleiadian and you've experienced Arcturian and many, many more that are even unknown. And you've been looking like that: "Well what is the answer to life? What is it?" Until you decided at this time, "Well I'm going to try Earth, because what Earth has is this interesting potpourri, this interesting mixture."

Now interestingly enough, you had to apply for a position here. You applied for a position here and you were accepted as a student. And you agreed, when you signed the contract if you will, to come here, you agreed that you would utilize what you found for the Highest Good of All. You had reached a place where you had agreed that you were not going to use it for selfish purposes.

Our job is to wake you up. To say that you have had a lot of time that you've been studying, you've been learning, and it's time for you to expand out a little bit more, continue your work on yourself, but not so much in solitude. Reach out a little bit more. Don't worry that people won't understand you, or that you don't fit in. It's going to be beneficial to get out of the solitude a little bit more. You'll be guided. Now the next thing to this is: "Let go and let God." You'll be guided. In other words, don't try to plan it, just make intention: "I am willing to go where I need to go, to learn what I need to learn to be what I need to be in service to something higher than self." And allow the stream to move you, as those fish did not. It's easier that way.

JOHN: So, there is, as you've discussed, there is a tension between intuitiveness and logic and the logic's attempt to structure a smooth transition or pathway through life. So at this point, where I don't think I have the strongest intuitive sense, it is a little difficult, right, to just simply surrender and allow things to be. I guess I am trying to have some ability to influence or shape the course. Maybe, I shouldn't but...

ANGELS: Well, guess what? You don't know anything. Really, like those fish, they are swimming and all they see are those rocks and all they know is that little view, but they don't see where they came from, and they don't see where they could go. It's the idea that if you've learned as you said to just be in the NOW. What does that mean to you to be in the NOW?

JOHN: For me it is keeping the attention focused to what is immediately occurring as opposed to being physically present in one place and thinking about other matters or events.

ANGELS: Yes, you are correct, that is what it means. But there is something else; if you are truly holding that space of what you are calling the Now, you can access everything. It is quite fascinating. It is hard to put into human words. But, let us put it this way, first let's say this, if you are in your mind worrying about something to come, then your mind is already filled and cannot receive intuition from your Angels or your Higher Self. Correct?

JOHN: Yes.

ANGELS: And if you feel guilty about where you've been it's the same thing. Now if you stay right in the moment, it allows you to forgive. First of all, everything disappears. You don't hold on; you don't even remember what happened. It doesn't have any weight to you because it is not Now. And, so if somebody said something to you that hurt your feelings, an hour ago, it's no longer there, so it's gone. Do you understand what we are saying?

JOHN: I understand what you are saying.

ANGELS: That's what you have to do. It doesn't matter Now. It didn't perhaps even matter then. But even if it did matter then, the further you get from it: Now is Now—you will even forget what it was they said. It will come to a point where it is not even in your consciousness because you haven't carried it with you, and that is one of the things that you need to learn, is not to carry things with you. Do you understand why we are telling you this?

JOHN: Well, I don't completely understand. But, I do agree I carry a lot with me. So forgiveness is essentially staying so focused that the mind doesn't keep going back and recreating it and therefore carry it along?

ANGELS: Yes, because those who are at peace, if you look at your Enlightened Ones, Masters on this planet who speak about living in the moment of grace at all times, you notice that they are not always rehashing what happened to them, every hurt, you see? And they feel more peaceful. Why would it be hard to let go of something that was said? Let's give an easy example of somebody who says something that hurts you. What part of you is wounded? It is the Ego - yes?

JOHN: Yes.

ANGELS: And why is it wounded? It's wounded because you gave them your power, to hurt you. You gave it away and you believed what they said about you.

JOHN: Yes.

ANGELS: And you believed it more than you believed your own truth.

JOHN: Right.

ANGELS: So, either they were correct and you did something wrong and you need to look at it, forgive yourself and move on, or if it was just their "control drama," then you realize it has nothing to do with you at all, and you leave it aside, and you move on. Both ways are just ways of meeting it. If you carry it with you, you cannot be in the Now; you cannot be in the moment. For you are always going to feel some of that agitation or irritation, and so forgiveness absolutely requires the ability to experience what you are experiencing but resolve it quickly by allowing the Ego to release the wounding either by forgiving the self or forgiving another, and then move on.

If forgiveness hasn't been present, you cannot move forward. Its greatest example is when Christ said: "forgive them, they know not what they do," it freed him from returning, in terms of reincarnating, holding onto old karma. He was showing you that if you forgive at that moment you don't have to return to the wounding. So that is important, that you do not carry wounding, or what happened to you yesterday to today. Let it go and try to find resolution as quickly as possible in forgiveness either of others or self.

JOHN: But the concept of letting go, in one way you can say that I am going to stay so extremely focused that I am not going to let anything else to penetrate. It's not really pushing out the old thought, but it is attempting to keep it out.

ANGELS: Yes, but that is war.

JOHN: Right.

ANGELS: And we're not talking about war. We said find forgiveness, in other words, we're not saying don't pretend that your ego wasn't hurt, or don't pretend you didn't wound another, we're asking you to look at it and move it to forgiveness.

In other words, if you were unfairly wounded by another, realize that it is just their projection onto you, so why would you hold it? And forgive them, for they are just acting a drama of their own wounding. So, why would you have to hold their wounding? You would not, and you could let it go.

It's not that you pushed it out, or had to deny it. You know it hurt you, but when you recognize that it only hurt you because you were allowing someone else's wounding to become your wounding, then why would you do that? You could say: "That is not my wounding; I am not going to carry it."

Now, if you have acted out of your ego, or lower nature, and wounded someone, and they come back with words that wound you, you then need to look at your own wounded place, and say: "You are correct, I did say that out of my own wounding. I ask you to forgive me, and I forgive myself, I realize that I am human and I acted from ego or my wounded place, I ask for your forgiveness and I forgive myself, and then you can move past it. That's not being at battle trying to hold something out; it's recognizing it and then moving past it.

That's what you can teach others. You see? It's not a left-brained device—getting your brain so conditioned as if it was a warrior to fight every battle. It's a surrender that leads you to the ability to know peace and that is what you are trying to teach, because as we said, ultimately you have experienced all of these intergalactic wars. If you can learn it here, you're hoping you can teach it to others who do not know how to find peace, so we are helping you in that way. But you cannot just push it out. You know, imagine if you go to a conference, where everyone is using bitter words and warring, you can't just push it away, it won't go away will it? So what has to happen is what? Everyone has to take a moment of silence. Yes? Stop the words.

Step One: Stop the words when you see conflict. We are helping you to put together some of the teaching methods that you're going to ultimately be utilizing. Number One is: Stop the words and stop the fists and stop the action. Number One is—stop. When you see conflict around you, number one is stop. Humans call it "count to ten." You know that one. Yes? Everything must be paused. It must be paused long enough so that then you can go into your body. Number one is pause and, number two is to go into the body. You will notice that if the body has been in conflict, it does what? It vibrates.

It has a vibration. So Step Two is: go into that vibration. Sit quietly and bring a feeling of that white, peaceful light to it. Sit quietly and bring a sense of peace. Use your mind to take your body to a peaceful place—calm the emotions. That is Step Two. Essentially what you are doing is calming the nervous system. Do you understand?

Step Three, which will take as long as it takes; there is no time limit to any of these. Once the body has been calmed, once the vibration and the nervous system have been calmed, the next step is to listen. Now, you are listening to your Higher Mind, and you are not ordering it around. You just listen. And then you say in Step Four: "What does it feel like to be the other person, the other person who you are in conflict with?"

That is Step Four: put yourself in their place. Think what is it that they are feeling? That is your next step. Once you have quieted your nervous system, you listen, you put yourself into their place, and you begin to try to understand what fear place they are acting out of. Once you do that, you ask your guides and God, to give you the correct action.

What is the action? Is it to move to them immediately and say, "I'm sorry?" Is it to give them space? What is the correct action? You begin to feel yourself doing those different actions, and see which one feels right. You use your intuition, your body, your kinesthetic feeling. What is it that sits on your shoulder—your consciousness? What is it telling you? What makes you feel less guilty? What makes you heart feel free? Where do you feel your heart being freed up? I notice my heart becomes free if I say: "I'm sorry." I am going to go to that person with calmness and I am going to say that I am sorry. Ahhh... That frees my heart.

And then you teach how to find peace. You can spread that and help others as you will be doing to understand that they must stop, and then they must go within, and then they must learn how to connect and then find peace. Then they will know right action. It truly has to come from the moment of Now, which is why you are interested in studying that—you can't find peace if you are yelling, and screaming and blaming. You can only find if you are forgiving, going into the moment of Now so that you can forgive and then move past the anger.

These are all things which you are actually trying to learn on this planet and teach yourself. So, you are a student, in a sense. Do you understand what we are saying? You do, yes?

JOHN: Yes, that was very useful. Can we go back to surrender?

ANGELS: Yes.

JOHN: The difficulty that I imagine with surrender is, to distinguish if, when you set out on a course that you believe is correct and a difficulty arises, how do we decide whether we surrender to the difficulty, because it is somehow an indication that we are now off-course or how do we decide that we are going to push though the difficulty?

ANGELS: Like the little fishes. Yes?

JOHN: Yes.

ANGELS: Pushing through difficulty will get you somewhere. So, let us give this fish example. They keep fighting and fighting and they do get somewhere. From that point, they get there, and they learn their lessons from that point. And, it's not that if you fight you won't get anywhere and you won't have lessons to learn. Whatever you do is going to take you somewhere and there is going to be value in it. So, the first thing to do is to understand that. If you are going to fight and struggle you are going to get somewhere and you are going to learn something.

Let us give an example at a job. It might be that at the job, if you fight a little bit at a job, or you push a little bit harder than the other fishes and step on the other fishes, you might be the one who gets there; back to where you think you want to be. Maybe you'll be the first one. But if you are struggling and fighting more than likely what you are doing is putting yourself further back, into a place that at some point later on you are still going to have to escape from. In other words, it is only a temporary housing. You think it's safer. You think that "Oh good, I'm the one who didn't get fired." You see, "I'm the one who didn't get let go." But you're the one who actually ended up trapped in a situation of enslavement that you assumed or thought with your ego mind was liberty.

You redefined it incorrectly. If you got fired or laid off—if you could just trust the Angel to pick you up—you are going to be grasping for air for just a few minutes little fishy—but believe us, your Angel sees a bigger lake for you. She is going to put you there, you see. Don't go into your instinctual panic mode but just surrender so that you are not fighting all of the time with your guides, and your Angels and your Higher Self.

You are going to end up someplace, of course, you'll always end up someplace but the new place you end up, you won't have to fight so hard, and you will be in place where it's a little bit better, a little bit easier, and you are going to be further along in your lesson plan if you will. You won't be back in the old place now having to repeat the old lesson. Wait a minute, you were just liberated from there, you fought over the rocks to get back there, and now you are going to have to just swim back over those rocks. Eventually you are going to liberate yourself from that old enslavement.

You are going to always end up somewhere. If you fight or don't fight, it doesn't matter. But it is a lot easier if you don't fight. If there is too much pushing—it is not the right time. What's very difficult for humans is "It's not the right time." That is an okay answer. Do you understand what we are saying? They don't like that.

Human beings don't like to hear that's ***not*** what they should have. "I want to have this job—right now" "I want to have this child—right now" "I want to get married—right now" " I want, I want, I want, I want—right now." The truth is it is not going to happen for that person right now. But they don't want to hear that. Do you understand that?

JOHN: Absolutely.

ANGELS: They don't want to hear that. They are not going to have it right now because it is not in their best interest. To have that child—right now—is going to cause a lot of difficulty. Now, they could find a soul, often, who will agree to enter into a womb at a bad time. But what the Angels see, and what God sees, is that in six months, your husband is going to have an affair and leave you, and if you have a child with him now, you are going to have a lot more difficulty. But you don't want to see that or know that, so you are going to push through and possibly even destroy your marriage by trying. Maybe you will even get pregnant and the child will be sickly. Maybe it is not going to be a soul who chose well, and if you had just waited another year, or year and a half, or two, you would have found the perfect mate after your husband leaves you. You would have remarried and you would have an easy birth, and an easy child. Right now—it wasn't the right time.

There are very few humans, when they are set on having a baby, who would want to hear that—do you understand? They don't want to know that their husband will be cheating on them in six months and they don't want to hear that.

As Angelic guides, it's very difficult, what do we say? We say if you will let go and let God, you are going to get, eventually, absolutely the perfect thing. If the baby is not coming to you right now, the baby is not meant to come. Trust it and have faith and let go. If in your job, you are being fired, then there is something else that you are supposed to be doing. Let it arise for you. If that person doesn't love you in the way you want them to love you, let go, the right person will come to you.

But humans have trouble, and so they assert their Will, but what you are seeing in this human race now is that the human race is in terrible trouble, because it has been nothing but, "My Will be done," and very little "Thine Will be done" in terms of God Consciousness. Yes?

JOHN: Absolutely.

ANGELS: That is what surrender is about. Just, knowing it in faith and trusting that if you are not getting it – you are not meant to have it right now. You can get it for yourself if you try hard enough, you can, but perhaps there was something better waiting for you. So always do the best to your ability to improve yourself, work hard, be a good person, do all the things you believe are in your best interest, as a human and in the best interest of all humans and if something you think you want isn't coming to you easily and you keep having to fight it, chances are you are just going into a blind alley. And you have to turn around and just let the water take you to someplace else and in a little while something else will appear and you'll realize that "Oh my God, if I had taken that, I would never have been available for this." That is what surrender is about.

JOHN: Can there be too much surrender?

ANGELS: No, because that is different. What you are talking about is someone afraid of living. Of someone who is living fearfully so they are mousey. In other words they want everyone to like them, they don't want to make a ripple or they don't stand for or do anything; they are fearful, so they aren't doing much of anything—they think that will keep them "safe". But that isn't surrender. Surrender, is: "I will go out there and be the biggest, grandest thing I can be, knowing that God and trusting that God will care for me, that I will fulfill my soul's purpose."

I won't push it down the throat of anyone else, and if I'm steered here I'll go there and if I'm steered away from there, I won't go there, but I will make a stand and I will be in my soul's purpose—to us is not being a mousey human being. Surrender and mousiness in our estimation are two different things. Surrender in its true sense is being extremely fearless and mousiness is extremely fearful. It may appear to be surrender but really its intense fear. You haven't stuck your nose out of the hole, so there is nothing to surrender too.

So, that is the difference.

Now, well, you are also thinking what if a big mean bully comes along? We need to address this as well. And they try to take away my power. What about the "turn the other cheek" thing? That's another part that we need to address. So we are going to ask you, because this is right down the line of your mission. This is really about what you've seen has caused so many problems.

In the Arcturian world they have pretty much done away with all of their enemies. In other words, they vibrate from a very high consciousness. They are truly living in fifth dimensional consciousness and above and because of that they have a very controlled society, and they don't allow a lot of things, they truly control the birth, unlike the human race where it seems like every being known to the universe is allowed through the birth canal. They do not allow this, they do not allow inter-species marriage, and so forth, very controlled. And it has a high level of vibration, if you (in an Arcturian world) don't maintain that high level of vibration, all beings on that planet will actually work to bring you up to that vibration. If you cannot hold that vibration, you are not welcomed there, and that is how it works. All is done to support all.

Now, what you're feeling is, "That is easy" because then you don't have any enemies, so then you're not getting tested, and Earth is such a testing ground. So, there are a couple of ways, and again, we are not judging, it is a way. There is not a wrong way or a right way—it's a way and you learn from it, and that's it.

So if you want to go to the idea of being slapped, because that is a simple analogy of turning the other cheek, ok? What would be the two options there? One option is to lay your hands down and say: "I'm not going to slap you back." Correct?

JOHN: Well actually I see several options.

ANGELS: Okay.

JOHN: One does not have to have a physical retaliation, one could over-retaliate, or one could just attempt to ensure that that does not happen again. But, my understanding of turning the other cheek, it has to do with not necessarily the physical response, but more the emotional response, it's sort of like forgiveness, it's not getting pulled out of the moment by that event, not losing the sense of presence and getting angry because of this event that occurred, that's what I think is the concept of turning the other cheek.

ANGELS: Well it's both. Of course it can be physical or emotional. It doesn't matter whether physical or emotional in its response. Some have said, "If you allow this, if you allow someone to bully you, then they will continue to do this. And there comes a time you have to stand up for yourself. You have to say: You are not allowed to bully me." And you can't. You must say: "I'm sorry, but this is not okay behavior." And that is the idea that you are standing up for yourself. You are not allowing others to run you over, and you can see that there are many humans who need to learn that. In other words, they don't know how to, almost peacefully, hold the space and say: "I'm sorry, but you've hurt my feelings and that is not acceptable." Do you understand?

Now what they haven't done, of course, is strike back and they have not said something mean back, as you said, over-retaliate, or get revenge in its extreme. Yes, people get revenge. But they have also said that this is going to stop here. In other words, the idea is they hold the space, and again the idea of sensing and feeling why did that person do that? So, you don't take it personally, because often, when you retaliate it's because for that moment you've allowed their wounding, as we said before, to damage you, which causes you to retaliate. If there's no damage, there's no need for retaliation. If you don't give away your power, you can't be damaged.

Obviously, in its extreme, would be the example that humans often use with the Christed experience saying, "Well, he was able to transcend even a horrible crucifixion." Now it's important for you to understand that in that experience Christ did not experience the crucifixion as humans experience it. In other words, there are two, or more, actually, many different realities at play there. Now, what humans would think is there is the reality of suffering, pain and humiliation. But then there is a reality of what you might call the Christed Consciousness, where none of that can touch you, and that's when you align with what's called the God Consciousness. It doesn't even reach you, and the minute you do that, you step out, or above it, and you come into an Angelic, or Higher Consciousness, a consciousness where those vibrations can't even reach you.

That is the ultimate way to lift out of conflict; you don't even accept it as reality, because that is not even a part of your reality. That is the extreme that is experienced by those that you would call Christed. In other words, you would experience it in your human as suffering but a Christ, or God consciousness would be anywhere it wanted to be in relationship to the event. Do you see what we are saying? Creating another reality; or focusing upon another reality.

So the reality you create in conflict is your own. Decide what it is you want this reality to be. Do you want it to continue? Generally speaking with most humans, unless it is a human who is determined to take you to the extreme, and that would include torture, to get a response so they can feed off you, in that case, then obviously they won't stop, because they need to torture another human being to feed themselves.

But in the case of an ordinary human who is not pushing it to the extreme, what you tend to find, is that if you hold space and you consciously hold up a mirror so that whatever is being projected energetically at you is just being reflected back at them, because it is all coming from their own wounding, and you are peaceful, ultimately, there is nothing for them to fight against, they walk away, there is no battle there. They have to walk away and own their piece of it, their part of it. If you engage, that's what they want. If they engage you then they don't have to hold their piece of it, because now you've become the bad guy. You see? Even if they started it they can turn on you and say, "Well, look what you did, you, you ..." and they don't have to own what they did.

If you want someone to own what they did, and you want them to get it, don't engage. Hold up a mirror, and just reflect, as a blank slate, back at them. Look at them with Love in your eyes, and just sit there as a blank slate, and make them hold their words and actions. You see? For an average encounter it works much better than retaliation or holding on to the anger. Just become that blank mirror and see what happens when they have to look at their own reflection.

It's a whole different matter if someone is a sadist and truly needs to feed off others. In that case, whatever would be required to escape, would be required for the physical, and would be fine, because there would be no other means of escape. Or if you are Christed, and you could just experience a Christed Consciousness during such an experience as Christ did, then you would just go there. So, those two, would be the options given to someone in those extreme cases.

Does this assist you? Do you understand?

JOHN: Yes.

ANGELS: You could perhaps utilize the mirror sometimes too. Then you could neutralize things more easily. All of this, as we said to you, is part of your training ground, and you are going to be utilizing this in far grander ways than you will even be able to imagine. But we wish, to also say to you that you are going to start waking up, more and more, and you are going to begin feeling and discovering and finding that you are going to be having certain sensations in your physical body. You are going to be hearing harmonic tones, sounds, sensations and things are going to be changing for you from this day forth as a result of this waking-up.

So, shifts and changes will start happening and you will become more and more aware of what's called your galactic selves and your grand position. You have to just get that, what you call your old logical left brain, out of the way.

JOHN: Yes.

ANGELS: That's going to be the hardest. But it's interesting because it's serving you, because you are gathering information. It is helping you to analyze. It's like we said, you are kind of like that scientist—that archeologist. You've been like that, but at the same time, what you are trying to teach yourself is something, that in many ways can only be gained upon the Earth. And that is the idea that you can find peace in ways that were never possible to find peace on these other planets that you visited.

There are Masters that have said of spiritual enlightenment, essentially: "If you can find some enlightenment on earth, you can find it anywhere". But it is true because it is a free will planet and you are given the opportunity to go to the lowest lows or to the highest highs and on other planets you don't have those extremes. You see? Do you see what we are saying now?

JOHN: I think that is fascinating actually, that that exists here.

ANGELS: That's why everyone wants to be here, on this Earth. And they covet it because you can have such extremes side-by-side and it's a great teaching tool for the soul. It is quite extraordinary. There are many who line up to experience these extremes. But, of course, once you get here it can feel quite different because it is full of self responsibility, you see. You are not having a community telling you and taking care of you. You have to make the choices and there is an easy slide into victimhood on this planet, into believing you are the victim, when in fact you are actually quite a consciousness co-creator. And the awakening comes when one comes to realize that.

JOHN: I think that I see that in myself, in that sense of moving out of victimhood, that I am starting to acknowledge that I have to take responsibility, and in effect that I am responsible for events that go on in my life, so that is something I am beginning to realize.

ANGELS: And understanding how to forgive others and how to say: "I'm sorry" that's a good one for you too. You see that? Learn about how you can hold that without it being such a big deal. It's not a big deal. It is: Okay: the conflict doesn't have to upset you. Do you understand what we are saying? The conflict can just ***be***. There are ways to deal with it. Humans are going to find disharmony at times. There are ways, as we said, to mirror back and let go, and then to teach that to others.

You are definitely not a victim. You are actually quite an interesting soul, quite different from others, and your path is not traditional. You have not taken in any way a traditional path. And that is part of the reason that you feel a little homeless. Do you agree? Do you feel homeless?

JOHN: Oh yes.

ANGELS: Let us explain one more thing to you, which is important to understand. Most souls take a, we're just going to make it simple, for the sake of this conversation, take a planet, and go into their consciousness, their path, their consciousness path, within that species or that planet. They, for example, they spent their time in Earth soul progression, or Arcturian soul progression or Pleiadian soul progression, or Sirian soul progression, or Lyrian soul progression or Orion, and so forth, they have these different soul progressions, and they have done their soul progressions and they identify with that particular group. When they wake up they say: "Oh, I can recognize that I am from the Andromeda Galaxy, and I have these strengths and weaknesses and I relate to that, I've done my soul progression there and so forth."

Now, as we said, that isn't what you have done. You haven't completed a soul progression in one species, in one body. You've been a little bit of a "hopper."

It's been interesting, and you've learned a lot, and it makes you quite useful to groups, to the motherships, the Arcturians and the Ashtar Command, it's made you extremely useful. You are actually, whether you know it or not, used in many ways as a resource, because you do have the ability to speak a number of different languages and to understand, so, for example when they need to ask about a certain species sometimes they call on you.

But it's left you feeling homeless and while it's interesting, there is a longing in you for the idea of the security of a home, or a species or being, belonging. And that you don't have. Yes?

JOHN: Right.

ANGELS: That's what we sense. So we would suggest, that you, let's see this is a tough one, even for us, to help you with. Well you feel somewhat at home with the Arcturians, although as we said the uniformity rubs you the wrong way. You enjoy the Pleiadians but the Pleiadians tend to be a little bit too emotional for you, they are extremely emotional and their emotions have gotten them into trouble. Just the opposite of the Arcturians who keep the emotions within a certain range, the Pleiadians are the ones who are the artists, and the dramatists, and you like that, and you admire it, and you have actually enjoyed them, but sometimes the extreme drama makes you uncomfortable. You can see that, yes?

JOHN: Yes.

ANGELS: Now, that's problem, in a way, nothing has quite fit. The Andromeda Galaxy, are closest, to give you the human image, you know on Star Trek, Mr. Spock? That's the kind of the idea, a lot of logic. And you like that, and you do resonate there, but since you've seen the other ways, it seems a little cold. So there you get stuck. And the warring, the Reptilians, you understand, and their warring nature, and their mastery, but you see how they have caused so much trouble. So, that has disturbed you. And you have done others as well, we could mention. But what we sense is that it's very hard for you and you don't know where to go to find a home or to find belonging. You are going to have to find your home, or belonging, out of a physical species. In other words, that also is what is attracting you to the idea of moving up into like an Angelic realm or the Ascended Master realm is the idea that, "Well, maybe I can finally find a home there"

And you are not Angelic, and you knew that. Yes?

JOHN: Well, actually someone had told me I was, but I can't say...

ANGELS: No, we don't sense you're Angelic. What they were picking up is all this; these other things That you work with us, we know you, you are familiar with us as you've done your searches, but you are not, you have not taken, and committed to, the Angelic path of evolvement. In other words, that has not been what you have said: "Okay, I am now going to be, and study as, a guardian Angel, and be Angelic. You associate with us, we know you and you work with us, but it is not your home either. Do you understand what we are saying?

JOHN: Wow, that's, I guess I understand it, yeah—

ANGELS: Okay, now the Ascended Masters is another path of evolution. There are souls that choose to work with the Ascended Masters and they are "Seekers." And you are more closely aligned with them.

JOHN: Seekers.

ANGELS: You are more closely aligned with what we call the Seekers and the Ascended Master path, than with the Angelics; but you work with us. Does that resonate for you? Do you understand that?

JOHN: I once had a dream, where I identified myself as a Seeker.

ANGELS: You are, yes. You are a Seeker. That is what you are. It does not mean you don't work with us. So, what we sense is that person who told you that you carried angelic energy sensed this specialness about you, that we're talking about, but didn't know quite how to explain it, and so the closest thing that they could get, was that higher vibration, so they called it Angel, but it is not your chosen path, that is a different frequency. Your chosen path is, as we have said, and as you have known, is the Ascended Master/Seeker path.

So, you are an interesting one. Are you having any other questions for today, or do you feel like we have hit you with enough for one time?

JOHN: Certainly, a lot of information, I do have one question.

ANGELS: Okay.

JOHN: I had a dream that really resonated with me, and, it was a very simple dream, and the character was named "Longnight" and, I was just wondering if you could help me, tell me, who Longnight is?

ANGELS: Well, you probably know, it's you.

JOHN: Well, there's some connection, but it's, you know, can you help me—

ANGELS: What did you sense that it was? Tell us more about this dream?

JOHN: It was one of these dreams where, just intuitively, through some cognition, there's not much, not a great deal of visual, but there is this sense that a very subtle shift has occurred, sort of like a very subtle shift has occurred in nature, and systematically events have shifted, sort of like a drought coming on, or something like that, and the animals that are dependent on that eco system are suffering and suffering and eventually dwindling, and then the only real, that was a sense, and then the only real narration, was this, there's this picture, or this vision, of something between the cross of a wolf and a bear, and then the narration was: "...and Longnight dies." And, I woke up.

But, it was very impressive.

ANGELS: That is quite interesting. Well from our perspective, what you, what we sense is that you were putting together many, many, many, different things in that one long night. And what we want to say is that its, it is a pun in many ways for you, that you created for yourself. Not only long-knight as you are a tall, K, N, I, G, H, T, and so you are the Long Knight. But it is also the idea of the long night, as in N, I, G, H, T, as in a long period of darkness, so what you were telling yourself was that you are going through a long period of darkness. You have gone through the long night, and what is happening is that the long night is ending, and the shift that is happening is the waking up, or the ascension. That is what we sense. Do you understand what we are saying?

JOHN: Yes, thank you.

ANGELS: But you were remembering all sorts of information from your different experiences in other planetary systems, putting it together almost into one short image, but the long night is over, that is the ending. But it is also that the Long Knight, you, is waking up, you see? It is a bit of a pun there. That is what we sense.

It was like a wake-up call for you—out of a long night of sleep or darkness. But you also sensed the Earth herself has been going through a long night of darkness and was now going to be waking up. That is what we sense. If that helps you.

JOHN: Thank you.

ANGELS: So have we helped you today?

JOHN: You have, and I wanted to start, actually, by thanking you for the assistance, not just for today but throughout the course of this life, and also for the teachings that come through Margaret. I find them very, very, useful. The perspective that you share is novel to the way I normally think, and I find it very, very helpful. So I thank you.

ANGELS: Well, its novel to your human, but what resonates with it, is all these other selves, and certainly the Seeker. We have very much enjoyed working with you, we have put a lot your plate and we are going to explain to you, that the long night, as you have said, is over, this is your wake-up call today, and from now on you will not be walking through the world in a state of unconsciousness; you have no more excuses, you are no longer a victim, you are aware now of your greatness, and so we expect you to walk the path of your own greatness. You have no more excuses for your victimhood and sleepy consciousness. Do you understand our meaning?

JOHN: Absolutely.

ANGELS: We thank you so much. We will be speaking with you again. As a Seeker, you are on a noble path, and you have done this job well. You need to now become, as you know, your higher and greater self. You will find yourself being called for more and more extraordinary journeys in your soul's growth, so thank you. And thank you for trying to understand and learn how to bring peace to the incarnate world, for we are very grateful that you are on that path and mission.

CHAPTER SIXTEEN

ARCTURIAN SEEKER

ANNE A.

The following channeling was done for a woman who progressed primarily in the Arcturian soul progression before choosing the human consciousness path. She too is a Seeker, but as you can see her experiences have led to very different experiences than the previous gentleman.

ANGELS: We are delighted to have this opportunity to be with you and to speak with you in this way. And as always, this is Ariel and Michael and Gabriel who are with this conduit and working in this way. And we wish to remind you of your noble heart and your noble task, and to help you to remember why you are on this Earth, and why you have chosen this path.

Your soul has evolved through numerous incarnations, in numerous forms, shapes, ways. You are what would be called a Seeker. You are advanced enough as a soul to have been accepted into the school of the Seekers. It is traditional for Seekers to go where they need to go to find what they need to discover, to do the work that they need to do. They do not like to be limited particularly to one species, to one kind of—one way of being.

It took you awhile to begin incarnating at all as a soul. You stayed away for a while. But once you started, you took it on with a bang and became curious or excited about the possibilities of life in a denser form. You had a number of different ways of expressing. You did settle, as you are well aware, for a long time in the Arcturian soul progression, and you lived a vast number of your lessons through that soul progression. It is, as you are well aware, one of your most comfortable.

What you liked about the Arcturian soul progression was its orderliness and its purity, and you liked the fact that they had found a way to keep chaos at bay and to function at a very high level; to keep a community consciousness working. It is extremely difficult to keep a community consciousness operating at a high frequency, for it doesn't take much for a number of the members of that society to bring down the entire community. The Arcturians learned through their soul progression as a species how to prevent that from happening One of the ways that the Arcturians do this is through thought regulation and by focusing always on the members of the society that need the help and assisting them to raise the vibrational consciousness, to rejoin the group.

There are many gifts and talents that you carry onto this planet from your Arcturian studies, teachings, learning and so forth. Those Arcturians who are esteemed were allowed to incarnate on the Earth and to bring the gifts, because the fear of getting lost, of losing yourself on the Earth was great. This Arcturian desire for purity is where we're going to begin. It is a difficult task to summarize a soul's long progression but we are going to put it this way: because you have been studying the energy or essence of purity you were hoping to bring to the Earth the idea of purity as it was developed in the Arcturian societies. The struggle to achieve purity has been at the forefront of your human karmic struggles throughout time. It is something that has plagued you; both your own purity and lifting your own self up, and also the idea of lifting others.

You have had times where you were punished in other lives for essentially being impure. You have had times where you have gotten what would be called today this idea of OCD—of almost obsessing over releasing your purity. As you progressed in your soul studies, what you've become interested in is the understanding that perhaps it isn't about destroying impurity. Perhaps it isn't about taking the light—the white—and eradicating the dark. But, perhaps there's something about living side-by-side with the light and the dark and the purity and the impurity that is currently at the forefront of your studies and your learning.

This wisdom that you are gaining through your many searches, your travels, your experiences is offering another perspective to you at this time. What the human perspective is offering you is different from the Arcturian perspective: this is the thought that perhaps it isn't about eradicating the dark but somehow coexisting with it; in the self or outside. You question whether or not that's possible; for it seems impossible. Yet you've begun to understand that perhaps there's some wisdom held somewhere in the shadow, that perhaps it isn't useless, that perhaps there are teachings there. But you don't know quite how to integrate or what to do, and it does butt up against your Arcturian sensibilities. So, we're just going to stop here for a moment and make sure you're with us so far.

ANNE A: Yes.

ANGELS: And tell you thank you for being here today, and seeing if you understand our message thus far.

ANNE A: Yes, it's very helpful.

ANGELS: What we want you to do is step away from yourself and begin to see and understand that there are a number of issues and things at play. Yes, you are human. You are. We are not denying your humanness. But you're approaching the human experience from your own point of view. And your own point of view has a couple of things: One, as we said, is Seeker, working with the Ascended Masters. All Seekers are apprentices of the Ascended Masters, but all apprentices of the Ascended Masters are not Seekers. It is a division, if you will.

Those who are in a particular line of study or have decided they like that way of soul expression is perhaps how we like to look at it, and are evolved enough, as you are, to begin to work at a higher level of consciousness, are working to evolve eventually to be a Life Carrier or Creator. Those kinds of jobs, if you will, often have been taken by Seeker souls, because Seekers understand—have studied and understand varied and various ways of incarnation and expression and have a scholarly nature, quite often, enjoying learning, studying and interpreting their experiences when not incarnated, when in spiritual body, sharing with others what they have learned.

One of the things you bring to your human experience is a curiosity and a willingness to experience a variety of things which would be outside of the Arcturian experience. The Arcturians have not experienced a wide variety of things for quite some time now in their evolution. They have limited, not through their minds—their minds are far more unlimited—but through their physical bodies. The extremes are pretty much gone. You understand that, yes? By that, we mean they don't experience the pain, the suffering and the death and all of these physical extremes, okay?

Human life gives you the opportunity to experience these extremes, to study them, to understand, and then to figure out what teachings you can offer to help human beings in their own way, to live comfortably with being human; with being in a culture and society and a world that has had so many extremes. You're beginning to realize that perhaps there might be a little value to it, and that perhaps your job, as we said, is not to just come in with purity's wand, magic wand, and purify everything. Perhaps there is something else here, there's something else to be learned and understood from the human experience that has value. Perhaps it isn't about eradicating, perhaps it's about integrating and understanding what has value.

So, we will pause and see if you understand that idea.

ANNE A: Yes.

ANGELS: So, you could see or resonate with the idea that you have experimented, is the best way for us to put it, with the idea of purity? Do you understand that?

ANNE A: Yes.

ANGELS: Okay. And purification, purifying the self. You had a life where you were made to feel, as a spiritual novitiate, in a sense, that you weren't pure enough and it wasn't "good," shall we say. The way that they tried to purify you had a bit of the punishment to it, the purification through punishment. You've experienced the idea that you need to be punished to be purified. You understand that's a human thought, right?

ANNE A: Right.

ANGELS: And you don't like that.

ANNE A: No.

ANGELS: But you know it. Do you understand? You know it. It's not foreign to you. As you've studied purification, you've asked, "Where is the value in the darker experiences? Where is the value in the pain? Where is the value in the separation consciousness? Is there a value?" If there is a value, how to integrate it and purify it—rather than by eradicating it and purifying it.

From our perspective, that is where you're at as a soul. We're going to pause and ask for your comments on that and how you feel about that idea.

ANNE A: Well, that's good because that's the central conflict. And I wondered, you know, where did it come from? I find that it resonates with me and that in many ways, maybe this impure proclivity has made me more receptive to just entering into the world and counseling. I have thought about this idea in a different way since learning about the Reptilians, the intergalactic wars, and a kind of reconciliation in an interplanetary, universal way. That's how I'm kind of trained—to kind of "take in" and not to face things. It's not that I dig in against them; it's just that I don't face them. To be able to purify myself. So, I really have been wondering what to do. I'm glad to hear that I'm—

ANGELS: Well, the idea that you could—.

ANNE A: That I'm not damned to hell.

ANGELS: No, you are not damned to hell. You are a student and you have understood that a student—as we said, as a Seeker, you have sought out many different experiences, in your desire to understand more fully what makes life tick everywhere throughout the universe. Because ultimately, as a Life Creator, one who learns to take the energy, in a sense, from God and create life with it, how could you do that unless you had understood life. You see? It would be ridiculous to not have to experience everything before trying your hand at creating anything.

What we're going to say is that the Arcturian model of sameness, all looking the same, all within a particular range of expression, perhaps is not the perfect model for the human. It isn't a template that you can just put on top of this crazy Earth, you see, and try to force this crazy Earth to fit into it.

What you're beginning to understand is that if you don't want to be at war, if a species is not going to be at war and is always working in duality, that it's important then for a species to be able to understand the gifts inherent in everything, to see everything as having a gift. Once you do that, whether in the self or in the world around you, you shift the energy from war to a benevolent cooperation. Immediately, the duality is put aside. It is the idea that you fight the Reptilian within you or fight the Pleiadian DNA within you and so forth is what leads to the discomfort.

But the idea that each and every part of you, or all others, has something to value, to learn from, is a way of enriching a soul and certainly completing that whole circle, that yin, that yang, the dark and the light, the light and the dark. You're not at war; you're unified. "Oh, well, that is the part of me, that's the Arcturian part," or "Oh, that's the part of me that's the Pleiadian part," or

"That's the Reptilian in me" and so forth—beginning to realize that you can live with all of those inside of you. It's when one thing becomes too aggressive or doesn't see itself as a teacher or on a path of evolution as a student that the arrogance sets in and the difficulty occurs.

Arrogance is the biggest downfall for the evolution of any species. The Reptilians have the signature—they can be awarded the most arrogant because they are impossible to teach. They don't want to admit that they don't know it all or can't see it all or aren't perfect. And Human/Reptilians are often subject to exactly the same problems. The Reptilian part of any human tends to express itself in defended arrogance. And, that is where the evolution stops. Evolution, as you know, is not denied to any species, whether Reptilian or human or any other species. But any species stops its evolution profoundly at the moment of profound arrogance.

So, the human gift to the Reptilians is to be humble—is humility. The DNA is so wedded; you can't find much purity on this planet. Everyone is so intermingled. So, when the Reptilian enters the human soul progression cycle and they are mutated with human DNA, they go to war with it. Yet eventually, the karma, the karmic cycle and the war that they've been creating leads them into a downward spiral. It is often the Reptilian track in the human that leads them into the idea of "getting down so low there's nowhere to go but up." The arrogance has been beaten, you see. That is when the Reptilian part inside the human says, "Help me, I can't do it myself." In that moment, the Reptilian arrogance is released and the human part of the self lends a hand to ascend that being, you see?

So, there are gifts, because in the Reptilian, there is of course strength; and they are very bright. They are not stupid by any means. Their intelligence is actually behind much of the scientific work that is done on this planet and there are gifts. If their arrogance and rage is controlled, they can be profoundly brilliant gifters to this planet, and it is not right to say that every Reptilian or human/Reptilian intermix is an evil being; this is wrong. It is only when their arrogance and their negative or dark side fights against the human that they get controlling and horrible in their action. But once that is under control, there have been many gifts that can be given to the human race. If they can learn to surrender and be in community through the human experience they can progress in their evolution.

The Arcturians also have given gifts and are giving gifts: gifts of healing, gifts of community consciousness, and gifts of relationship. They understand very well how to help each other get along. And of course, the Pleiadians give the gifts of the arts and as you know music and so forth. So, all these gifts are intermingled now in the human being, in the human species, and to each one to varying degrees. There are much "purer" or less "intermingled" Pleiadians, Arcturians and Reptilians, for example, and there are those that have a little of everything.

But, it is important to realize that as this relates to you, that your understanding and gifts are focused a great deal on the Arcturian experience, but you have an understanding of other creatures as well. You know the insects, the insect species. You know that there are very intelligent species that look like insects and so forth. You're not limited in your wisdom, but you're focused at this time on the Arcturian gift of purification and how it can live alongside the darkness and the impure parts of the human race. As we said, you're trying to figure out how now not to work from a place of eradication of self and others but a place of coexistence and mutual harmony, knowing that all gifts—that gifts are given with all of these expressions, rather than duality and the idea of separation.

What we would suggest is that always when you see lessons learned through darkness, whether in yourself or others, please to first think of the great gifts rather than the way to eradicate the darkness.

ANNE A: Is this why—a friend once channeled that my spiritual name is Mayakaya . And when I asked a Sanskrit scholar about it, she said it means divine and everything that isn't the divine all in one word.

ANGELS: The dark and the light.

ANNE A: Yes.

ANGELS: But the dark is also the divine and that is very hard, because for some to understand, because they don't see the gifts in it, they think that God will only be in some things. But you had better hope that God is in all things, because how would the dark ever transform itself if it did not have the spark of God in it? You see? Some beings are choosing one path and some beings are choosing another, but they all are given that spark which is a transformative energy, a creative energy, which means that at any moment, anything can change. And of course, change is not comfortable for the human race because too often, of course, you've seen change bring trauma. We understand that much change occurs and has occurred through trauma on this planet because human beings do not want to change, so trauma comes in and changes them. You understand.

But then the change—even the trauma has to be looked at as good, you see, because it couldn't go on as it was, so something had to happen. So, if the energy was low vibrational, then the change will be perhaps of a low vibrational nature. Change itself is not bad. It can be done at a high vibrational level and be quite pleasant. Because humans do not often operate from that level, they are in a state of difficult or traumatic change. But it still has the spark of the divine in it. Even someone who is drug addicted or so forth, as horrifying as it is, at some point, even that terrible way of learning lessons, whether it is in this life or in another life or in- between life, at some point, the soul says, "That isn't working for me, enough, enough! I want something else. "So, if that's what it took for the soul to embrace change, well, we see it as a blessing.

ANNE A: I see so many people who have been through so much and it's extraordinary, because it's helping me understand how they can be so open to the traumas that they have had and bring in some Light.

ANGELS: Those who do not utilize that are in the victim consciousness that is disempowering. It is important, as you well know that every human, in order to heal, in order to ascend, must embrace and accept their own Mastery. It is very, very hard, even for souls such as you who are highly evolved, to be on the Earth and remember that, correct? It's easy to be a victim, yes?

ANNE A: I've been a victim myself. I'm just crawling out of that consciousness, I hope.

ANGELS: You can understand why it would be hard for a less wise soul, a soul who has less wisdom than you to do that. You can see that your understanding of how to move from victimhood to Mastery is a beacon of light for others. You needed those experiences so that you could, as you say, teach others, reach others and fully understand the human experience. It would have done you no good to come to the human soul progression and incarnational cycles and to not immerse yourself in it. You cannot lift it from outside of it. You must lift it and lift the self from within. You see what we're saying.

ANNE A: Right.

ANGELS: So, it's important. When we in this dimension, when we "lower our hands," often, they are slapped away. It doesn't feel real to the human. Well, they think, you don't have anything to give me; you're an angel, so you don't get it. But we can be a human like yourself and say, "Well, I get it, but I can help you because I've got the escape route." They're more likely to listen to you as human though.

ANNE A: Well, I hope that I'm on the right path for trying to help others. One of the things I wanted to know is am I being too complacent? I'm studying some things and thinking about getting another degree.

ANGELS: That Seeker in you, huh?

ANNE A: The researcher. But I don't know—I have a therapist who was very forceful with me. He said, "You really ought to be doing your creative healing center." It doesn't seem like the right time.

ANGELS: Well, your problem is that, in part, you don't want to stay around on the earth a whole lot longer. Do you see what we're saying? It's hard for you to hear that but—we're not telling you that we're taking you off, okay? So don't worry. But can you close your eyes and envision a future? You don't see very much. Do you see what we're saying? It kind of just goes into a mist, doesn't it?

ANNE A: Yes.

ANGELS: That's what we're talking about. You're not really committed to a long haul here at this point. You feel—you've come, doing what you set out to do, and perhaps taking this planet through that 2012 Ascension and the work perhaps into 2013 might just be enough for you. So digging your heels in and making a commitment to anything longer than even a year or two, it doesn't really resonate for you. Do you understand what we're saying?

ANNE A: Yes.

ANGELS: We don't mean to make you afraid because it's not that you will be taken off by this side; it's a choice you will make of your own free will. If you choose not to make it, that's okay. You can stay. But it's certainly an option for you coming up in the relatively near future. We have trouble with linear time but we're seeing in the next two years. You have about a two-year vision scope. Do you understand that? You can feel that.

ANNE A: Now, is that because I'm not being well cared for or pure, as it were, about my diet or—

ANGELS: No. That's all your purification fears.

ANNE A: Okay.

ANGELS: That's all your purification fears. You decide whether you stay or go at any time.

ANNE A: Some part of me—because I would like to stay but I gather some part of me is ready to check out.

ANGELS: Well, you can feel—it's not right away but you can feel that there isn't sort of a long-term vision, and that's because you're leaving your options open. We feel that once you make a commitment between your Higher Self and your human self to stick it out: "Hey, maybe I will go through what are going to be some difficult transitions for this planet, and I'll stick it out and work through and help on this side of the curtain"—once you make that grounded, you'll start to open up your future plans. What we feel is it comes from having not quite made that decision yet. Does that resonate for you?

ANNE A: Yes.

ANGELS: We think it does.

ANNE A: Yeah.

ANGELS: It's totally up to you. You will be deciding what you want to do and nobody will tell you what to do. There will be some coaching because you will ask of your teachers and so forth. You will ask Vishnu.

ANNE A. Vishnu!

ANGELS: Yes.

ANNE A: Really?

ANGELS: Yes. Vishnu is one of your teachers. You know this.

ANNE A: No, I didn't know.

ANGELS: Ask your teachers and they will say, well, it's up to you.

ANNE A: I am hearing the word faith.

ANGELS: Vishnu teaches you to trust.

ANNE A: Yeah.

ANGELS: Vishnu is working to teach you trust, and that is good. Lakshmi is helping you with your prosperity and working in the flow and feeling good about being on the Earth. But you're just not quite settled into a future plan yet. All of the Starseeds, all of the Ascended Beings who are assisting in this leap, in this time of transition, will be making a similar decision, whether to stay or whether to go and how to assist. Each one is asked and what the decision is by the individual is adhered to. Those decisions are not made by others but made by the self. It's too important a decision for another soul to make that kind of decision for you.

ANNE A: I've just completed my studio to be able to make art. I would like to be able to create a good vibration through the artwork or through teaching or something, to maybe anchor in energies to be useful now or perhaps in the future.

ANGELS: You do have the ability, if you develop it, as many Arcturians do, to scan a body with your third eye. It is a particularly developed Arcturian gift. If you wish to develop that as a healer, you would be able to use your third eye to scan a human form and to be a medical intuitive, perhaps is the best way to put it, to see and notice areas of blocks that are problems. That would be a gift that you do have as a healer; should you wish to develop it. But you're not sure because the commitment to do this is a lot of responsibility. You understand?

ANNE A: Right.

ANGELS: That's why you haven't developed that to the extent you could, because once you can really see inside, then you have to take responsibility for that person and help them and assist them to move and to heal. That's a lot of responsibility. Do you understand what we're saying?

ANNE A: Yes.

ANGELS: That frightens you a little. You also—we need to address—you need to work on your lack of feeling worthy, your feelings of worthiness. You need to really work on this because sometimes you doubt yourself a little too much. In other words, you can do that; don't even question it. You have a great number of gifts. You could work with your art, as you have suggested. But what we sense—this is going to be a very strange thing for you and we don't have a model to give you, but your ability would be as an artist to combine your Arcturian sight, as we call it, and to paint the perfected soul—the human moving from imperfection to perfection or, from impurity to purity.

Because that is what you're studying you could use your third eye to see the human in what you would think of as their impure expression, and gradually paint them, almost in slices, as moving into their perfected form. The human would look and see the journey to their purity and their perfection. That ability to bring what you wish to do as an artist to help others to see—your painting would say, "You can move from this to this." You can be all of those things. As a visual, it would be an interesting way for you to express your gifts.

ANNE A: As in individual portraits?

ANGELS: As in individual portraits for people, yes, showing them their shadow to their light.

ANNE A: And that would—I've experienced as a kind of spiritual guidance as I make art. I assume I wouldn't have to deal with a feeling of unworthiness as I get that guidance.

ANGELS: We are not telling you what to do, but we are telling you what your strengths are. You study life forms. You are interested in beings of all types. Painting beings of all types and the lesson of impurity to purity in a particular evolution of one being would be a beautiful expression of all your studies. Soul portraits in a sense.

ANNE A: Yes. I've seen a few and I was just bowled over by them. Beautiful works. So human.

ANGELS: Well, there were some DNA experiments that were done combining horses and humans. There's a reason that you have that in what you call your mythology. That was a species that was created. It is a tragedy when species are intermingled through DNA experimentation, for they lose their identity. Am I a horse or a human? You see? It is terrifying to them. And we consider that to be one of the worst things that can be done is to use DNA to intermingle a species in a way that creates a lost soul.

ANNE A: So, I guess it's no coincidence that certain movies that I've seen, books that I've been interested in reading, all resonate with these ideas that you're talking to me about. I'm so grateful to Supreme Consciousness for that guidance.

ANGELS: Because you're trying to remember who you are, yes?

ANNE A: Yeah.

ANGELS: Actually that is what it really is about. You're trying to remember who you are. It's as if, from our perspective, you're standing and you're looking—there's a little shadow, as if almost the mirror still has some shadow, and you're trying to get a clear picture—as are many humans currently. They're trying to find out what is truth for them and beginning to understand that there are many, many, many truths upon this planet and that all truths need to be respected side-by-side. And they can be. They do not need to eradicate one another. That is why you are doing so much of this study.

One of the reasons is because it is very difficult, too, for you, as a soul who is much expanded, who has a lot of information within you, to be human. It's very tough. There's not very much room in the human body currently or human template for all that information that you contain. It's as if all the material—there's not enough chest of drawers to stuff it in, in your human body. It's very limited. As the DNA awakens, the ability to carry more information awakens–in a sense, you add more drawers to yourself, to hold more information. It's exciting but you have to be careful that you don't burn out by trying to move too quickly. Allow the human body to go along for the ride.

This is the ascension of the human being. The human body was destroyed. It was originally a template of perfection. It was—we're going to put it this way—messed with. It was dumbed down until now—it's a shell of its former self. What is trying to occur is the repair of the human form. Many Lightworkers want to go out of their body. They just want to just go away. But that's not why you're here. You're here to help the human form awaken. As you all know, to awaken more strands of DNA, to help humans hold more information, to live in less fear, to destroy the old templates; everything that is not working.

It's not about dying and leaving your body. It's about helping the human body regain its splendor, its glory, and learning to love it once again—most people do not like the human body. They hate their body and they curse their body, and their body pains them. It's too skinny or it's too fat or it's too old or it doesn't run fast enough, it doesn't ski fast enough, it falls down too often. How often do humans bless their human body? Very little, you see. Trying to ascend that which has been so broken and abused is quite the task.

ANNE A: So being lazy to the degree I am is okay?

ANGELS: Well, we don't see you as lazy. What we feel is that you are integrating. You need the time for integration. You understand? You need that time to integrate and it's not easy. Once you make a decision whether to stay or to go, a lot will shift for you.

ANNE A: I hooked up with the Oneness movement about five years ago in India. It's really pained me that they've gone through somewhat major hits and difficulties and things like that. I'm just wondering if I need to leave that behind and move on to something else for my own development, to some of the temporal avatars. But I love the blessing and I'm able to channel this energy that they're anchoring to help people. I have questions about it.

ANGELS: Well, you have been drawn to it for your own purposes, yes, to serve you first, yes? Which is okay. Which is good. It needs to serve you. If it did not serve you, then how could it serve anyone else? We're not calling you selfish; we're saying that was correct. But you've changed, yes?

ANNE A: Yes.

ANGELS: It's done its job. As it does its job for you and as it does its job for others, it needs to evolve into the next stage. Do you understand?

ANNE A: Okay.

ANGELS: If you are evolving as a result of what you have done so far, then allow the evolution to happen into a new thing or a new form. It's okay. Do you understand what we're saying?

ANNE A: Yes. So should I meditate more, to get out of my ordinary thinking?

ANGELS: Well, we don't think of you as an ordinary thinker. Do you really think you're an ordinary thinker?

ANNE A: Well, I can get pretty mundane.

ANGELS: Well, you are human. You are human but perhaps you don't know what the other humans are like. (Laughter)

ANNE A: Okay, I get it. Point well-taken.

ANGELS: We think you're intriguing.

ANNE A: I do have fun with my thinking. This is so refreshing because I was involved with the Gurdjieff group, which pretty much said that you shouldn't be thinking and just be in this receptive mode all the time, which was kind of neurotic, I thought. What you were saying before explained a lot of my rebellion with that. Saying that you're only close to higher consciousness in one state seemed to me to not be the whole story.

ANGELS: Well, what we feel is what you resist persists, what you deny, will make you ill. What you hate, what you deny, what you push away, what you refuse to see, what you think is worse than you, what you put in duality, what is not worthy of you, however it is expressed, is a separation of the God force. Who is doing the separation? Not God, the human. The human is saying, "Well, this will be godly and this will be not." What is the difference between that and a religious who says, "This act is Godly and this act will put you into hell." So, every time you touched yourself "impurely" you went to hell. What is the difference? It is not different.

Any organization that would say, "This is God and this is not God," runs the risk of creating anxiety and disassociation on the part of the practitioner. For every time they do that thing, which is natural to the human, they immediately hate themselves and have separated themselves from God. So, they go into OCD behaviors out of anxiety and pushing part of themselves away. There's no peace there. This is not pure and this is pure. That is what caused your OCD in past lives; because you did do that. You said, "This is pure, this is not pure." You believed it when they told you that, and it came from an Arcturian point of view and started to fit in quite well in the beginning. Well, in the Arcturian society, it works to keep everything pure, but it's not working on the Earth. It's a different species and a different way of learning. There are gifts that the Arcturians can give but at this time, as we said, the template doesn't fit perfectly.

ANNE A: Right. Can you enlighten me as to why it is that I am thinking of not wanting to stay around? It's not a fear of...

ANGELS: It's boredom.

ANNE A: Boredom!

ANGELS: You're bored at times. Don't you know how bored you are?

ANNE A: No, I didn't.

ANGELS: Yes. You're a Seeker. You like traveling. You like going off to this place and that place. You've stayed on this planet for a long time and it's getting a little old.

ANNE A.: But I haven't even been to Egypt in this life!

ANGELS: Oh, in this life, it doesn't even matter to you. It doesn't even matter. It's so small compared to what your Higher Self is dying to work on on the other side. This is getting a little old for you. You must know this.

ANNE A: I don't know it.

ANGELS: Yes, it is old. It's old for you. You've done this, been there.

ANNE A: And the 2012, is that…

ANGELS: Yes, that's okay. Once you get through that, it's like okay, enough. That's enough.

ANNE A: I'll be disappointed?

ANGELS: It's enough already.

ANNE A: Maybe I should be checking out in a few years?

ANGELS: There are *no shoulds*; it's what you wish to do. But there is a level of boredom. You call it laziness. You call it laziness, we call it boredom. You've been everywhere throughout the galaxies.

ANNE A: If I meditate, I might be able to do some more interesting travel?

ANGELS: Certainly. Go visit your little insect friends—your big insect friends. They look like Praying Mantises, sort of. Go visit them. Talk to them. They'll hang out, they'll blink at you. They'll communicate.

ANNE A: Are you telling me that those things in my garage and my basement, with the horns?

ANGELS: Yeah. They will talk to you.

ANNE A: I'm afraid they're after me because I tried to exterminate a few of them.

ANGELS: Getting rid of the darkness, are you? (Laughter) It's only a little piece of you here at this time and there's a lot more of you elsewhere, but this piece is doing some important work, in purifying the self and teaching others about purification. You're also teaching others or hoping to teach others about self-acceptance. You chose to learn self-acceptance, trying to really learn and work through self-acceptance; to teach others the same. A big lesson for you, yes?

ANNE A: And I'm in the perfect place for it.

ANGELS: You're doing quite well. And, again, when you come into the spiritual realm, you will analyze your data and say, "Let's see, how can an imperfect species learn to come to self-acceptance, love, and to live side-by-side with the goodness, the love and the purity but holding simultaneously the shadow, the knowledge of those parts of the self that are evil, without acting on it, you see, through self-acceptance?" These are all lessons that you will be bringing to your studies for a long time and sharing with your friends on the other side of the curtain, too.

ANNE A: You mean in other galaxies?

ANGELS: Both spiritual realms or other galaxies—whether incarnate or disincarnate.

ANNE A: That's why community is so important.

ANGELS: To all Arcturians; they work with community. Arcturians always are drawn to communities.

ANNE A: And yet I've had such a feeling of disconnection for the past nine or ten years in this job, and there was a little voice inside that said that things would change, and they are changing.

ANGELS: You are here as a Seeker, studying. Do not forget, that is one of the aspects of who you are as we said, as you study yourself on this planet. You experience things and when they no longer suit your studies, you change or let them go. That is true whether it is the Oneness blessings or it is a work situation or the work you do or the relationships you have. They suit you and then you change and you let them go. You've immersed yourself in your studies well. You tend to do that. That is what your guides are asking us to tell you: "You tend to immerse yourself very powerfully, no matter where it is you are assigned, whatever planet you go to study. You have done your job well and it's time to come out of the belief that you are that limited human and remember now the Big Being, Seeker that you are, so that you can really finish your studies off with a bang, so to speak, and not buying into the smallness. But really bring all parts of yourself, all wisdom that you have. It's time to really open up all the leaves that have closed up so tightly, all the leaves and all the parts of you, as you start to access and you start to realize and know intuitively the gifts that you have, and you can begin to integrate them slowly, so that you can bring more and more of them through you"

ANNE A: Thank you.

CHAPTER SEVENTEEN

THE ARCHIVIST

KARLEY K.

We thank you and welcome you here today. We wish to begin today by reminding you of your soul purpose—your *interest* is really how we see it, for you are selecting and choosing where you focus your energy, what it is you choose to study and to learn about and understand. It is you who determines that course of study.

When you are in your spiritual body you are an Archivist. That means you work in the Akashic Records archives and are interested in information and soul history. You select the past lives and the information which is then presented to incoming souls when they pass; when they are beginning life review and working to understand and see the images and pictures of who they have been. You work with the guides and teachers in selecting and piecing together the information. From your perspective it would be that you select holographic images of previous lives or experiences to assist the incoming soul to understand the issues that are being talked about or looked at and not overwhelm them with too much information. It is a result of that work that you became very interested in understanding, from the human perspective, when you are on the earth, some of the issues that are brought to you when you are between lives. You are interested in conjoined souls, the interaction and interplay between soul histories and soul stories, soul groups themselves—mass reincarnations and how the karma is spread among many souls in a particular soul group and where and how an individual is responsible for a karma and when and how a collective, group or few individuals become karmically linked. These are studies and interests of yours.

You are not particularly interested at this time in being the teacher as much as you are interested in being the Librarian or Archivist. You enjoy working in the archives because it gives you a broad access to profound amounts of information and you realize that working one-on-one as a teacher or guide would limit you to a particular soul or issue and you like being able to move freely in the Hall of Records.

You love to have your finger on so much information. That is something that also profoundly impacts the choices you make when you incarnate—your focus on whom you will ask into your life, who you will incarnate around will help you to understand better so that you can help incoming souls and assist with soul retrieval and so forth. So, we just pause for a moment and welcome you and thank you and ask if you understand and how it resonates with you.

KARLEY: Yes, I do.

ANGELS: So, you can see that this would be applicable to your soul purpose.

KARLEY: Yes.

ANGELS: You enjoy information coming in, things coming in, stimulus coming in that causes you to act. You actually like that. It feels exciting to you. And you can see that it mirrors what you do between lives when guides come to you and say, "I'm bringing you a soul—Go to it." It gives you the freedom to decide what the best method would be to handle a situation that has been presented to you. That impacts you in your earthly life because events come to you and you enjoy the challenge of how to get the information or do what needs to be done. That is your soul impulse. As a result of that you often ignore yourself—you don't interest yourself as much as other people interest you. You tend to forget that you too are on a soul journey, a soul progression and are learning things and evolving for your *own* sake. For your sake—not for the sake of the archives, not for the sake of the others; but what are you doing for your own sake?

That is another area that we wish to talk about today. Sometimes you forget to do things for you and your own sake. We understand that you do believe that when you do things for others you do them also for you and we understand and agree. Yes, when you do things for others you do learn and grow and progress; you learn by what you do, by the energies you call to you, the potions you mix and what energies and what ideas serve you. But, there are times when you do manifest illnesses—or events—which occur and suddenly stop you and ask you to focus directly on yourself.

And so when you get too "out there" in terms of your focus, an event will arise which will draw the focus back to you and it's helpful because it also helps you not to be too scattered. The external focus can leave you scattered and you need to be drawn back to you; feeling and sensing in your own body. The body, as you know, is a beautiful divining rod—a frequency generator and a frequency receiver and being in the body to you is a way to help both yourself and other people. If you get too "out of your body," events come in to focus you on the body itself.

So, we are going to pause again and see if you are with us so far and if you have a question about what we've said.

KARLEY: Yes. I understand.

ANGELS: Do you feel it is a resonance for you?

KARLEY: Except that I know that I have been a guide too. Although I know that I have probably also been in the archives in-between lives I think that I also have been a guide too, hopefully

ANGELS: You are a guide and a teacher but what interests you is not so much the idea of sticking with one soul and taking one soul through many, many, lifetimes in great depth—what you are interested in is taking one soul and assisting them with a particular lesson or looking at a particular lesson or a series of lives that deal with a particular lesson and then moving that soul on to another. You want access to more information than just working with one or two souls would give you—you would rather guide them and work on an issue but then send them on their way so the next one comes in. Do you see what we are saying?

KARLEY: There is a being here. Her name is a Joan. Is that what I did with her?

ANGELS: Oh, that's interesting. You feel there is a being here that is named Joan? What we sense the energy you are picking up on isn't so much—although you have helped her and worked with her—you have worked also *with* her; in other words as an "equal" more. It's not just that you help her but that you work *alongside* her. It's an "Alongside of" relationship is the best way to put it.

KARLEY: They say our DNA almost matches.

ANGELS: Well, that is the idea of "alongside her."

KARLEY: I understand. Okay.

ANGELS: But your mind is a very active mind and you often enjoy challenge; so you will take up new challenges, new souls and so forth so you can keep that active. You don't sit in one place with your soul or your mind—on both sides of the curtain. You enjoy activity in your working. That is what we sense. We would welcome any questions you brought with you and anything you would like to get clarification on.

KARLEY: I would like information about the two beings that would have been my twins. My son's twin. To find out what he needs from my son or what he needs in general. Whatever it is they need—honoring their needs for each other; and also so my son can get to the point where he can move into his purpose because I believe he does have a divine purpose for being here. At this point I see that the point where he is at he may not be able to do that; it's going to be harder for him to get to that point. I guess that is the question.

(Explanation of what she is asking about: In the womb one twin absorbed the other. One died and one lived; but the soul of the dead twin is still present around the living twin. The living twin talks to the dead one. The twin in spirit form is named Mark. The one who remains alive in body is Roy.)

ANGELS: What we sense is that the one in spirit needed a body to work through. That spirit (named Mark) was not able to take a third dimensional body himself. It would have been too dense and the fear of "getting lost" in the human arena—drama, density—did not serve the purpose. What you are calling the purpose. So, the idea is that one energy—what you call a Higher Energy or spiritual energy—can remain pure. We are going to use the word pure although we are not entirely comfortable with the word. What we mean by pure is less dense; can remain less dense but have a vehicle or body through which to operate without completely losing itself in the third dimensional density. Do you understand?

KARLEY: Yes, he needed to be lighter.

ANGELS: But still needed a vehicle.

KARLEY: They have this attachment then?

ANGELS: They have an agreement.

KARLEY: That's a better word.

ANGELS: What we sense the agreement is: One says "I will stay in the density and be that bridge between heaven and earth" and the other one stays in the spiritual realm and says, "I will be that bridge between heaven and earth. With two of us operating the bridge can be complete." The idea was: which one would operate better in human form and which one would operate better in spiritual body? That is how we sense or feel it. The energy in the spiritual realm that you call Mark is an energy that does better when it is not incarnate but needs a physical human body in which to operate if it is to reach the earth and affect the earth. So, the soul purpose of the one on the earth is to be a vehicle for the one off the earth.

KARLEY: The reason Roy incarnated I think is because he had a strong connection to me.

ANGELS: We would not put it that way. We feel that both of these souls have a connection with you. Obviously that agreement has to be between all the energies, or souls, in order for it to be realized as it has been on earth. We don't feel that one is closer to you. But, perhaps you might say that you feel the one who is on the earth understands and can handle—still it's a struggle for him—but can handle better the earthly frequencies than the one who chose not to incarnate. You, who are comfortable in both realms, earthly and non-earthly, feel that you can help the "earthly one" to anchor and to hold and be on the earth as long as he feels he needs to be to do the soul agreement with Mark. That is why you would feel closer because there is an earthly tie or agreement going on; so your human would feel connected. It's not really closer in the spiritual body. In your spiritual body you don't feel one is closer than the other. We feel that you are concerned about the earthly son—you are concerned about the ability of the human son to anchor.

KARLEY: That's along the lines of grounding? Yes?

ANGELS: Yes. Grounding. Anchoring. Being able to anchor the human part concerns you. But, there is also a need for you to help your son to understand the gift of the human body. The GIFT of the human body. Not just that spirit bodies are better; but truly what are the gifts of being embodied or human. We are going to pause and ask you to tell us what you believe the gifts of the human body are.

KARLEY: The ability to help and love each other. The ability to enjoy the normal things. To enjoy being connected to this planet; even though the frequency is not what they are used to it is still a beautiful place.

ANGELS: Of course the helping and the love can be done without a human body. But perhaps if your son would understand that there are feelings and experiences and energies which the human body can understand and receive and interpret which lend the soul growth experiences. In other words that feeling, that emotion, that density sometimes even, complexity, even pain in the physical body, elation in the physical body—these experiences such as the anger and the joy and the wide gambit of emotions to fully be experienced by humans offer information that no other realm can touch. So, while in human embrace those wide ranging experiences rather than feeling that at a moment's notice one wants to go out of body—but allow oneself to sit even with that which is difficult. You understand although you may not like it, that even in difficult experiences you gain a great deal of learning and wisdom but it is hard to pass that on to someone else and to say, "Wait a minute, if you are willing to sit here and really feel, know, learn from and ask the physical body, 'what is it that you are trying to teach me?' What is it that you are teaching me abdomen? What is it that you are teaching me? That grounding or anchoring in the body has some lessons that perhaps are worth gaining. You see? It can be hard to ask someone who is more comfortable out of body to do that anchoring. Do you understand? But sometimes that anchoring is worth doing.

So, we are going to again ask you how you might assist not only your son but anyone else who is having trouble. As a teacher or guide what would you say to them to be comfortable and be willing to embrace their body or their human experience?

KARLEY: What I would probably say is that whatever you feel is something that needs to be felt and it will teach you and bring you to a better place…

ANGELS: Stay with it. Stay with the feeling

KARLEY: Exactly.

ANGELS: Stay even with the pain, anger and sorrow because each one of those emotions is a gift. And that is difficult. That is not comfortable in the human experience and expression. Stay with it to understand its origin. Stay with it to transform it.

KARLEY: In the case of my son, Roy, he has allowed things and circumstances—he's "wired" differently than the rest of us. I guess the brain is different. It was done purposely to protect himself from the feelings, from the anchoring. Does that make sense?

ANGELS: Yes, because many of the autistic children are choosing the autism to keep themselves protected and safe while the world is still in density. Yes, this is correct and they will wake up in a fifth dimensional world that is "safe" for them. We understand. But, it is essential that while they are still embodied as a human that they are not afraid of the human piece or the human part; they don't push it away. It's okay to be human. It's okay. You are strong enough. You can be with a feeling and not have to run away from it. You can sit there and be at peace with it; rather than having to run away.

We do understand the cocoon and we do understand, as you do, that so many are choosing autism for that protection of the cocoon and to awaken when the fifth dimensional earth is established. But, at the same time it is important while human to feel that the human experience—we don't like humans to be at war with anything—because the irritation that develops creates disharmony. We like humans to feel and embrace, "Oh, I'm feeling this now. Why did I draw that to me and what do I have to learn from it?" Then they can integrate the experience and release it. Simultaneously with understanding: Yes, there is a protection there, but also not to be afraid of the human. It's okay, you are stronger than any of those emotions you are afraid of.

KARLEY: Does he understand that he doesn't have to be afraid of those emotions? He's better than—

ANGELS: —he used to be.

KARLEY: He used to be.

ANGELS: Part of that is the energy that is connected with him. If you wish him to feel less fear and difficulty say to the energy (Mark) tell him to tell Roy, "It's okay, you won't drag me down."

That energy might, we sense, be contributing a bit to the idea of "don't get too low or you'll pull me down," so it's important that Mark understands that part of the job of his other half on earth is to BE on earth. You know? Is to be on earth. And not to be always pulling him off the earth; or to be afraid of the earth. You can be safe on earth. The thing which the Masters understand is that you can be safe on earth; you can be spiritual and safe simultaneously. Learning that for both Mark and Roy—or the earth and the heaven part is how we would put it—is also a good lesson. You don't always have to be pulling off the earth to be safe. There is a way to achieve Mastery through feeling; through being on the earth. You can learn to trust yourself—no matter what is thrown at you, you can still find your heavenly or spiritual self. So, there is a lesson there as well. You might want to communicate that to Mark as well. Just in the everyday. No rush. Nothing intense. We don't mean to give any feeling of intensity or anything; but just feeling in a gentle or generous way that one can have a foot on the earth and one can be safe. Do you understand that perspective? Does that assist you?

KARLEY: Yes, that's pretty much why I had gotten ill and gotten cancer. I didn't feel safe here. It was as if I had to make a decision which was, "Do I want to really stay or do I really want to go?" I decided to stay. My Higher Self was, "You have a choice. You stay or your go; that's it." Once I made the decision to stay here I felt safer.

ANGELS: To teach others that idea—not to reject the human and all these experiences that you call the Dark and the Light—the human duality experience and the energy of Unity are all ways of gathering information and ways of learning that have interest, that have merit. And once you decided it was okay and it interested you and you were willing to embrace learning in that way you can teach others that no matter where you are there is something to be gained and learned. You don't have to leave or exit or reject it; that's how we would put it. And that benefits your work on the "other side" of the "curtain" as well; of course it would have to.

Everything you do here is connected to everything you do on the "other side of the curtain" as well—there is no separation there. And you know that.

KARLEY: When Roy was very small I can't remember but I think about eight months old, he did try to exit I believe. Was that true?

ANGELS: We sense it was the other soul pulling him off.

KARLEY: The decision to stay; wouldn't that have anchored him a little bit? Because I do believe as a very young soul, of course it wasn't a conscious decision, but there was a decision made that he would stay.

ANGELS: That he would carry that "piece," but it doesn't mean it's easy.

KARLEY: Right. Right.

ANGELS: It's still difficult.

KARLEY: He chose to stay and yet not to anchor.

ANGELS: Yes, because it is still difficult for this soul. Being high vibrational. There are other homes, galaxies and planets that he is more comfortable on than this one. But, it is part of the learning, the teaching and this experience and you have agreed to assist him to gain that experience and so it is a beautiful thing that you are doing.

KARLEY: The way that I see his brain being wired there are certain chemicals and impulses that are almost like a "misfiring" of neurons or chemicals or whatever; that stops him from making connections with people. Take for instance myself. There are times when he shows love and there are times when I look in his eyes and it is very empty when I'm showing him love or whatever. Will that change with the anchoring or will that not change until we hit fifth (dimension)?

ANGELS: It will help a little but also he is more comfortable with what we would call an "Andromedean brain." What you call "wired" to the Andromedean galaxy, and he receives his information and is much more comfortable to receive his information from that Frequency Generation "Station." (The angels laugh uproariously about this and say: "We laugh because there are so few human words to describe what we are trying to explain that we have to use these terms. And they make us laugh. But you understand what we saying even though it is a limited vocabulary. Humans have yet to develop the words they need to describe the ideas they are discovering.")

This Andromedean brain is what you are sensing or feeling to be "cold." It is not "cold" actually it is more what you saw in Star Trek in the character of Spock. It is not cold but it is not wired the same. It tends to be more analytical. That is what we sense you are feeling when you connect and you don't feel something back that is quite human or in the same way.

KARLEY: It isn't feeling something back but I look in his eyes and they are distant and glazed over—kind of.

ANGELS: Connecting somewhere else.

KARLEY: Like an emotion whether positive or negative it is like he is connecting there; he is connecting somewhere else.

ANGELS: It can help you to think of Spock on Star Trek as a humorous and light way to understand that kind of processing.

KARLEY: I do understand and I think that's a way to think of my experiences with the little Gray people with funny eyes—I forgot what they are called. The almond-shaped eyes.

ANGELS: The Grays.

KARLEY: Yes, my experience with them is that they only have one emotion which is survival.

ANGELS: Yes, you are correct.

KARLEY: They don't have any type of emotion. The one time they appealed to me for anything was because there was a woman who needed to survive and they asked if they could have a piece of skin from my finger so they could help her; because obviously there was some reason she was in danger. That was the only time I saw any emotion coming from them. They are very much the same way you are talking about; they are anchored somewhere else.

ANGELS: They are quite an interesting story. Well, way back—we'll tell it like a fairy tale story because some information appears to people to be fairy tales. You understand about the galactic stories—you know there have been a lot of divisions and a lot of war.

KARLEY: And destruction.

ANGELS: And destruction and so forth. The Grays come from way back at the time of the Arcturian ascension. At the time when the Arcturians did their ascension into the Fifth Dimension like the earth will be doing those who could not "make the leap," and hold the higher vibration were cast-off.

KARLEY: They were put into ships.

ANGELS: Yeah. They were cast-off is how we will put it. They are searching for an identity; they are searching in their deepest part. They feel that they have an injury in some way. They are trying to find a method of healing their species and their own personal wounding; and outside of that they don't care about anything else. It appears cold. But, as you are saying they say, "We need to survive and we will do what we need to do to survive." And that's where that comes from.

They are less destructive by far than the Reptilians. The Grays do not conquer for the sake of feeding off a created hell realm. The Reptilians conquer for the need of a hell realm to feed off of. It's a different agenda so to speak. But, at times if the Grays could serve the Reptilians or the Reptilians could serve the Grays they would join forces, but not because of a common agenda except at that moment.

KARLEY: Yes, it does come from there, because they have needed our DNA to keep the species going.

ANGELS: Yes, but for the Grays it isn't out of hatred. It isn't out of an emotion of evil so much as it is out of survival, which can lead to an act which appears to a human as evil but it is a different motivation than the Reptilian motivation.

KARLEY: Like when I met this woman they made sure that I met this woman and when they took the DNA from my finger they asked. I still have a wound from that. But, they asked.

ANGELS: And so you agreed because you believed it was a good cause? Or was it done by force?

KARLEY: It was not done by force. When I saw this woman I felt compassion for her and when they took the piece out of my finger I agreed because of her.

ANGELS: But, we sense they had been "working" with her, that this was not a random soul. In other words it wasn't just a random soul—it was someone they had been "working" on. They don't just go around helping every sick human.

KARLEY: No, it was that I was helping her. She was odd looking. She had long dark hair and they don't have hair. She had their funny eyes. She looked like them in some respects but she also looked human. That seemed to be why they needed human DNA. If it had been their species they could have helped her.

ANGELS: She was a DNA splice. You understand? You understand how much DNA experimentation has gone on.

KARLEY: Oh, yes.

ANGELS: What we are saying is she wasn't just a random, "Oh, let's go help the human race." They don't go around helping the human race.

KARLEY: She was one of them but they needed human DNA to help her. I was in a room. There was a man in there; he reminded me of a magician the way he was dressed.

ANGELS: Kind of like a Merlin figure?

KARLEY: Sort of. And there was a star on the floor. I went into this room—he didn't touch me he didn't say anything. He just walked around and showed me around and there were almost like parts—what seemed like parts of humans. They were using DNA. For some reason they needed mine. But I agreed to it because I felt compassion for her and felt if I didn't she might die.

ANGELS: She was one of their DNA blends.

KARLEY: I must have been a close DNA match or something.

ANGELS: But, also they are trying to bring into this "clone" some of the psychic abilities that you carry. And that is why. And the information that you carry as an "archivist," so that it can get inside this being so that this being will have the knowledge and the information that you carry. Do you understand?

KARLEY: In fact you use the word cloning. The man who was like the wizard I think he was showing me test tube babies; that is what it felt like.

ANGELS: Absolutely. Absolutely. And we understand the fear carried by the Grays about their annihilation. We understand that. What we are always concerned with and have witnessed with this DNA experimentation is that it can be very difficult on a soul—an energy— because there can be no soul group alignment. For example, if you clone or you combine together a cow and a pig the confusion of, "Am I cow or pig," is powerfully disturbing. Where do I go? Everything needs to be "ensouled" in a group identification in a vibrational way. Without it the "lostness" is profound.

KARLEY: Yes.

ANGELS: Now, one of the things that is happening currently is that those who were a result of past DNA experimentation for example between the Reptilians and the Pleiadians or the Reptilians and almost any other group you want to put your hands on; there have been beings who have been created who are lost.

KARLEY: Do they have a soul?

ANGELS: Well, the werewolf. The idea of combing a wolf and a man you see. Some of these creations must be pitied and they feel extremely lost. The only thing they have been able to try and do is to try and create some kind of group to belong to which is one of the reasons they will try to draw others into their group so that they feel less lost. The "lostness" is not okay to the Angelic Beings. We do not feel "comfortable" with humans and other species pretending they are "God," and playing freely with God's energy without Love in their intention. Because those who are learning Life Creation at the level of the *highest* Merlin work are doing it in a path of great love and would never create an energy or a species that was not fully ensouled. But those who play at Wizard, such as the being that you saw, can often create and wreak havoc, as you know and saw in Atlantis. On Earth there has been a lot of playing Wizard with energies and it has not gone well when that happens. So, we understand the sympathy that you feel but it is also important for you to understand that your willingness to do so, "Yes, I'm going to try and help this poor being who is experimented on and try to save them," perhaps you understand that now you have created a karmic link with that soul.

KARLEY: Right.

ANGELS: There is a responsibility that you will have with that soul. To help that soul find its way home. All people create karma by action and it's important when you do something that you are in clarity and willingness to take on that karmic agreement and that you understand it is not something you are able to walk away from once you have "stuck your finger in it."

KARLEY: Literally.

ANGELS: Literally. Thank you so much for sharing that with us because it is important. Is there another question or two before she grows tired?

KARLEY: What would be the best way in everyday life—nothing I would have to really work at or do any real healing—that would make Roy and Mark feel safe so that Roy could really anchor if that's in his Highest Good?

ANGELS: First of all you must feel safe yourself. You said that you are feeling safer since your illness you said.

KARLEY: It's been twenty-five years since my illness but, yes. Especially in the world. I never felt safe in the world. I go out into the world and there are no butterflies in my stomach. Where I work I deal with people who have just gotten out of prison but there is never an issue of my feeling safe; at the end of the day I know that I'll be protected and everything will be fine.

ANGELS: And it's important for you to help all of those you come in contact with to begin to feel and touch and understand that Divine Spark that IS the safety. Because at the end of the day, as you say, when something comes at you if you have that Divine Spark, that safety.

KARLEY: Right, they can't touch you.

ANGELS: And what we are talking about with the clones is that unless they can find their safety it is a horrible existence. Each and every being that you talk to you remind them that that is where the safety is. It is not outside of you, it is within you. What you call or humans call God, which is of course far too limited for the Truth of that energy, but it is in the end that thing which will keep you feeling safe.

It is essential to teach them how to connect and re-connect with that piece and that part; knowing that whatever comes at them it is never impacting that piece. That is a sacred part, a sacred piece which will never be allowed to be destroyed or corrupted; it can certainly look like it is and it can certainly feel like it is, but ultimately anyone who contains that piece when God breathes in, will find their way back home because it is a piece of the energy which, once again, when inhaled back home will return to the Source. That's the piece we are talking about. That's the piece that keeps you safe and connected. And when you work with any children, with what you call prisoners, that awakening, that safety is the only thing—that ensoulment—which will help an individual get through the most trying time. It is one of the reasons we are going to say that there have been many black magic experiments to divide or destroy the soul.

When they take the heart out beating—the idea is: I will control you now, I will own a piece of your soul, I will consume it, or I will destroy you. Destroying the Divine piece can't be done through taking the heart out. If you convince the person that it can be done then the person will struggle with it for many lifetimes but they will eventually be able to find the divine core. Another thing which has been done—piecing-up bodies. Trying to destroy the soul by cutting up a body as was done in the story of Osiris. That was done to try to destroy his soul

KARLEY: That was Seth wasn't it?

ANGELS: Yes, and he actually ate the penis to gain the power he could get through the act of eating it. But even that did not work because that soul did not—it thought it had for awhile—it got lost here and there but it is not lost now.

The only place we get concerned is in these clonings or mish-moshed pieces which confuse a soul. Then it can be hard for that soul to find identification. But, what we want to tell you is that the trick is always to go back to the original DNA piece. If a soul has been pieced together like a Frankenstein's monster which is essentially what that story is about—when a soul has been "pieced together"—find the original piece. And you as a healer if you want to help these souls that you saw; find the original piece of DNA and let it call to you. Enter right through there and PSHHhhh….. enter right through there and regrow the soul from there.

KARLEY: So, the original DNA piece from which—

ANGELS: From which everything else was attached on to.

KARLEY: If I send them Light and Love the original piece of DNA will come through that connection?

ANGELS: You'll feel it right away. That's a Reptillian soul, that's a Pleiadian soul, that's an Arcturian soul, that's a human soul or whatever.

KARLEY: Okay. That little piece from my finger.

ANGELS: That piece will come right through to you and speak to you and you will move it back to its original soul group and "re-ensoul" it and that's the best way to do the re-integration work.

KARLEY: Okay. The being on this planet called my mother. There was an issue of a beating. I was probably about twenty years old. With that beating there seemed to be a piece of me that was lost or left or whatever. Is that a correct statement?

ANGELS: Again it is correct for your human experience. This may seem very odd and we apologize for the "oddness" of it—much of what have said today may sound odd to many people.

KARLEY: Not to me.

ANGELS: But, first of all do you understand the energy that we are going to call Vlad Dracula?

KARLEY: No.

ANGELS: You have heard of Dracula, yes?

KARLEY: Yes.

ANGELS: Well, the energy that is called Dracula does exist. It is a fourth dimensional energy. Okay? You are pretty aware there seem to be a lot of vampires in the world. That energy did incarnate as a human in a life called Vlad the Impaler. A very dark life with torturing and impaling and so forth. We think of him even as the darkest incarnated soul; which is quite a statement. And that energy works from the fourth dimension through humans. It needs human bodies in which to operate in which to create a Family of Dark. He is the leader of the Family of Dark. He worked through your mother to try and get and vampire you to get you into a state of fear where you could be attached to and sucked dry. Does that help you?

KARLEY: Yes.

ANGELS: It's a different way to look at it; but from our side of the curtain that's what it looks like.

KARLEY: Yes. Did they succeed? They obviously did to some extent.

ANGELS: Well, you've always had an interest in the Family of Dark. You've always had an interest in what they do.

KARLEY: I've played with the shadow.

ANGELS: You've liked having a foot in both worlds. But, what we would like to tell you—you're doing it again! You like to be the Archivist. You want to know it all. What's the Family of Dark up to and what's the Family of Light up to? How can you retrieve information from the Hall of Records if you can't retrieve information from ALL the Hall? You see?

So, rather than what humans would say, "Oh, she is so dark," or "Oh, she is so Light," your motivation doesn't come from—you wouldn't wed yourself to a Family of Dark and you wouldn't wed yourself to a Family of Light because you want to wed yourself to ALL of it.

KARLEY: That balance.

ANGELS: It's more like a librarian that wants access to all the stacks. It would drive you crazy if they said, "You can't go there. That's the closed stacks." You would say, "I'm getting in there." That's more the motivation for you.

KARLEY: Well, the Dark actually carries a lot of intelligence about their situation.

ANGELS: They are smart. Because the Family of Dark does not have fear—not of the same things. Perhaps they fear the Light; but they don't fear some of these places. So they can get to certain information more easily. You know this. And so does this conduit. Not many humans understand this.

KARLEY: Something you brought up in the beginning. Why I've stayed with my husband.

ANGELS: As a study.

KARLEY: Exactly.

ANGELS: But, you've also begun to step a little bit out of neutrality because what you are beginning to understand is that the pain that has been caused by the Family of Dark is getting to you. That is creating little bit of havoc in your soul.

KARLEY: Right.

ANGELS: That's a discussion for another time. Let's close on this note. One of the things you are beginning to see happen is that people are having to "choose sides." Are you with the Family of Dark or the Family of Light? The reason is because the energies of destruction and creation are starting to feel pulled apart. That's another discussion but it is the idea that the creational light energies and the destructive dark energies are squaring off. And you've had a foot in both worlds and now your legs are being pulled apart; like an earthquake gap opening up between them.

We laugh with you to give you an image you can understand. And that is where we feel you are right now. We hope this has helped to clarify some things for you.

KARLEY: Thank you, it has.

CHAPTER EIGHTEEN

A SEEKER QUESTIONS THE EXISTENCE OF "OTHER"

HAROLD P.

ANGELS: We are most delighted to have this opportunity to be with you and to work with you in this way. As always, this is Archangel Ariel who is speaking with you, and all the other angels are also in attendance. We wish to thank you and to remind you of who you are today and also to have a joyous occasion of sharing and speaking with you. The opportunity to share and to work with you in this way is our joy as well as your joy, and we look forward to this exchange.

We want to remind you, of course, that you are a Seeker. As a Seeker, you have acquired and gained information from many different places, many different civilizations, planetary experiences and galactic experiences outside of this universe. Throughout God's creations, you have been gathering information. You have come here on the Earth at this time to gather information as well; to study, to learn and to seek.

One of the things that you want to begin to understand is this question: Can there be anything outside of the Self? Is the idea of an "other" a lie? Is it possible for an "other" to exist? And this question is what your Higher Self is posing at this time. You are searching, because it came through your searches for you to begin to feel and sense and to understand that perhaps there can never be anything other than the Self; that everything which one perceives is always continually a projection of the Self. It is not possible to be looking at or perceiving anything which does not in some way reflect the Self.

As a result of that, you became very interested in this planet called the Earth because of its profound separation consciousness. The idea of the "other" is very alive on this planet, and you've witnessed and understood how other beings, other life forms perceive the Self in relationship to "other," and you understand how it is construed and how it is set up. You understand that advanced civilizations understand that concept, that there is no "other" than the Self, and as a result, come to the conclusion that in order to treat the Self well and to love the Self and like the Self, one must treat others with the same values, the same ideas because it is you.

And you understand that if you look at a painting or a picture and someone next to you looks at the same painting or picture, you are looking at a very different canvas. You are looking at a reflection of yourself and you cannot look at a canvas from a point of view other than the Self. You cannot perceive a painting outside of the Self and only perceive it as the Self perceives it. You understand that the person standing next to you can only perceive that painting or that work of art as their Self sees it. You will never know how they perceive it and they will never know how you perceive it. But you make an agreement to perceive it and you make an agreement to call it a painting, and you make an agreement perhaps even to call it a portrait. But how you truly perceive that and how it sets up inside of you is your own individual self-reflection.

That idea is quite fascinating to you. So, we believe that the philosopher in you, the Seeker in you, the sage in you, the wizard in you, all of these parts of you are coming to this time and this place to perceive the nature of reality as it pertains to the Self versus Other. So, it is an interesting study that you make, and of course it is also one that could drive you insane because of its chameleon-like reality.

But we also understand that somewhere inside of that, you believe and know it to be the essence of the God that resides within you. And it is fascinating. You feel that if you can get through that portal, if you can solve that question and get through that portal, then somehow, the reunification with All That Is will occur. So, we are delighted to have this discussion with you today. We are delighted to work with you today about that question and that topic, and we welcome you and thank you for the opportunity to share.

We're going to ask you if you understand our opening message and how you feel about it and how you relate to it at this time.

HAROLD: Yes, I do. I don't think, growing up, I ever realized that I could do this. But I agree with you and I had a number of questions I was going to ask you. One of them was to ask about some experiences that I had and one of them relates, I think, to what it is that you were just talking about.

I was with—I didn't know then who they were—but I was with Tibetan Buddhists in Brooklyn on a three-week meditation retreat. While meditating, I had a number of different experiences. But one of them was very, very significant. Some were with my eyes open and some were with my eyes closed, and this is one with eyes closed. This was what I was aware of: I mean I saw it as if my eyes were open and I was falling through a hole, a well. And I remember thinking so clearly, now I'm going to die. Then I just went into—I'm going to say it this way but then I'm going to change it. I went into whiteness. It was just whiteness. There wasn't me. I wasn't seeing white and white wasn't out there. It was just whiteness. There was no sense of myself, there was just whiteness. And then I came back, if that's the right word. I think for me that was just so experientially significant.

I think my question is going to be, what happened? Was that time a suspension of my sense of self? Was it whatever people mean by a mystical experience? What happened? I know it was significant and I know there was no sense of myself or what was going on. I had no sense of what I was seeing or what I was experiencing; just whiteness was occurring.

ANGELS: You went through the rabbit hole, yes?

HAROLD: Yes.

ANGELS: And of course, there are many who talk about going through the rabbit hole or going through the vortexes and so forth, the portals. But it relates exactly to our opening message and was in fact another example of your studies. You were trying to again answer the question if there was anything truly outside of you. Is there anything inside, outside? What are you in relationship to All That Is?

HAROLD: Yes.

ANGELS: And what it is that you begin to perceive is that if you go through yourself—for that is how we view that journey; you went through yourself—if you go through yourself in a state of complete and total willingness to surrender, what you will always get to is that state which we will call, for lack of better words, where Nothing and Everything reside. Where you were is a state of pure potential. In other words, you were at a state before creation, the state where all is possible; pure energy before it is formed. And at that moment is the idea of, "And then there was the Word."

HAROLD: Right.

ANGELS: What created or called you back to you was the Word. So it was that you disappeared to your experience before you were created and became created by your Word, by your intention to create yourself again. Now, at that moment or at that time, you could have created anything. You could have, had you really decided to push the boundaries, if you will, you could have become anything at that moment. All potential, all possibility exists in that White Space.

But you felt, and your Higher Self felt, at that moment that you wanted to return to you. So you spoke the word of you and from the pure matter, the pure energy, you recreated you. But if at that time you had wished to shift yourself wherever it was, you could have done it. What you were only interested in, though, was the idea of whether or not you as human could reach a state of you as All That Is. So you wanted to bring the information of you as All That Is back to you, who is human.

And if you had chosen to shift into "other," you who is human would have felt the experiment had failed. It's a strange way to put it but you were satisfying your human in that experiment, so you wanted to bring the information back to your human. So it was absolutely decided by your human to come back with the information of what it felt like to be All That Is or at the point of complete and total potential or possibility. Now your human carries that information, for at this point in time, it is your human who is doing the seeking. So, you honored your human, who is seeking, by returning with the information and the experience, so it could be integrated through your human. Do you understand?

HAROLD: Yes.

ANGELS: So, it was a beautiful moment of disappearing and then returning and bringing with you what it was you experienced and learned. And what it was that you experienced and learned is the Formlessness; and you understood why, out of formlessness, God wanted to create form. You forgive God for creating form. You understood that the formlessness is nice but doesn't feel quite as exciting as the form. Do you understand?

HAROLD: Yes.

ANGELS: So often, many who are formed are angry at the Formless Self for creating the Formed Self. But once you had experienced the Formless Self, you truly understood the pull to create the formed self. And so it is that you understand why life and form were created in the first place. If you had died into the formlessness and disappeared, it is as if you would have felt that all those many hundreds and millions of years of Seeker studies would have been lost, too. So you weren't ready to disappear into formlessness. You felt that you still had questions that you wanted answered. So your experience was an answer to your question. Do you understand?

HAROLD: Yeah. My first question was going to be, who am I? I must have had past lives. I have no idea what they might have been. But you're actually providing some answers to that, in terms of speaking about how it is that I got to—

ANGELS: Well, you are a very, very old soul, of course, and not just old in terms of human, for humans usually mean that old soul as human, but you are more than a human old soul. You are what we call a Seeker soul, and Seekers have decided that they wish to study life forms everywhere. They're very, very interested, very curious souls, and they want to study it everywhere, so they don't just stop at one outpost. They go to a lot of outposts.

Now, the problems that Seeker souls sometimes have is that even a Seeker needs to settle on a soul progression through a sentient form, and you did this in the Arcturian. So, you did choose to stick around for a while, if you will, to put it that way, in the Arcturian form and to teach and to learn and to study and to be and to experience what it meant to be Arcturian. And through that experience, through your lives in the Arcturian forms—again it was a way of your understanding Other and Self through the Arcturian perspective.

The Arcturian perspective of Other and Self has grown through its evolutionary process, so that when an Arcturian looks at another, it comes closer and closer to seeing the Self. So when an Arcturian is looking at another Arcturian, there's very little difference in the physical appearance. They look alike. An Arcturian is always reminded by the fact that when they look at Other, they are truly looking at the Self, by the fact that the appearances are very alike. And they like that because it is a constant reminder. If everyone on this planet looked like you, it would be much harder for you to harm them.

And it is a way that the Arcturians have pulled together to remind themselves to love one another as the Self, and you liked that. You thought that was a good idea. But you did understand the limitations. If all are looking like the self, you began to think, well, maybe it's a little bit of a cop-out, because it's easy to love when you look at another who looks like you, but what about a planet where nobody looks like you? Can you still learn to love them? And then you chose to come here, on Earth. You see?

You decided that it was all well and good to understand and to be at peace and to be among those who thought like you and looked like you and cared about each other like you and worked together in community like you. Boy, it was harmonious and it felt good, but your Seeker soul began to get a little bored and it started to think, 'Well, I'm going to just go to a place of greater chaos and I'm going to study there.'

So, you came to the human soul progression and decided to experience it. It was a tough go for you for quite awhile because it was such a shock, coming from the Arcturian peace to the human chaos that you got kicked around a lot in your earlier experiences. You came here with interest and you learned quite quickly that if you thought as an Arcturian on this planet you were going to be in big trouble; that if you thought that every human was looking at you and caring about you as they cared about themselves, that wasn't going to lead you anywhere good fast, because there were plenty of humans out there seeing you as the idea of "a sucker born every minute." And you learned that you didn't want to be a sucker to somebody else's hijinks.

So after getting taken quite a few times, you decided to wise up. And one of the reasons that you took an intellectual approach to operate from was because you decided very quickly in your incarnations that being an intellectual, being a scholar and learning as much as you could, you decided was going to be the safest route for you and would protect you the most on the Earth.

Some others chose a big body. They thought, 'Well, if I'm going to be a safe, I need to be a warrior.' Their desire to be safe on the Earth, they thought, was going to happen through the warrior self. So they took warrior lives and warrior identification. Now, once one is identified with a particular vibrational signature such as warrior or scholar or server, it is how you learn your lessons—through that progression. So you identify with that and you stick with it. You can be at war as a scholar but you're going to be at war as a scholar soul, not as a warrior soul, and it's a different way of approaching it.

And your choice to take on the scholar soul approach was because, as it is for all humans, you thought it was going to keep you the safest. So you chose that.

You said, "I'm going to acquire as much knowledge as I can," because you were one who believed knowledge is power. You could see how a warrior would say, power is power, but you believe knowledge is power. Others might think that a quick wit and good looks and being able to talk your way out of a situation are power. They're the ones that are good manipulators. Often entertainers are the ones who tend to incarnate with the good looks; and they figure that's how they're going to keep themselves safe, you know?

Others think that the spiritual route is going to keep them safe, and they do it that way. The servers feel that if they are humble and loving and align themselves with their heart center that is going to be the best route. Each and every one of you found that your choices kept you safe to some extent; but you also found yourself in great danger and paid heavy prices for those choices. Each one has a strength and a weakness.

HAROLD: I was in the seminary for a while and then I left. And then I guess being in the seminary on this go-around made me aware of philosophy, and that's eventually what I pursued. So is there some kind of interrelationship between the priestly and the scholarly?

ANGELS: Yes. As you know, the priests were in control of many of the manuscripts.

HAROLD: Right.

ANGELS: It was through the church that knowledge was gained, and it was the only way to be safe. Scholars were always attracted to the church through human history because it was where esoteric knowledge was held, even pre-Christianity, by the priests or the cults.

HAROLD: Right.

ANGELS: So esoteric knowledge was always held that way. But the approach that you took was that you enjoyed the knowledge, whereas the priests often enjoyed the power of saying, "I am closest to God," and that was not your way. You enjoyed being closest to the knowledge, so you would often seek out priests and temples but you were seeking it out from the intention of wanting the knowledge that was held there, not from wanting the power that was held there. It was a different intention. Often, the priest souls would seek it out and get addicted to the power of the priesthood, and those priest souls would then find themselves in dark places.

Now, you of course know that, often, what scholars did, in their shadow side or dark side, was they had knowledge and they hid it. They understood knowledge is power and they would start to hide the knowledge. They realized they didn't want all the riff-raff having it, and so that would be the shadow of a scholar.

HAROLD: It's kind of interesting because I think that in my teaching career, my focus was to enable the kids to be able to acquire the knowledge themselves and then be able to utilize it for themselves. It wasn't that I was giving it to them as such; I was trying to enable them to do it for themselves.

ANGELS: Right. So you weren't working at it from your lower self, you were working from your Higher Self as a scholar. But the shadow side of the scholar, you could see, would not have that point of view.

HAROLD: Right.

ANGELS: But of course, you're working in the Light in this life. So you understand that you want to empower others.

HAROLD: Yes, and as a result of the courses I taught they were empowered and they could do whatever they wanted to with their lives.

ANGELS: Yes. You wanted them to know and understand not only what you knew and understood but also, again, what their own Self would perceive. And you began to utilize your study of Other and Self, wondering will those others ever acquire the same knowledge that you knew? No, because your knowledge is your self-knowledge, their knowledge is their self-knowledge.

HAROLD: Right.

ANGELS: And that leads us back, of course, to your original desire, which is to teach others how to understand that they are the portal.

HAROLD: Right. I would like to ask another dimension of myself, which is what is my own sexuality?

ANGELS: Well, Arcturians are very asexual. The Pleiadians are very sexual. It was the Pleiadians who taught tantric sex. And Mary Magdalene and Jesus were coming in, particularly Mary, to teach and understand the route of sexuality as a route for God consciousness. That was a Pleaidean gift.

The Arcturians, on the other hand, are very asexual. And what they did is they evolved themselves—again, they understood that sexuality often leads to war and violence and misuse. So what they did is became more and more gender neutral as well. And they used reproduction as—it was sacred but in a very different way. There was no lust; there was only the idea of a spiritual—sacred, yes, in this way.

The mother or father were chosen by the elders, by the Arcturian elders as being the most prime examples of the highest energy, because they understood if you breed those who are at the highest, you create a higher species continually. So the mother/fathers were selected and it was a great honor. Reproduction did not occur with the idea of coitus, as you know it on this planet. It occurred from the idea of joining and intertwining DNA, in a sense, the cells, but not through the sexual act as you would think of it.

So when the child was produced from the two parents, it was actually given away to be raised by those who are selected to be the proper parents. So there isn't the same reaction to the sexual act, to the reproductive act or the birth of children. So of course, for an Arcturian to come to this planet, they are also often drawn to lives of celibacy and spiritual study, because it feels to them that actually, they see that reproduction and children is often a very karmic act. Do you understand?

HAROLD: Yes.

ANGELS: It almost feels to an Arcturian soul on this planet that it's not the way to bring a species up. To them it often seems that they're bringing the species down. So there's a lot of trouble even "getting it" as an Arcturian soul. So many Arcturians will be childless and celibate. Perhaps if they are involved in relationships, even if they have homosexual relationships, they will often be more like partnerships than strong sexual attraction.

An Arcturian soul such as you—scholars vibrate more neutrally—so it's a very neutral energy already. An Arcturian scholar would tend to be sexually a more neutral place to be, where the attraction would be toward the individual, regardless of the sex and would be about wanting partnership with someone who would fulfill the Self, regardless of the sex, and even perhaps regardless of age. It would be if the mind and if the soul seemed in alignment, well, what the heck? So we sense that this is what your sexuality is coming from and how it would express itself most comfortably.

You could find, for example, a male partner who would be 25. If that male partner was exactly old enough, evolved, to be a partner, to be a true life partner in a sense, what the heck? Or if it was a female who was even a few years older, if the woman was truly in alignment with you, what the heck? It would be so comfortable being around them, to share wisdom or knowledge or information, to travel, to share, to visit, to experience, that would be fine.

So you're going to see, that's you and that's beautiful and that's your expression, whereas someone who is, for example, strongly influenced by their Pleiadian experiences would want drama, would want that idealized idea of the Twin Self in a different way. Oh, we will spiral upward! Sometimes they spiral downward. But they like that. They like that feeling, until they get tired. And then at a point, the Pleiadian soul realizes that's exhausting and they look for a different thing. But the impulses are extremely different. Does that assist you?

HAROLD: Yes, it does. One of the things I always found so fascinating is just the multiplicity of orientations that people can have and how they express themselves at least on the Earth now. I think that's just so fascinating.

ANGELS: And so different than your Arcturian life. The Arcturian was peaceful and calm and community and building. But after a while you felt your Seeker soul was dissatisfied. It just needed a little more. It was like, okay, this was a good stop, I really learned a lot. I got it. I learned about love and community, helping, all for one, one for all. But I have to go further if I'm going to be a true Seeker.

And what we always tell the Seekers and we will remind you, is that at your final stages of your work, what you are planning or looking to do is be a life carrier or life creator. So you learn how—given all the studies that you do throughout the multiverse, you learn then how to take the energy directly from God and to create life forms, to actually populate a planet. So you make the butterflies and you sit with other Seekers and you say, well, how are we going to make this planet today? How are we going to do it? So God doesn't create all life directly. God creates life through the forms that are created from God.

Then you say, how was it first created—form? If God doesn't create all form, how was form ever created? The chicken or the egg, right? You say, well, that doesn't make sense. What happened is this consciousness that was God, it started to—this is the only way we can explain it—it started to "irritate" itself. The energy—imagine that you're in that formless state; be in that "white state" again and imagine that you start to rub together; imagine that your own energies start to rub together. Immediately upon the rubbing together of the Self, something arises and that rubs and that rubs and that rubs, and then all these things rub together—so what we're saying when we say, "God doesn't create," is that God creates but then all the rubbing together creations *they* start to create. What we think of as the Big Bang is God sneezed, you know. He rubbed together and he sneezed, and then they all take it from there. They're still God, though, you see, because they're little pieces of God, and they all rub together and they start to create.

So, as you evolve and you differentiate and you create more and more and you grow wiser and wiser, and this formlessness looks out at itself and sees and knows what it is, it looks all around and sees. And then pieces of that become more and more evolved. The first ones that ever experienced separation began to evolve and move out. And they learned how, in a sense, to take that energy and to act as God and to make form, and they started to have fun with it and play with it. The true Seeker waits until he or she is so aligned with the Divine Self that the true Seeker feels that the creations will be beautiful, the creations will be harmonious. But the impatient Seekers start to create right here, and they create things that are maybe not so harmonious—so you are patient enough that you are waiting.

HAROLD: I'd like to ask about two other similar experiences, not the white experience but in a sense unusual for me. One of them is, I was doing some Reiki stuff and an M.D. came to talk to our group and she was tired and I wanted to give her some energy. So I put my hands in front of—I'm not sure if I touched her but we were close. We created literally a white ball of light and a rainbow between her heart and my heart. The energy was so strong that I actually was like standing on my toes, like my feet weren't—it was not comfortable. But there was such incredible energy.

And it happened one other time where I had—again, it was a workshop and I had my hands on this woman's shoulder. Again, the energy just came through my legs and out my arms, and I was standing on my toes. I could feel it. I had no idea what it was.

ANGELS: Well, do you know that the Arcturians are some of the greatest healers?

HAROLD: No.

ANGELS: The Arcturian are supreme healers. So Arcturians are—the idea that you saw in your movie E.T., where the little finger lights up.

HAROLD: Right.

ANGELS: That is the Arcturian healing. The Arcturians know how to heal, to make that which is out of alignment into perfection. So as you are coming into your integration of your soul—we need to pause for a moment because you need to understand that's what you're doing. You, in your human, as we said—remember we said this—are integrating all the pieces of who you are through this human self.

HAROLD: Right.

ANGELS: Your Arcturian gifts are awakening through you. What are also awakening through you are your Sirian gifts because you have experienced life in the Sirius star system. And the Sirian gifts are the understanding—it's more your esoteric knowledge and wisdom, and also the idea of sacred geometries and how to play, as the Seekers like to, with sacred geometry and creation. So, your Sirian understands some things, if you will, your Arcturian understands other things and so forth. Your Andromedan understands other things and so forth, and you have gained wisdom from many of these other Selves, and you are beginning to integrate them, to create a bigger and higher Self.

What is interesting again is that you realize that it's all the Self; there is no "Other." So you are not "Other." All of these are you; all of these are through you and integrating through you. And you are realizing that you could not give to that woman or any other person unless you had understood truly the idea of Other and Self—that she was you. Because as an Arcturian self, understanding that all others are the Self, it makes it easier for you to heal others, because the separation that exists between a patient and a doctor is what stops the healing from occurring. The doctor always, in traditional, human medicine, looks at the patient when the patient comes in, and the doctor says, you are sick, I am not, I will heal you. I am powerful and knowledgeable, you are not, you see? So everything that has been done from the moment that patient walks in has been done in a consciousness of separation. Then humans expect healing to take place, and they don't understand that in that state, they have created disease. And from a state of disease, they're asking healing to take place.

What you, in your Arcturian self understand is that if you draw a patient to you as the Self and you treat that patient in a manner of healing as you would heal the Self, in a sense, you are already a further step on the path of healing. When you connect to anyone, if you connect to them with the consciousness that you are one, you are all one and you are just bringing that person into a higher alignment with the One, you immediately have created a much stronger human force. So your Arcturian consciousness helps you to go immediately into union and not to go into a separation consciousness.

In other words, when you heal, you don't feel that you're healing someone who can't do it for themselves. You feel that you're lifting yourself as you lift them. It's the idea of all for one, one for all. That's why it's so strong and why you always feel a connection between you and the other.

HAROLD: That makes sense.

ANGELS: That is really where you get the strength to do that and the wisdom is from your knowledge that you're bringing through you from your other selves. It's not Reiki really.

HAROLD: I'm not saying no. I'm just saying that's what we were doing.

ANGELS: But you understand that you have—that you are utilizing Reiki as a vehicle for your Arcturian Self to emerge.

HAROLD: Right.

ANGELS: And your other Selves as well.

HAROLD: I think what was helpful with Reiki is that there's a structure, you know, you do this and you do that.

ANGELS: Absolutely.

HAROLD: So somehow that's helpful for me. Then once you have that, then you can just do it.

ANGELS: Now, the Andromedan Self would be much more likely to do a quite different thing. The Andromedan Self uses a machine. So the Andromedan would be much more likely—and it is not that the Arcturians don't use machines, in a sense. They don't use them in the same way. In other words, the Arcturian might create a room or a space or a place where one would go to receive frequencies to heal, but the Andromedan would be much more likely to say that they would want to create a machine which, utilizing highest wisdom could reintegrate the self when the self moves through it. So an Andromedan approach is a very different approach.

Now, a typical Pleiadian approach to healing, as you can imagine, would be very different. The Pleiadians would use their own bodies as a vehicle, as sound or music or vibration, to bring it into a sense of beauty and peace and to lift up, so that everyone is feeling a joyful, fairy-like energy.

HAROLD: It's kind of interesting, too, because I think the last couple of weeks, stuff has just been going on with me, and I know that's going to happen because I don't listen to music. I like to listen to music but I think somehow I'm changing significantly. I need to just be quiet or be with myself or whatever. I don't know exactly how to express it. But when there are changes, that's one of the things that happens; I just stop doing that. It's not a difficult thing, you know, now I have to stop. It's just that the interest is not there, and that's when it clicks to me that stuff must be going on.

ANGELS: Could you talk to us about the changes you're speaking about?

HAROLD: I'm not even sure I know what they are. I went to Lillydale (spiritual retreat center) and that was another question that I was going to ask. There was a kind of a meditation thing, and during the meditations that were led by this woman, I fell asleep. That just doesn't happen. I don't fall asleep. The last one, I had an image of the face of an old man, and the face was silver and it sparkled. I have no idea what that was.

ANGELS: It was you.

HAROLD: It was me.

ANGELS: There is no other than yourself, you see? As we said, when you stare, you always see the Self. That's what you're learning. That was you.

HAROLD: That's kind of interesting.

ANGELS: You were saying in Lillydale, you had the visions.

HAROLD: Right, of the silver man—myself. Since I had a heart attack, these last few weeks or month or so is the first time I'm kind of getting back to, I don't know, feeling how I did before I was sick. One of the things that I thought was so fascinating is that when I started to teach, in addition to my traditional training, I did other things that were a little bit unusual, and they formed the structure of my traditional work. I was in a wonderful and supportive environment.

What seems to be happening, with meeting Margaret and doing a little bit of Reiki, is that now that I'm retiring and I don't know how long I'm going to be here in this mode, stuff is coming in again. Different kinds of things are coming in. I've also written a manuscript for kids called, "What I Do When I'm Thinking," which I haven't pursued to get published yet. Then I'm going to ask you about another "person" because recently I channeled something or someone called Wah. I have no idea who Wah is. So it was like when I started my teaching career, in addition to the normal teaching, all this other stuff came in. And now, when I'm retiring, all this other stuff is coming in and I'm saying, "Well, it's very nice. I have no idea where all this is going". So that was going to be my other question.

ANGELS: Is that not delightful for your Seeker Self?

HAROLD: I love it.

ANGELS: All these new opportunities to study and learn and acquire knowledge.

HAROLD: Absolutely.

ANGELS: Arcturians will often make themselves very sick and then heal themselves. It's very common for an Arcturian to experience at least one major healing crisis in their life, at least one, because Arcturians are very interested, as we said, in healing. So when they come to the Earth, they will often give themselves cancer or, in your case, you say heart problems and so forth, in order to study the human healing systems and to experience them. But they usually will recover not because of what the humans did but because of what the Arcturians were doing to help themselves. Often, we will say to an Arcturian, "You can stop experimenting on yourself now. It's okay, you did enough." So remember that even that was an experience that you had given yourself to learn from and to study, and to see and to know, and to feel what it felt like to be helpless.

HAROLD: Yes, it was. I don't think I've ever felt that way before.

ANGELS: And there's no better place than the Earth certainly to feel helpless, because in the Arcturian realms you can't feel helpless because, first of all, disease is eradicated. Second of all, there's always someone there to help you. So you needed to come to the Earth to understand helplessness.

And one of the things that you wanted to learn is whether or not there's a benefit. Is there something to be gained or learned by the experience of helplessness? And one of the things that you did like about it or you felt might be a benefit is that through being helpless, one does learn to empower one's self and be strong. You can pick yourself up by your bootstraps, in a sense. And you see that so often on the Earth, everyone falls into victimization. They say, "I'm so weak, it was your fault, I can't do it, I need you to do it." And you said, "Wait a minute, if one is feeling helpless, one has two choices; either to die and succumb to it or to just get stronger. You do it yourself."

You realize that in some environments, some souls who are so used to having everyone else do it for them and give up their power they need helplessness to re-empower themselves. So you needed to experience it, so that you would understand that aspect and that facet to it.

HAROLD: I think it was so interesting, too, because I did it right after I finished my career. I retired and I gave the invocation, and the next day is when I had the heart attack. So it sounds awful but it was an appropriate time.

ANGELS: Yeah, because you were ready to experience—with the next phase, to go on and keep seeking in a new way, as you put it. So it's interesting. But you are not so self-destructive as to leave yourself in such a vulnerable position of helplessness that you would have died or, you know, been harmed or suffered beyond your capacity. It was carefully controlled—which suited you just fine.

HAROLD: Right.

ANGELS: But you did feel enough that you understood, "Well, it's either me or nobody." Nobody is going to get me out of this. I'm going to have to do this for myself and do what I need to do and it did help empower you and help you to feel that, yeah, that's quite interesting that I learned that. You asked about that and about the illness and so forth. You asked about Wah and about some of the shifting that you're doing. One of the realizations that the Earth has to give you is the understanding that there's a limit to the mind.

HAROLD: Yes.

ANGELS: And what is interesting again in your Seeker studies through your human incarnations previously is that the mind, of course, had been your seat of power. If you are around the knowledge, if you are around the wisdom that people hold and the knowledge, you are always close to the power center. Isn't it interesting that you're beginning to feel that somehow, those who have the greatest knowledge are not getting it in the old ways that humans used to? They're not getting it from books, they're getting it directly.

HAROLD: Right.

ANGELS: It's quite fascinating, and that is in a sense what's happening on this Earth. Why it's happening is because there's an understanding that unless humans learn how to do self-empowerment and knowledge, if they don't learn to do that, they will always be enslaved by those who do. So you're beginning to experience and understand that there's a way to get knowledge that isn't through a book or through another person, and you can do it in your own way, through your own self. That's why you're choosing these routes such as channeling and such as Reiki or hands-on healing work. You yourself are taught to get out of the way and allow something greater to come through, so that knowledge is acquired in a different way.

HAROLD: Right.

ANGELS: Both of those routes are exactly that. You're taught to get out of the way so that knowledge and wisdom and healing and light and so forth can come through—and you like that. It's a new way of seeking.

One of the things that you're interested in is whether or not you could be involved in creating a planetary system of forms where knowledge is gained directly. This is going to be complex. We're going to try to help you understand and get it through this conduit. There are universes or places where each and every person gains knowledge directly. That is done. But in those universes where each and every form, each being gains knowledge directly, there is profound separation. So in those places where there is profound separation and each and every being is gaining knowledge, they don't even know the others exist. The others are next to them, in a sense, but there's no knowledge that they exist. That expression of "beingness" exists in that universe.

You're in a universe currently where you know everything that's around you, and there's a shared, collective consciousness. Do you see the difference?

HAROLD: Yes.

ANGELS: What you are studying and interested in is: Can an individual gain knowledge directly in a universe of shared collective consciousness?

HAROLD: Right.

ANGELS: Can direct knowledge happen simultaneously with a collective consciousness?

HAROLD: Right.

ANGELS: And you have come to the place as a Seeker, in the idea of creating life on another planet, where the idea of doing that is fascinating. Can we—you and your soul group—when we get to that point where we are life creators, can we create life that has the best of both worlds, so to speak, where people understand knowledge directly and simultaneously understand the existence of other. The problem is that once you let outside information in, you also let in the potential for chaos. Although chaos also creates learning, you are interested in figuring out a way to create a more peaceful world. And you have been, by the way—this doesn't affect you at all now but just for your knowledge—you have experienced "beingness" in your cone. It's as if each being exists as a cone of light and receives information directly from the cone—the world is in that cone. The entire world is in that cone; so you are creating all of your world. But you don't even know, you see?

But here on earth knowledge is gotten from others and humans don't know how to get it this other way.

HAROLD: I had an unusual experience. I was at the wedding of a kid that I babysat years ago. And before the wedding I was involved in some kind of meditative practice. But what I remember so clearly, because I was very relaxed and everybody was very relaxed—it was almost as if I could be aware of how some of the kids that I babysat were experiencing what was going on. Does that make any kind of sense? I wasn't reading their minds. I wasn't saying, "I know what he's thinking." It was almost as if I was having that person's experience.

ANGELS: Do you understand how that matches with our opening message about the Self?

HAROLD: I know.

ANGELS: You are studying Other and Self. So you are trying to figure out if they exist, or are they all just you?

HAROLD: A projection of my mind.

ANGELS: So, you might drive yourself crazy. But you are so deeply enmeshed in that study of: "Is there another outside of the Self, or are these Selves that are around me—these 'Others' that are around me—are they me? Are they really just me and my creation or are they having a creational experience opposite or different or separate from me, and is that possible?" So you are taking your studies to extremes.

You also know that the one known as Jesus was a mirror, absolutely a mirror. So think about it for a moment—particularly once Jesus became the Christed Self. He became pure mirror. Once he integrated more and more of his Higher and Highest Self and became like his Christed Self and had fewer and fewer "trigger buttons" of his human self and was more and more in alignment, it became more and more that he was just Pure Light.

So what is pure light? It is the energy of creation. So when you look at a being of pure light, you see them as yourself, because they are nothing more than creational light. You look at them and create what it is you are; you understood that that is why, simultaneously, everyone sees the experience called Jesus Christ as completely and totally different. And why, even now, there are some who will swear he was crucified and some who will swear he was not. So what is truth? Was he crucified or not? Well, the question is, "Who are you? Who are you?" That's how you answer that question. And where were you in the moment of your consciousness when you witnessed it and where are you now in the moment of your consciousness? And why is it that you need either one of those creational existences to be? Why do you need that even?

And you understand that as a perfect mirror, he was the perfect gift. So God, again, cannot know His/Herself until God sees you—formless/form. So what you're beginning to understand is, in a sense, even though this sounds a little odd, but we're going to put it this way: Words are limited but what do you think? When Jesus looked out from his eyes, his Christed Self—we've told you what others thought of when they looked at him, right? When he looked at others, what do you think he saw?

HAROLD: Beauty expanding. Does that make sense?

ANGELS: He saw himself.

HAROLD: Yes.

ANGELS: He saw himself. So what are you seeing when you look out and see others? You're seeing yourself.

HAROLD: Yes. I know I'm saying beauty but beautifulness. Do you know what I mean? I don't know if that makes sense.

ANGELS: He saw himself.

HAROLD: Yes.

ANGELS: The more pure you are—

HAROLD: Yes.

ANGELS: And he never denied the darkness. He did not live in an illusion—he said to the last, "One of you will betray me," or did he? But he was able as God to hold all. He could see the dark, he could see the light. He could see the children; he could see the old people. He could see the weak, he could see the strong. He could see himself in every single one of those beings, because if you are the All, you are in all those beings.

HAROLD: So, could a metaphor of that be—a visual metaphor be—a group of holographic beings? In other words, not solid the way I see ordinary reality, but that there is this structured luminosity. I don't know if that makes any sense.

ANGELS: Well, first of all, we want to say that Christ would say to you, I was the soldier who put the nails in. I was all these beings.

HAROLD: Right, exactly.

ANGELS: Because if Christ was truly in his Christed Godself, he would be all those beings.

HAROLD: Right.

ANGELS: He would see no separation. Christ would have no problem with that. Humans have a problem with that. Humans get angry at that. Christ would have no problem. Well, what you must understand is what you're asking about is two things. First of all, it is all holographic. It is all an illusionary creation realm. From your Higher Self perspective, everything is a hologram, if you mean it as everything is a projected consciousness illusion.

HAROLD: Right.

ANGELS: Secondly, what you are asking is, are there holograms set up to deceive within the projected consciousness illusion? You are asking, within my reality, as I have created it, is somebody interfering and setting up things in order to make me believe that's a reality, in order to manipulate me?

HAROLD: Right.

ANGELS: And the answer to that is yes, because those who wish to control the collective human reality have at times resorted to creating illusions or holograms, what you call holograms, in order to convince humankind that something existed on the third dimensional plane when it didn't. But that was only possible during the density of the human race. The human race has been fooled over and over again and each and every one of you has experienced betrayal. Each and every one of you has been fooled, has had experiences where you believed something and later found it to be completely false, and you believed it with your whole heart. You might feel your whole world has been a false, illusionary hologram, creating for you experiences of control and fear in order to enslave you. It's all been done to create separation consciousness, and it's done well. You have believed in war and hatred and famine and destruction over and over and over again. That's fear. So, those have all been done over and over and over again.

Have beings with higher technological civilizations come down and created, particularly when it was easy to fool people, particular experiences or scenarios? Absolutely, absolutely, like mirages. But you can't do that to the human race to the same extent anymore because human beings are now frequency sensitive—many, not all. But there are too many humans on this Earth who are frequency sensitive now, and there are too many humans who are able to feel or douse their way through an experience. That doesn't feel right. That's not feeling right. Something about that feels creepy. Something about that doesn't have an energy or a frequency of love. And you say, "I'm not going to buy that. I'm not going to buy that because it doesn't feel right."

And because the idea of human beings "waking up" means they cannot be fooled, those who wish to keep you asleep will desperately try to trick you. But the light is returning and the tricks are working less and less. What if a project was conceived to create a holographic reality to fool the human race into believing in the event of 2012? Christians and the Jehovahs and everyone are looking for the Rapture, the 2012, so why not give it to them? They're expecting it. Give it to them. How are you going to know whether it's real? What if the skies start to show rainbows and light like you've experienced? There's the rainbow of my heart. It's the rainbow bridge I've been told I will cross. And what if the Messiah comes down and declares himself, and you see him in the sky as clear as can be? Will you believe it? 2012, it's happening, you see? They're counting on you believing their holograms as you have in the past. But what you don't know and understand is that you are not asleep like you used to be, and what they're counting on is you being asleep. You can feel with your frequency generating machine called your body and your frequency receiving machine called your body what's real and what's not, what's in alignment and what's not. And you're going to say, "Wait a minute, that's some illusionary thing." You're going to feel it. Are you feeling from a truly spiritual and essential place the rapture of your heart or are you being talked into an experience, you see? That's the difference. That's where you're beginning to go. That's what you're beginning to investigate.

Just remember, please, that your studies really are about Other and Self. So remember that when you have these experiences, always look at them as a relationship to where you are in your studies, that you are giving yourself these experiences to try and answer the question: Is there really an Other?

HAROLD: That's so interesting because I think that's how I try to formulate—maybe that's exactly what it is—whatever was understood as a different experience was to somehow suspend, which evidently happened when I saw the whiteness—to suspend the ordinary sense of myself, so that there would be consciousness beyond the boundary of me. I think that's what I was trying to do.

ANGELS: Expand your ordinary self so there would be consciousness beyond the boundary of you?

HAROLD: Suspend.

ANGELS: Suspend your ordinary self?

HAROLD: Yes. You could say expand but suspend. In other words, there is this vastness and then there are these things here. If we suspend that, then we are the vastness.

ANGELS: Yeah.

HAROLD: Or I am the vastness.

ANGELS: In the vastness, you are all.

HAROLD: Right.

ANGELS: So in that moment, you become both the One and the All simultaneously, and that is what you are also studying.

HAROLD: I think so, and I think that's where it was going. I don't know that I knew that when I started but at least in this go-around—

ANGELS: You don't usually know what you're doing. In a sense, when you get the best results, you often don't know where they're going to come from. You don't control.

HAROLD: Right.

ANGELS: For you to get out of your own way tends to give you the meatiest pieces or morsels of your study.

HAROLD: Right, exactly.

ANGELS: Have you felt you have enough information for today, or are there any more questions you would like to ask us before we release her?

HAROLD: Yeah, I do. Who are you? That's my next question.

ANGELS: We are the angelic expression of the human soul. We are the beingness of you humans, who know and understand everything through the eyes of love. So, when this conduit taps into that realm, she taps into a wisdom and a knowledge and a beingness of All That Is through the eyes of love. And then that frequency or that being or that knowledge is directly sent through her to you, in the proper way to give you exactly what it is you need in the loving manner at that moment. So, again, from our perspective, human and angel are the same but at different places in the vibratory realms. The angelic is the Higher Self, and the human is in a sense the lower self, meaning the denser vibrational expression of that which also exists in the higher vibrational realm.

HAROLD: Very helpful.

ANGELS: So we will release her now, if that is okay?

HAROLD: Yes. Thank you so much.

ANGELS: We love you and we thank you for all your searches and "seekings" for truth.

Printed in the United States
By Bookmasters